DIFFERENTIATED INSTRUCTION
in Literacy, Math, & Science

The Best of Corwin Series

Classroom Management
Jane Bluestein, Editor

Differentiated Instruction
Gayle H. Gregory, Editor

Differentiated Instruction in Literacy, Math, and Science
Leslie Laud, Editor

Educational Neuroscience
David A. Sousa, Editor

Educational Technology for School Leaders
Lynne M. Schrum, Editor

Equity
Randall B. Lindsey, Editor

Inclusive Practices
Toby J. Karten, Editor

Response to Intervention
Cara F. Shores, Editor

THE BEST OF
CORWIN

DIFFERENTIATED
INSTRUCTION
in Literacy, Math, & Science

LESLIE LAUD
Editor

With contributions by

Carolyn Chapman · Rita King · Lois A. Lanning

Sheila Alber-Morgan · William N. Bender · Leslie Laud

Paul J. Riccomini · Bradley S. Witzel

Douglas Llewellyn · Gayle H. Gregory · Elizabeth Hammerman

CORWIN
A SAGE Company

CORWIN
A SAGE Company

FOR INFORMATION:

Corwin
A SAGE Company
2455 Teller Road
Thousand Oaks, California 91320
(800) 233-9936
Fax: (800) 417-2466
www.corwin.com

SAGE Ltd.
1 Oliver's Yard
55 City Road
London EC1Y 1SP
United Kingdom

SAGE India Pvt. Ltd.
B 1/I 1 Mohan Cooperative
Industrial Area
Mathura Road, New Delhi 110 044
India

SAGE Asia-Pacific Pte. Ltd.
33 Pekin Street #02-01
Far East Square
Singapore 048763

Acquisitions Editor: Carol Chambers Collins
Associate Editor: Megan Bedell
Editorial Assistant: Sarah Bartlett
Production Editor: Melanie Birdsall
Typesetter: C&M Digitals (P) Ltd.
Cover Designer: Rose Storey
Graphic Designer: Nicole Franck
Permissions Editor: Karen Ehrmann

Copyright © 2011 by Corwin

Printed in the United States of America

Library of Congress Cataloging-in-Publication Data

A catalog record of this book is available from the Library of Congress.

978-1-4522-1733-8

This book is printed on acid-free paper.

11 12 13 14 15 10 9 8 7 6 5 4 3 2 1

Contents

Preface

Leslie Laud

Historically, students of all ages learned together in the one-room schoolhouse. Teachers had no choice but to teach in a way that addressed the different age groups. Differentiation "was how they did school" (Tomlinson, 1999). Students used varied materials and often tutored one another as they learned. As schools expanded, students began to learn with peers in their own age group. Out of this emerged the whole-class teaching model. Unfortunately, so did the problems that come with this model—mainly boredom and frustration. Research has shown how essential it is for students to be taught at the appropriate instructional level and through varied pathways so that they are appropriately engaged (Huebner, 2010).

Instruction must be differentiated in these ways to engage students so that they can learn optimally. Fortunately, we have come a long way since the one-room schoolhouse; this book does not advocate a return to that model, though its reliance on differentiation serves as the guiding premise. In these chapters, current research on the most effective differentiation practices is brought alive through the many suggestions and examples for how these practices might play out in the each of the three major content areas: literacy, mathematics, and science.

Several themes permeate the three sections in this book. The first theme is the differentiation of content. The authors call on teachers to develop common understandings by offering students varied materials, presenting present numerous alternative options and specific examples for doing so. The second focus is on instructional methods. These authors describe in-depth research-based practices such as curriculum compacting or scaffolded support models that demonstrate the kinds of alternative methods that can be used for teaching the same material. They eschew the domination of teacher-directed activities, instead providing innumerable examples of how students can be systematically empowered to drive their own learning. Finally, the pacing of material is another major theme. These authors recognize that not only do students operate at different instructional levels and learn best through multiple varied experiences and pathways, but that they also move at different paces.

In Part I, the authors address the full gamut of how to differentiate literacy instruction. In Chapter 1, Carolyn Chapman and Rita King cover the arena of reading comprehension, emphasizing diverse options for structuring reading experiences. They describe how to support students with emerging reading comprehension skills bymodeling increasingly complex strategies until these students master those skills. They also describe advanced approaches, such as independent projects and extensions, as well as options for students who fall between these two ends on the spectrum of learning needs. Chapter 2, by Lois A. Lanning, takes differentiation to the next step, demonstrating how to use a guided release of responsibility model so that teachers can prepare students to become more self-directed and self-propelling readers. In a differentiated classroom, teachers often work with small groups and cannot directly guide the full class at all times; students must learn to self-regulate their own learning. Preparing students to take fuller responsibility for directing their own learning is challenging, but with Lanning's guidance, this goal becomes far more attainable.

The first section concludes with Sheila Alber-Morgan's chapter on writing instruction. Continuing the thread of structuring instruction so that students are empowered to take more of the lead in their learning, Alber-Morgan describes the most well-researched writing methods, including the self-regulated strategy development (SRSD) model. Citing the large-scale research that underscores its effectiveness, she provides examples that make the SRSD approach easily accessible to readers familiar and unfamiliar with this model. In Chapter 3, she also describes other writing interventions with the same clarity and extensive research overviews.

Part II gives an overview of how to differentiate mathematics instruction. In Chapter 4, William N. Bender reminds the reader of the traditional model of mathematics instruction in which all students work on the same problem set, taught via one method to the class as a whole. In sharp contrast, he then presents a model for mathematics instruction that is based on the latest brain research about how students learn. This model shifts toward offering students problems to solve that are differentiated, all based on evidence the teacher has gathered about where the students are in their thinking, as related to each new topic they study. Bender offers a teacher-friendly model that acknowledges the busy realities of teachers' lives.

The two following chapters, both by Leslie Laud, cover how to fine-tune how teachers differentiate for students who struggle with mathematics and for students who excel and therefore need additional challenge. Following informal pre-assessments such as those described in Chapter 4, some students with greater needs may require more formal assessments to help uncover specific areas in which they can benefit from additional assistance. Chapter 5 provides these more fine-tuned assessments along with research-based strategies for addressing the three main areas in which students may struggle: basic facts, conceptual understanding, and procedural algorithms. For each area, specific examples, activities, and reproducibles are offered for teachers to use to strengthen students' understanding. In the next chapter, strategies for stretching students who show greater capability are provided; many are similar to those described in the literacy chapters in Part I. Laud explains how these strategies can be applied to the mathematics curriculum, and addresses unique issues that arise when differentiating in the area of mathematics.

In the final chapter of Part II, Paul J. Riccomini and Bradley S. Witzel detail how to differentiate mathematics instruction within a response to intervention (RTI) model. In this practical and comprehensive treatment describing how to implement RTI in mathematics, these authors cover the research base and address the most pressing and common questions on teachers' minds. They also offer abundant realistic suggestions and resource lists of many of the most strongly research-supported options for tiering mathematics instruction.

Part III, the last section of the book, addresses differentiated instruction in science. Chapter 8, by Douglas Llewellyn, provides an in-depth model of a differentiated lesson, while the second chapter in this section, by Gayle H. Gregory and Elizabeth Hammerman, gives a bird's-eye view regarding how to differentiate across the many facets of the curriculum. Llewellyn's model lesson on motion energy presents the standards addressed in the lesson and the pre-assessments to use, and then demonstrates several different ways in which the lesson can be experienced through different activities that all culminate in similar learnings. Gregory and Hammerman's chapter shows the bigger picture of varied options for differentiating each area of the science curriculum and all the diverse cognitive areas that come into play. The many options they overview, along with the in-depth model Llewellyn offers, leave science teachers well equipped to begin differentiating their own curricular topics.

When one-room schoolhouse teachers differentiated to meet the needs of the multi-age student populations they served, they used practices that are well-supported by today's research findings, such as providing different leveled materials and cross-age tutoring. However, they did not have the benefit of much of the current research on more sophisticated models for differentiating such as curriculum compacting or models for systematically building self-direction in students. Moreover, they often worked in isolation and did not have access to the creative suggestions and models currently available to educators, and reflected in this compendium. Today's teachers are fortunate to live in an information age that makes the kind of teaching described in this book so widely available.

Introduction

Leslie Laud

This volume is an overview of the concept of differentiated instruction in literacy, math, and science, featuring excerpts from eight works by recognized experts. The following is a synopsis of what you will find in each chapter.

PART I. READING AND WRITING

Chapter 1. Differentiated Models and Strategies of Reading

Carolyn Chapman and Rita King

Now that I have collected assessment data, how do I use it to differentiate how I help students learn to read? In Chapter 1, Carolyn Chapman and Rita King provide a comprehensive array of options for accomplishing this feat, describing various options like curriculum compacting, projects, guided reading, read-alouds, stations, problem-solving tasks, cubing, and shared reading. Moveover, they provide examples and templates that busy teachers can use immediately.

Chapman and King recommend practical strategies for tiering instruction so that activities can be adjusted to meet specific instructional levels; they also provide diverse options that allow students to learn through varied pathways. For example, they recommend independently driven creative options, such as book making, as well as explicit choices like directly modeling certain reading comprehension reasoning processes. Such diverse activities strengthen alternate capacities and pathways and are more likely to meet the needs of students with diverse learning preferences. The breadth of suggestions provided in this chapter enable teachers to differentiate in creative and varied ways, using student data and their own judgment to determine which of these strategies will best meet the needs of their students.

Chapter 2. Gradual Release to Accelerate Progress

Lois A. Lanning

Teachers can differentiate the content they teach as well as the instructional strategies they use to deliver the content. Lois A. Lanning addresses how to do both in the area of reading comprehension. In this chapter, she focuses on how to differentiate the specific instructional strategy of using a "gradual release of responsibility" model when developing reading comprehension skills.

Teachers experienced with differentiating instruction will appreciate how Lanning addresses the dilemmas that may arise. For example, teachers often ask, "How do I fade the differentiated scaffolds (or supports) that some need to comprehend what they read?" Abundant strategies exist, and Lanning makes a strong case for four of the most powerful: (1) summarizing, (2) making meaningful connections, (3) self-regulating, and (4) inferring.

Chapter 2 takes the important next step of differentiating not only how these strategies are taught, but how students can be equipped to use them independently. Lanning describes specific, detailed, and comprehensive steps that teachers can take for offering individualized levels of support, and also addresses issues such as how to help students transfer the strategies they learn to all settings. Finally, she addresses the most common challenges teachers face, including how to facilitate the transfer of skills from one task to another and how to accommodate differences in the pace at which different students transfer and generalize the strategies.

Chapter 3. Implementing Multi-Tiered Writing Instruction

Sheila Alber-Morgan

What can teachers do to make fluent writing possible for all students, particularly those who struggle the most? Differentiating writing instruction is the key. In Chapter 3, Sheila Alber-Morgan describes the most stringently validated evidence-based strategies for differentiating writing available. She offers an overview of how to address the five major and timely areas within the writing curriculum—handwriting, keyboarding, spelling, applying the writing process, and using technology—and describes how each can be addressed in the whole-class setting, or Tier 1 instruction. She then describes how writing instruction can be differentiated to meet the needs of students who may require additional Tier 2 and Tier 3 support.

Alber-Morgan's recommended strategies all have powerful research bases that validate their potential, but what makes her work unique is how she brings this research to life by carefully explaining, in easy-to-read terms, how to carry out each step of the recommended methods. In one section of this chapter, the six-stage self-regulated strategy development

(SRSD) model is clearly described, along with almost a dozen different ways in which this model can be differentiated to meet the individual instructional needs of varied students. In another section, extensive resources for differentiating writing instruction, particularly with the use of technology, are offered.

Not only does Alber-Morgan offer a wide array of detailed suggestions, she also provides specific benchmarks students should be expected to achieve in the various areas of writing. For example, she describes how students should grip a pencil, the exact language students should use to direct themselves when writing letters, and even how many letters proficient writers should be able to write per minute. Using such benchmarks enables teachers to monitor and differentiate instruction with far greater precision.

PART II. MATHEMATICS

Chapter 4. Differentiated Instruction and Response to Intervention in Mathematics

William N. Bender

"Differentiated instruction represents a drastic paradigm shift that fundamentally changes the way teachers teach mathematics . . . ," writes William N. Bender. In Chapter 4, Bender contrasts traditional direct whole-class instruction with a model based on adjusting instruction to meet the needs of individual heterogeneous students. His central model for differentiating mathematics instruction, "Guess, Assess, and Tear Out," provides a clear and feasible framework that teachers can build on and customize as they determine how they will differentiate instruction.

Bender acknowledges the challenges of differentiation; teachers frequently feel overwhelmed with all the perceived demands that would come with "teaching three separate lessons," a concern I have often heard teachers express. Bender recognizes these concerns with a "start where you can" and "don't try to do it all at once" position. He shares general global recommendations and tips such as subdividing the class early and often and planning for several activities, both fundamental premises to differentiating instruction that move away from full-class instruction. Through these recommendations and examples, he demonstrates how teachers can shift toward using the diversity in their students as the driving force in lesson planning and instruction.

Bender also provides a simple yet comprehensive five-step plan for implementing response to intervention (RTI) as a route toward differentiating instruction, illustrating how to implement each step through a detailed case study. Throughout this chapter, Bender offers a teacher-friendly vision for differentiating mathematics instruction, one that is grounded in step-by-step plans and classroom examples.

Chapter 5. Supporting Students Who Are Low Achieving

Leslie Laud

Chapter 5 opens with the reminder that each child is a unique mystery, emphasizing the need for preassessments for each unit. Students who struggle in one area may surprise us in unexpected and exciting ways; pockets of unanticipated understandings may surface during preassessments, and the gains that students are capable of making may be all the more striking when scores on preassessments and post-assessments are contrasted.

When students struggle with mathematics, teachers can differentiate instruction for them by identifying the underlying learning profile issues that complicate their learning, such as challenges with working memory, fact retrieval, or visual processing. How these difficulties play out in each discrete unit, ranging from topics such as algebra to geometry, should be assessed. Teachers then have the dual role of strengthening underling capacities and addressing the specific curricular skills needed for each unit.

There may be no magic wand for successfully differentiating instruction for these students so that they can attain proficiency within the same timeframe as students who are average or high achieving; these students require additional time as well as research-validated practices. However, this chapter demonstrates how to differentiate instruction and develop basic skills, conceptual understandings, and procedural routines through research-validated approaches and specific steps and activities. Also woven throughout the text are tips on managing time—a precious resource that these students need to use as efficiently as possible. Many reproducibles and suggestions support teaching for proficient understanding while helping students compensate more effectively for the underlining areas that cause struggle.

Chapter 6. Challenging Students Who Are High Achieving

Leslie Laud

Differentiating instruction for students who are high achieving in mathematics is a task filled with rich and rewarding possibilities. This chapter presents research on two basic methods: providing exemptions and cultivating higher order thinking capacities. Leslie Laud provides detailed descriptions of strategies as well as models for structuring these exemptions (and the replacement tasks) when students master basic curriculum at an accelerated pace.

Chapter 6 offers an overview of the specific patterns of strengths to expect from high achievers and how these students process information in qualitatively different ways. Using this framework to help identify the common cognitive patterns these students demonstrate, teachers can tailor tasks so that they better challenge and stretch students' learning. Teachers can use the models provided as a framework for evaluating and modifying the kinds of enrichment and curricular adjustments they offer their students who benefit from additional challenge.

Chapter 7. Mathematics Interventions Overview

Paul J. Riccomini and Bradley S. Witzel

Widely used in the field of literacy, response to intervention (RTI) provides a model that enables many struggling readers to excel. Given the success of this model, educators have sought to use the same approach in mathematics, but differences between the fields complicate this transfer. While acknowledging and addressing these differences, Paul J. Riccomini and Bradley S. Witzel provide a comprehensive overview on differentiating mathematics instruction within an RTI model. This approach is informed by the authors' backgrounds as both practitioners and researchers who have contributed much-needed current empirical research to the field, enabling them to provide a quick up-to-the-minute overview of the research along with clearly stated implications for guiding instruction.

In Chapter 7, the authors describe both evidence-based instructional and curricular approaches for tiering instruction to meet the needs of diverse learners. They raise and respond to the major questions on the minds of mathematics teachers: *Who needs intervention? What do I teach for intervention? Who should intervene and for how long?* Riccomini and Witzel's responses and extensive resources provide a structured jumping-off point that can expedite the process of differentiating mathematics via an RTI model, focusing on promising full-class instructional strategies along with options for differentiating support in more targeted, tiered interventions; providing detailed descriptions and examples of specific curricular approaches; and offering a list of mathematics interventions and programs resources for teachers.

PART III. SCIENCE

Chapter 8. Differentiated Science Inquiry

Douglas Llewellyn

In Chapter 8, Douglas Llewellyn provides an in-depth description of a model for differentiating science inquiry through a hands-on science lesson on motion energy. He lists the standards and goals addressed and then suggests starting the lesson with an embedded preassessment about prior conceptions surrounding motion energy, explaining how teachers can quickly analyze this information and use it to drive the next instructional decisions to be made as the lesson continues. Llewellyn also describes several learning stations, each designed to develop different facets of understandings surrounding motion energy and to help students come to certain fundamental shared overall outcomes.

Llewellyn's model can be replicated and used to teach most areas of the science curriculum. Built into the model are opportunities for students to feel safe (they get to choose the station), to feel challenged (supports and extensions exist within each), and to become active meaning makers—all essential components of effective differentiated instruction. This lesson also brings to light two essential qualities for the person designing the lesson: deep content proficiency combined with expertise in differentiating instruction in ways that are most likely to build this proficiency in students. Llewellyn presents an ideal but also acknowledges that the ideal may not always be possible, offering progressively scaled-down options and versions that teachers can use based on available resources and where they are in mastering the differentiation process.

Chapter 9. Methods and Effective Practices for Increasing Student Achievement

Gayle H. Gregory and Elizabeth Hammerman

Science learning draws on multi-faceted capacities. Just a few that students are expected to master include logical thinking, synthesizing new understandings or insights from data, memorizing definitions, and using guided inquiry processes to confirm or disconfirm hypotheses they have generated. In Chapter 9, Gayle H. Gregory and Elizabeth Hammerman tackle a comprehensive overview of the many areas that come into play in science instruction. They relate all of these areas to the latest research on effective practices and brain research, but they don't stop there—they then provide detailed lists of examples of how these practices can actually look when used in science classes. Woven throughout are suggestions for how teachers can adjust instruction to meet the needs of students who excel through strategies such as curriculum compacting. Structured options for how to adjust tasks to offer differentiated support to learners who might struggle in some areas are also provided.

Gregory and Hammerman ambitiously cover tremendous ground in this chapter, ranging from the varied methods that can be used to teach the different areas of science learning to the latest and most compelling research that supports the effectiveness of how best to do so. The many examples demonstrate the kind of assistance that some students will require and the extensions that will stretch others, with the goal of enabling each student to experience what the authors refer to as "flow" while they learn about science.

About the Editor

Leslie Laud, EdD, has differentiated math instruction in her own classroom and in her coteaching with her math colleagues, and has been doing so for almost two decades. She teaches an online course on Differentiated Middle School Math Instruction at Bank Street College of Education. In addition, she has presented at many conferences both nationally and internationally, including The National Council of Teachers of Mathematics annual conference. She has also published many articles in leading journals such as *Educational Leadership* and *Teaching Exceptional Children.* She currently leads staff development groups with teachers in school systems in the Boston area. She received both her doctorate in curriculum and instruction and her master's in special education from Teachers College, Columbia University.

About the Contributors

Sheila Alber-Morgan has been an associate professor of special education at The Ohio State University since 2005. She was also a faculty member at The University of Southern Mississippi for eight years. After teaching for several years in inclusive classrooms in both urban and rural South Carolina, Dr. Alber-Morgan began doctoral training at The Ohio State University and earned her PhD in 1997. For the past 15 years, Dr. Alber-Morgan's research has focused on examining the effects of various literacy interventions on the learning outcomes of elementary and secondary students with and without disabilities. Additionally, her research incorporates strategies for programming for generalization and maintenance of academic and social skills. Almost all of Dr. Alber-Morgan's research has been designed and implemented in collaboration with classroom teachers, and she has over 50 research and practitioner publications including peer-reviewed journal articles, textbook ancillaries, and book chapters.

William N. Bender is an international leader who focuses on practical instructional tactics with an emphasis on response to intervention (RTI) and differentiated instruction in general education classes across the grade levels. In particular, Dr. Bender has written more books on RTI than any other author in the world, two of which are best sellers. He has now completed seven books on various aspects of RTI, as well as a professional development videotape on that topic. He completes between forty and fifty workshops yearly in the United States, Canada, and the Caribbean. In the fall of 2010, he was selected to work with the Ministry of Education in Bermuda to establish their nationwide RTI framework. One of his recent books, *Beyond the RTI Pyramid*, was a 2010 finalist for the Distinguished Achievement Award for Excellence in Educational Publishing.

Dr. Bender uses practical strategies and easy humor to make his workshops an enjoyable experience for all, and he is frequently asked to return to the same school or district for additional workshops. He consistently receives positive reviews of his professional development workshops for educators across the grade levels. Dr. Bender believes his job is to inform educators of innovative, up-to-date tactics for the classroom, rooted in current research, in an enjoyable workshop experience. He is able to convey this information in a humorous, motivating fashion.

Dr. Bender began his education career teaching in a junior high school resource classroom, working with adolescents with behavioral disorders and learning disabilities. He earned his PhD in special education from the University of North Carolina and has taught in leading universities around the nation, including Rutgers University and the University of Georgia. He is now consulting and writing full-time and has published over sixty research articles and twenty books in education.

Carolyn Chapman continues her life's goal as an international educational consultant, author, and teacher. She supports educators in their process of change for today's students. She has taught in a variety of settings from kindergarten to college classrooms. Her interactive, hands-on professional development opportunities focus on challenging the mind to ensure success for learners of all ages. All students *do* learn. Why not take control of that learning by putting excitement and quality in effective learning? Carolyn walks her walk and talks her talk to make a difference in the journey of learning in today's classrooms.

Carolyn authored *If the Shoe Fits . . . How to Develop Multiple Intelligences in the Classroom.* She has coauthored *Multiple Assessments for Multiple Intelligences, Multiple Intelligences Through Centers and Projects, Differentiated Instructional Strategies for Writing in the Content Areas, Differentiated Instructional Strategies: One Size Doesn't Fit All,* and *Test Success in the Brain Compatible Classroom.* Video Journal of Education, Inc., features Carolyn Chapman in *Differentiated Instruction.* Carolyn's company, *Creative Learning Connection, Inc.,* has also produced a CD, *Carolyn Chapman's Making the Shoe Fit,* and training manuals to accompany each of her books. Each of these publications and her trainings demonstrate Carolyn's desire and determination to make an effective impact for educators and students. She may be contacted through the Creative Learning Connection website at www.carolynchapman.com.

Gayle H. Gregory is an internationally known consultant who has specialized in brain-compatible learning and differentiated instruction and assessment.

She presents practical teacher- and student-friendly strategies grounded in sound research that educators find easy to use. Her interactive style and modeling of strategies help teachers and administrators transfer new ideas to their classroom and school with ease.

She has had extensive experience in elementary, middle, and secondary schools, and in community colleges and universities. Gayle has also had district leadership roles, including the role of curriculum coordinator and staff development director. She has worked with instructional leadership teams in many schools and districts throughout the country, focusing on data analysis; using assessment, both formative and summative; and differentiating instruction based on readiness, learning profiles, and interests.

Her areas of expertise include brain-compatible learning, block scheduling, emotional intelligence, instructional and assessment practices, differentiated instructional strategies, the use of data to differentiate, literacy, presentation skills, renewal of secondary schools, enhancement of teacher quality, the use of coaching and mentoring, change management, and creation of professional learning communities.

Gayle believes in lifelong learning for herself and others.

Gayle may be contacted at (905) 336-6565 or (716) 898-8716, or by e-mail at gregorygayle@netscape.net. Her website is www.gaylehgregory.com.

Elizabeth Hammerman is a dedicated Science Educator. Her background includes teaching science at the middle school and high school levels, instructing elementary and secondary science methods courses at the university level, and working extensively with K–12 science teachers in the field. She has served as a consultant, workshop facilitator, project director, instructional designer, and professional development provider for school districts, regional centers, state offices of education, and professional organizations.

Elizabeth is the author of numerous articles, instructional materials, and books. Recent publications—*Eight Essentials of Inquiry-Based Science* (2006), *Becoming a Better Science Teacher: Eight Steps to High Quality Instruction and Student Achievement* (2006), and *Differentiated Instructional Strategies in Science* (2008)—provide a vision for high-quality, standards-based science and offer practical, research-based tools and strategies for effective teaching and learning

Her Science Achievement professional development programs for teacher leaders and classroom teachers are designed to build leadership capacity and strengthen expertise needed to achieve excellence in teaching and learning in K–12 science.

Rita King is an international trainer, keynote speaker, consultant, and author. She conducts training sessions for teachers, administrators, and parents. She served as principal and director of the teacher-training program in Middle Tennessee State University's laboratory school. In this capacity, she taught methods courses and conducted demonstration lessons. Educators relate to Rita's background as a teacher and administrator and her experiences in preK–12 and classrooms. She has been recognized as an Exemplary Educator by the state of Tennessee.

As an international consultant, Rita conducts training sessions for teachers; administrators; and parents on local, state, and international levels. Her areas of expertise include differentiated strategies for reading, writing, management and assessment, multiple intelligences, practical applications of brain-based research, creating effective learning environments, and strategies for test success.

Rita coauthored *Test Success in the Brain Compatible Classroom, Differentiated Instructional Strategies for Reading in the Content Areas, Differentiated Instructional Strategies for Writing in the Content Areas,* and *Differentiated Instructional Management.* She also coauthored training manuals to enhance professional development sessions using the reading, writing, management, and assessment books. Multimedia kits are available for use on-site.

Rita's sessions give educators and parents innovative, engaging activities to develop students as self-directed, independent learners. Participants enjoy Rita's practical, easy-to-use strategies, sense of humor, enthusiasm, and genuine desire to foster the love of learning.

Rita may be contacted through the website for King Learning Associates, Inc., at www.kinglearningassociates.com, by phone at (615) 848-8439, or via e-mail at kingrs@bellsouth.net.

Lois A. Lanning is currently the Assistant Superintendent of Schools in Pomperaug Regional School District 15, Connecticut. In addition to being an assistant superintendent, other roles in her career include classroom teacher, K–12 reading consultant, special education teacher, elementary principal, district curriculum director, and adjunct professor. These positions span urban, suburban, and small town school systems, giving her a wide view of literacy practices.

Lois has extensive background in district-level curriculum work and staff development training. She stays actively involved in the trends and issues in reading instruction through professional organizations, by presenting at state and national conferences, and by working with other school districts and state departments. She is the author of several articles published in professional journals and of other reading resources for teachers. First and foremost, her passion is helping all students become lifelong readers.

Like many of you, **Douglas Llewellyn** wears several hats. One hat is his teaching hat. Doug teaches science education and educational leadership courses at St. John Fisher College (Rochester, NY). Previously, he was the K–12 Director of Science at the Rochester City School District, a junior high school principal, and a middle school science teacher. Recently he codirected a program to develop K–12 teacher-leaders in mathematics and science. Llewellyn's research interests are in the areas of scientific inquiry, constructivist teaching, and teacher leadership.

His second hat is his author and presenter hat. He writes on science education and leadership for the National Science Teachers Association and other professional journals. Llewellyn is a frequent speaker at state and national science conferences on constructivist and inquiry-based teaching. His book, *Inquire Within: Implementing Inquiry-Based Science Standards in Grades 3–8,* Second Edition, is published by Corwin. Accompanying his *Inquire Within* book is a *Facilitator's Guide* to help science leaders and coordinators plan effective professional development in science inquiry. His Grades 9–12 book, *Teaching High School Science Through Inquiry,* is copublished by Corwin and NSTA.

His third and favorite hat is his Boston Red Sox cap. During the summer months, he is usually either watching a baseball game or boating on the New York State Finger Lakes and the Erie Canal. He can be reached at dllewellyn@sjfc.edu or dllewell@rochester.rr.com.

Paul J. Riccomini, PhD, began his career as a dual-certified general education mathematics teacher of students with learning disabilities, emotional and behavioral disabilities, and gifted and talented students in Grades 7–12 in inclusive classrooms. His teaching experiences required a strong content knowledge in mathematics and the development and maintenance of strong collaborative relationships with both general and special educators. He earned his doctorate in special education from The Pennsylvania State University and his master's degree in education and Bachelor of Arts in mathematics at Edinboro University of Pennsylvania. Currently, he is an Associate Professor of Special Education at Clemson University. His research focus is on effective instructional approaches, strategies, and assessments for students who are low achievers and/or students with learning disabilities in mathematics. He has written several research and practitioner articles related to effective strategies for teaching mathematics to students who struggle and has coauthored two math intervention programs targeting fractions and integers. As a former middle and high school general education and special education mathematics teacher, Dr. Riccomini knows firsthand the challenges and difficulties teachers experience every day when working with struggling students, a motivation for writing this book. You can e-mail Dr. Riccomini at pjr146@clemson.edu.

Bradley S. Witzel, PhD, is an experienced and decorated teacher of students with disabilities and at-risk concerns. He has worked as a classroom teacher and before that as a paraeducator in inclusive and self-contained settings. Dr. Witzel received his BS in psychology from James Madison University and his master's degree in education and his PhD in special education from the University of Florida. He currently serves as an associate professor, coordinator of the three special education programs, and assistive department chair of curriculum and instruction at Winthrop University in Rock Hill, South Carolina, where he recently received the 2009 Winthrop Graduate Faculty Award. In higher education, Dr. Witzel has taught undergraduate and graduate courses in special and general education methods as well as a variety of other courses from transition to behavior support. He has written several research and practitioner articles, books, and book chapters on mathematics education and interventions, and served as a reviewer of the Final Report from the National Mathematics Advisory Panel. Recently he coauthored an IES practice guide on response to intervention in mathematics. You can e-mail Dr. Witzel at witzelb@winthrop.edu.

Part I

Reading and Writing

THE DIFFERENTIATED MODELS OF READING DISCUSSED IN this chapter provide a framework for planning instruction. Each model is designed for immediate use in the classroom within the content area curriculum. Adapt the suggestions and guidelines to your teaching strategies. Choose the reading model to match your students' needs and enhance their reading skills.

ADJUSTABLE ASSIGNMENT MODEL

Adjustable assignments are used to plan for the teaching of one topic, standard, skill, objective, or essential question to students who are on multiple levels of learning. The standard, skill, or concept is identified. An appropriate preassessment identifies the background knowledge and experiences of the students in relation to the new learning. In most classes, an analysis of the data reveals three distinct groups.

- One group has the proper background and is ready for the grade-level standard.
- Another group lacks the proper background knowledge or experiences for the lesson. This group has gaps in learning that hinder the ability to fully understand the standard. The teacher plans instruction to intervene and fill in the learning gaps for these students. Of course, all deficiencies cannot be addressed, so select the skill that fills in the most important missing piece for the standard. In Chapman and King's *Differentiated Instructional Management* (2008), this process is referred to as curriculum rewinding.
- The third group has the proper background and has mastered the standard. These readers need assignments that enrich, challenge, and fast-forward their learning.

When a teacher knows specific information about a student's background knowledge on a topic, appropriate actions are planned so all readers grow in learning.

With adjustable assignments (see Figure 1.1 on the next page), the learner begins with current knowledge and skills and moves into identified areas of deficiency. Analyze the needs of students, than make strategic plans for individuals and specific groups. Design activities and tasks that produce growth and improvement for each reader.

Figure 1.1   Adjustable Assignment Model

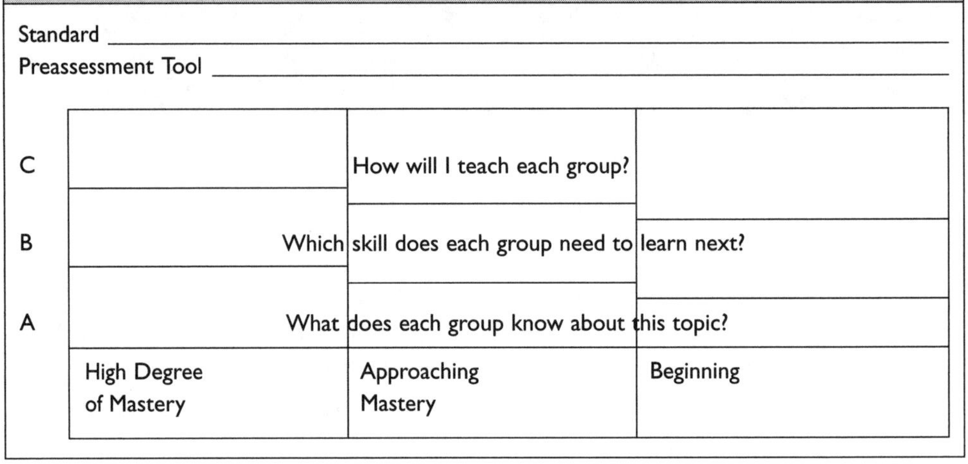

Standard _____

Preassessment Tool _____

C		How will I teach each group?	
B		Which skill does each group need to learn next?	
A		What does each group know about this topic?	
	High Degree of Mastery	Approaching Mastery	Beginning

SOURCE: Adapted from Chapman & King, 2008.

See Figure 1.2 for an adjustable model showing levels of readiness for research assignments.

Figure 1.2   Adjustable Model for Research

Has resources and uses them effectively. Clearly defines and expands the topic. Works independently and productively. Work reflects creativity. Uses accurate information.	Uses two or more sources to locate information. Stays on topic. Needs little assistance. Has some awareness of purpose. Shows some organization.	Uses one source for given topic. Ongoing assistance is required. Has inadequate awareness of purpose. Lacks skills to organize thoughts.
High Degree of Mastery	*Approaching Mastery*	*Beginning*

SOURCE: Adapted from Gregory & Chapman, 2007.

CURRICULUM-COMPACTING MODEL

To meet the needs of high-end learners in a particular topic, Dr. Joseph Renzulli designed the curriculum-compacting model (Renzulli, Leppien, & Hayes, 2000; see also Tomlinson, 1999, 2001).

Many readers study and explore the world as researchers and discoverers of information. If students are experts on a topic or have mastered a standard or skill, they need a special plan so they, too, grow in knowledge. These students deserve an alternative with an exemption for the grade-level tasks. Here are some examples:

- Students work with an agenda assignment containing a list of challenging tasks.
- Students who have mastered the vocabulary words receive a more difficult list to broaden their vocabulary.
- Students who read at a higher level go to another classroom for reading instruction. The reading teacher is responsible for the grade.

CENTERS AND STATIONS MODEL

Add centers and stations, labs, cooperative groups, and personalized instruction to your classroom. Design periods of time for hands-on experiences to make learning happen. Students work independently and in small groups at manipulative stations, experiencing content in meaningful ways. This approach allows students to take control of their learning.

Examples of Reading Stations, Centers, or Learning Zones

Stations are set up as an assembly-line process, with students working in each area. Center activities can be leveled according to difficulty. This way, the students are assigned to the center or station based on preassessment data that identify individual needs.

The stations can be designed for student selection so they choose a place to work. This gives readers responsibility and ownership in learning.

Here are examples of hands-on centers or stations to use with all subjects.

Book-making station	Manipulatives	Resource library
Center bulletin boards	Problem-solving puzzles	Skills centers
Computer games	Reading nook	Tubs with manipulatives
Folder games	Reading response center	Vocabulary-building center

PROJECT-BASED MODELS

Project-based learning fosters in-depth studies about a unit. Everyone is given the same assignment, guidelines, rubric, and time line, but the topics and products vary. For example, students receive an assignment to create a travel brochure with the same criteria and grading rubric, but each brochure will have a different appearance, because different destinations are depicted. In this example, students may use any media to design their brochures.

Projects can be assigned in different ways, depending on the model used:

- In a multiple intelligences model, the lists of the possible project assignments are created around targeted intelligences, with students choosing projects they prefer.
- In a student choice contract model, the student presents a proposal to the teacher for a project. This can include the idea, reasons, procedure, and product. The contract is approved by the teacher. Guidelines, criteria, and rubrics are set by the teacher to establish standards and expectations for the project.

Here are some questions to consider:

- Will the project be an ongoing part of the instruction in one or more content areas?
- Will the project be a culminating activity to show what the student has learned within a specific area of focus or topic?
- Will the project be a shared home and school commitment?
- Will the project be worthwhile?

Here are some factors to consider when making project assignments:

- *Experience appropriateness:* Will the student be able to process and utilize the information and resources?
- *Content:* How will the project be used to extend the learning process in a particular study area?

Remember to plan peer-to-peer conferences throughout the project process so the student is held accountable for progress on assignments along the time line. This encourages individuals to pace their work on the project instead of waiting until the last minute to complete it.

PROBLEM-SOLVING MODEL

The reader, a small group, or a class can identify a problem to solve or be given a problem. It is usually related to the school, local community, or world. The problem can be assigned to the total group (T), a student working alone (A), partners (P), or small groups (S) using the TAPS model. For instance, in one classroom the students stated that a traffic light was needed near the local community sports center. The teacher arranged for the students to work with a traffic engineer to gather information on regulations and requirements for installing a traffic light. The students created charts and graphs to share the information gathered.

The teacher arranged for the class to visit the intersection to gather more data. Students shared the collected data with the traffic engineer. Today that intersection has a traffic light.

INDEPENDENT CHOICE READING MODEL

Independent reading time provides students with opportunities to choose fact or fiction to read. A supply of ready resources in the students' areas of interest is available in the classroom for selection during this time.

Some teachers allow students to bring materials from the media center, the local library, or home. These materials may need adult approval. When the reading materials are assembled, the classroom shelves contain a variety of information relevant to the current topic, such as the examples in the following list.

Factual information   Readers' ability levels
Fictional accounts   Reference materials
Illustration booklet   Students' areas of interest
Materials written in different genres

Students need specific times to choose books and materials for independent reading. This is an ideal way to encourage reading for pleasure because students know they can find something on the resource shelf they are anxious to read.

GUIDED READING MODEL

The purpose of guided reading is to empower students with independent reading skills and strategies they will automatically use to interpret texts and related materials. Guided reading activities are teacher-directed learning opportunities. Conduct guided reading with a total class, a small group, or one student.

Engage each student in sharing and discussing ideas in the passage. Ask comprehension questions to determine the students' understanding of the reading. Use questions to elicit responses that require literal, inferential, and evaluative comprehension. Present the skills through modeling, explanations, examples, and discussions during this special reading time.

In most classrooms, the guided reading groups form with students of similar needs. While one group works with the teacher, other students work on specific reading skills in centers, with partners, or independently. As the students' needs and strengths change, so do the individuals who make up each group.

The Teacher's Role in Guided Reading

The teacher leads the students through reading passages modeling appropriate skills and strategies.

1. *Activate prior knowledge.* Use lead-ins, essential questions, graphics, music, or props to activate memories linking prior knowledge and experiences to the new learning. Here are some examples:
   - What do you think this is about?
   - What is going to happen?

- Today we are going to . . .
- How many of you remember . . . ?
- Remember a time when . . . ? Tell us about it.
- Look at this picture. What does the picture tell you?
- Do the topics and subheadings remind you of an experience you have had or something you have read? Tell me about it.
- What do you think when you hear this music?

2. *Teach vocabulary* words, standards, and skills related to the passages.

3. *Monitor readers* and respond strategically with cues, prompts, and assistance. These aids further refine understanding of the passage.

4. *Teach students how to monitor* their comprehension and how to fix a breakdown in understanding.

5. *Model specific reasoning processes* used by effective readers to construct meaning of the text. Give students step-by-step directions to follow when completing a task. Talk through the thinking process to demonstrate how to control thinking while reading.

Sample Model for a Guided Reading Session

1. Choose the reading selection and identify the group, using flexible grouping.

2. Match the text to the instructional level of the students.

3. Get ready for reading.
   - Assess to identify the students' background knowledge.
   - Arouse interest with hooks and anticipatory carrots.
   - Set purposes.

4. Introduce the new vocabulary and skills in novel ways (see Chapter 5).
   - Analyze the structure of the word.
   - Learn the word and its meaning as used in the text.

5. Make predictions.

6. Introduce the passage with prereading activities.
   - Discuss the title and subheading.
   - Preview graphics, charts, and pictures.
   - Present the essential questions and purposes.
   - Announce the focus for learning.

7. Read the passage.
   - Assign short passages. Some assignments call for note taking.
   - Provide time for independent reading.
   - Intervene with assistance as needed.

8. Discuss and develop comprehension skills (see Chapter 7).
   - Discuss answers to questions and facts discovered.
   - Review organization and sequence.
   - Redefine the purpose.

9. Reread orally with a small group, partner, or total group if oral reading skills are weak.

10. Use the information learned to differentiate assignments for individual need.

11. Employ intelligence and modality tools to customize activities and assignments.

12. Use follow-up activities to teach, practice, and review skills, concepts, and strategies.

13. Locate additional information and sources.

14. Use learned information in creative displays, portfolios, reports, or presentations.

Assessment of Guided Reading

Use a checklist similar to Figure 1.3 to assess the learner's progress.

Figure 1.3   Assessment of Guided Reading

Student's Name _____   Teacher's Name _____
Date _____

Learner Skill	Not Yet	Developing	Consistent
Reads orally with expression.			
Knows the vocabulary.			
Recognizes and uses punctuation to guide reading.			
Demonstrates understanding of text.			
Retells the story or information.			
Makes predictions.			
Interprets characters' feelings.			
Makes inferences.			
Comments			

LANGUAGE EXPERIENCE MODEL

In a language experience activity, the teacher selects a content-related topic. The students are given a prompt or questions about the topic to elicit oral responses.

As a student responds, the teacher writes exactly what the individual says, word for word. This activity demonstrates the writing-reading connection. Students gather near the teacher to see their words recorded and read. Chart paper is recommended, because it is easy to handle, display, move, and revisit as needed. It is important for students to see the chart, board, paper, or computer screen as their words are recorded.

During a language experience activity, learners observe letters forming words, the words making sentences, and sentences creating paragraphs. The teacher repeats the student's words, modeling how the spoken words appear in the form of writing. Often students do not understand that the words they say are the same words written on the paper. The teacher explicitly demonstrates that spoken words are now in a written form. Read each phrase as it is written. Read each sentence as it is completed. Invite students to read specific phrases and sentences. Lead the group in rereading the recorded information.

Learners may know what they want to say but have difficulty writing it. Language experience activities teach students the value of writing their words as they say them. Each experience demonstrates the writing and reading connection through content lessons.

The language experience is a vital tool to use because students can read their own words in writing and receive teacher guidance, which students often need while reading. The language experience is effective with an individual, a small group, or a total class.

Language Experiences in the Lower Grades

The teacher usually selects the topic for a language experience in the lower grades. The class can choose a title before the writing begins or select a catchy, clever title when the activity is completed.

The student gives the information to the teacher orally. The teacher writes the sentence, saying the name of each letter of the word as it takes form on the chart. The student repeats the letter's name. For example, if a student's sentence begins with the letter *T,* the teacher says, "Capital *T,*" while writing it. The student repeats it, saying, "Capital *T.*" When the letters form a word, the teacher and the student say the word together. For example, the teacher says, "T-h-e spells *the,*" and the group repeats it.

Using this method, the teacher reinforces each letter's name, the recognition of every word, and the connection of words to create sentences. When a sentence is complete, the teacher brings attention to each word by using a pointer while reading the sentence to the listening students. The readers repeat the sentence. As each learner becomes more proficient with letter recognition, spelling, and reading, individual progress is evident. Students join their voices with the teacher's as the letters and words appear in the writing. Upon completion of a chart, the class and the teacher read the entire story, passage, or list together.

Language Experiences in the Upper Grades

Language experience activities are effective for conveying topic information in the upper grades. A chart, blackboard, overhead, or computer projection screen is used to record student responses during a small-group or class discussion. The teacher reads each word, sentence, or phrase after writing it. This repetition reinforces word recognition and correct spelling.

Any time a teacher records a student's words, it is a language experience. This technique records student responses to questions during class discussions. For example, students realize that as they speak, the teacher is scripting their words. When responding to an open-ended question on a test, learners realize the need to write thoughts in words as they would say them orally. Often a student knows the answers but does not know how to transfer thoughts and information to tests. Language experience activities develop metacognitive skills the reader needs to record thoughts in all academic activities.

Teachers often misinterpret the students' information as they are writing it. The teacher continually asks for clarification, because the student may not volunteer to correct the teacher if thoughts are recorded incorrectly.

The teacher also encourages the student to give further explanations. If the information is not clear, the student can be asked to respond to probing questions. Encourage the student to use explanations that clarify the previous statement. Here are some examples of questions to use for clarification.

- Tell me more.
- What part do you not understand?
- Explain this idea.
- What does this mean?

Create an adjustable assignment similar to that shown in Figure 1.4 for a language experience activity. Identify and record the student's knowledge base in the lower section. Record what your students need next above the line.

Figure 1.4   Adjustable Assignment for Language Experience

• Can write and read the story. • Is a leading contributor to the language experience process. • Has a strong knowledge base of language and sentence construction. • Spells the word before the teacher writes it. • Is a fluent, comprehending reader.	• Contributes to the story or topic. • Recognizes and knows how to spell most common words. • Reads most of the words without assistance.	• Repeats letters and words after the teacher. • Reads a few words without assistance.
High Degree of Mastery	*Approaching Mastery*	*Beginning*

SOURCE: Adapted from Gregory & Chapman, 2007.

SHARED READING MODEL

During shared reading experiences, everyone has an individual copy of the passage selected for the activity. The students gather around the teacher. Selecting the right passage is important to making this activity successful. The pupils follow the words as the teacher reads to them. Students who know how to read some words join in the reading. During the shared reading, the teacher provides needed word prompts and cues. The students participate in a rereading and retelling activity. This approach is recommended for beginning readers and English-language learners of all ages.

Use these suggested guidelines for shared reading:

1. Choose an appropriate selection with interesting, intriguing topic information.

2. Use books with predictable language, such as a rhyme, rhythmic text, or repetitive phrases.

3. Begin with an exciting hook to build interest in the reading.

4. Let the students make predictions about the selection.

5. Read the passage aloud.

6. Discuss the selection.
   - Ask students to give the information in their own words.
   - Elicit and confirm predictions.
   - Describe the details and valuable descriptive information.

7. Repeat the reading using various reading designs.
   - Assign parts for the students to read with the teacher.
   - Ask students to join in the parts they are able to read.

8. Provide a follow-up experience.

During shared reading experiences, students see the connection between written and spoken forms of language. They learn to read a passage from beginning to end and see that print runs from left to right and from top to bottom. Students hear and see reading modeled. Listeners hear the story read with expression and fluency. As the book or selection is read again, students further develop their listening and sight vocabularies. The discussions and follow-up activities teach readers that meaning comes from print.

READ-ALOUD MODEL

Read-aloud experiences give students of all ages the opportunity to hear the sounds and rhythms of the language. Each student needs to be read to every day. Jim Trelease, author of *The Read-Aloud Handbook* (2001), says if every person were read to orally every day from birth until age 21, we would have a literate world.

Read aloud to students each day. Make this a special, daily routine in all classrooms, in all subjects, and in all grade levels. Choose passages that relate to the topic of study or a high-interest area. (See Figure 1.5 for suggested sources of read-aloud materials.) The read-aloud time gives the student the opportunity to see and hear a reading model. When adults read aloud, they need to show passion for the piece through their emotions, voice inflections, and feelings. Relationships of letters to words, words to phrases, phrases to sentences, and sentences to paragraphs are better understood when the listener views the printed material as it is read aloud.

Figure 1.5 Suggested Read-Aloud Materials			
Chapter books	Newspapers	Trivia	Riddles
Picture books	School newsletters	Quotes	Announcements
Fiction	Magazines	Sayings	Biographical sketches
Textbooks	Brochures	Brain teasers	Lyrics
Journals	Sports tidbits	Cartoons	Poetry
Reference entries	Movie reviews	Play scripts	Comic books
Articles	Spotlight a hero	Current events	Jokes
Game statistics	Weather reports	Fashion tips	Advertisements
Topic references	Editorials	News flashes	Travel Brochures

FOUR-BLOCK MODEL

The four-block planning format teaches reading in an organized manner, covering specific components, such as vocabulary development, guided reading, independent reading, and writing. Each block consists of a 60- to 90-minute period. A reading component is taught during each allotted block of time.

Some instruction is conducted with the total group. For example, the entire class may need to hear the directions and the introductory hook. On the other hand, some reading skills and strategies develop as the student works alone. For example, students need time to work alone to create their own interpretations of the information read. At other times, they find a comfortable place to work with a reading partner. Often instruction leads to small-group work. For example, the teacher may lead a group in a guided reading lesson. Guided reading sessions provide opportunities to model reading, teach skills, assess, and apply thinking skills in differentiated group scenarios.

Preassess the students to identify their background knowledge related to the standard. Design flexible grouping to tap into preferences and the potential of diverse learners. The four-block method is a structured way to plan reading instruction strategically. With appropriate activities in each quadrant (see Figure 1.6), fluent, comprehending readers develop through well-planned, meaningful lessons.

Figure 1.6 Four-Block Planning	
Vocabulary Development	*Guided Reading*
Design activities to . . . • introduce, assess, and review vocabulary words. • decode and pronounce words. • work with structural analysis clues. • apply phonics automatically. • master sight words. • study word origins. • learn and apply meanings. • teach mnemonics and hooks for learning new words. • use new words in daily conversations. • engage intelligences, learning styles, and interests. • entice and challenge with word games.	*Design activities to . . .* • provide a wide range of fiction and nonfiction materials related to the topic. • model and teach comprehension strategies and skills. • learn how to use context clues. • use a text or multiple copies of a trade book or literature (fiction, nonfiction). • teach reading skills and tools. • check for understanding of passages. • read in various genres related to the topic. • use different levels of thinking to check for understanding. • use explicit, inference, and evaluative questions. • develop the ability to identify the author's purpose, main ideas, and supporting details. • identify problems and find solutions.
Independent Reading	*Writing*
Design activities to . . . • learn how to select and read personal reading materials. • practice specific reading skills. • develop an eager, fluent reader. • develop opportunities to read a variety of materials. • allow reading text assignments alone or with others. • allow reading at one's own pace. • enhance comprehension and interpret information. • create a personal fit for success. • read materials in areas of interest.	*Design activities to . . .* • respond to and interpret in written form the information read. • record thoughts on graphic organizers. • express points of view and draw conclusions. • use different types of writing to respond to reading. • use various genres. • provide reflections. • engage in self-analysis. • process information. • critique, analyze, or summarize. • provide choice.

FROM MODELS TO IMPLEMENTATION

The following differentiated instructional strategies include agendas, cubing, response books, graphic organizers, and choice boards to use with content material. The flexibility of each activity provides options to meet the reader's individual needs during the implementation of a specific reading model.

Agendas and Menus

An agenda is a list of tasks for an individual or a small group of students to complete during independent work time. In many schools, this list is referred to as a "menu." Often while students work on their agendas, a teacher works with a small group, assisting students or assessing individual learners.

An agenda is an organizational tool for planning instruction that allows all students to work at their own levels. An agenda can be used with students of any age in any subject area across the curriculum. Small groups may have the same items on their assignment lists. The agenda is tailored to the individual's need and knowledge base.

The agenda for individual students or small groups may be presented in a folder or displayed in a designated area of the classroom. The tasks are determined from a data analysis of a preassessment. Before the work, begins the students know the due date for the completed tasks. Tasks on the list should be completed in a specified time. For example, during a unit of study, students☐are assigned specific tasks related to a standard. Before the work begins, the students know the due date for the completed tasks. Students who share similar knowledge, interests, or ability levels work though the same tasks.

The teacher and the students assess progress. As part of the information in the folder, the students are given an agenda log (see Figure 1.7) or an agenda checklist (Figure 1.8). The student can record each entry at the end of a work session.

Figure 1.7 Agenda Log				
Item and Date	*Today I*	*I need help on . . .*	*Completion Date*	*Comments*

Figure 1.8 Agenda Self-Check				
Student_____ Topic, Subject, or Unit_____				
Date of Assignment_____ Due Date_____				
TASK	*A*	*B*	*C*	*D*
Task or assignment				
Beginning work date				
Completion date				
What I learned				
Request for assistance				
Concerns and questions				
Comments				

Check Points   Identification _____ Signature _____ Date _____

Identification
S: Self   Identification _____ Signature _____ Date _____
C: Classmate
P: Parent   Identification _____ Signature _____ Date _____
T: Teacher   Identification _____ Signature _____ Date _____

Why Use Agendas?

- *Pacing:* Agendas teach the reader how to organize task sessions, use time wisely, and complete tasks within a set period. The teacher allots adequate time for the student to work effectively and efficiently on each task.

- *Sequence:* The student determines the order in which to complete the agenda items. One learner may complete the easiest tasks first, while another may complete difficult tasks first.

- *Independence:* Agendas foster independence. A student who is working on an agenda accepts personal responsibility for completing the assignment.

- *Time on-task:* Agenda assignments provide independent practice with and growth in the individual skills indicated as needs by the assessment data. This approach eliminates busywork and fosters efficient and quality use of time.

How Are Agendas Used?

- The teacher assigns all tasks.

- The teacher assigns some tasks, and the student chooses others from a choice board or a list of agenda ideas (see Figure 1.9).

Here's an example of how this can work. The teacher assigns one to three tasks and allows students to choose two to four tasks from a choice board. Students may design an activity related to the topic and submit it for teacher approval.

Reading Learning Zones, Centers, and Stations

Stations (see Figure 1.10 on page 18) are an important addition to any differentiated classroom. Preassess well so you know which activity each student needs next. Strategically plan activities that do the following:

- Teach the needed information. Select activities at the knowledge-base levels to teach the addressed standards, concepts, and skills. Also, remember to level the activities and tasks with a blending of grade-level and high-challenge opportunities.

- Intrigue students and hold their interest, making them anticipate and yearn to engage in the activity.

- Provide age-appropriate and stimulating tasks that intrigue and challenge the mind.

- Provide student-focused tasks that can be completed without adult supervision.

Try This Management Tip!

Color-code folders and activities to identify the knowledge-base or background level (see Figure 1.11 on page 18). Assign readers a yellow, red, or green activity to work on a standard, skill, or concept at the appropriate level to meet the individual's needs (Chapman & King, 2008).

Figure 1.9 Agenda Ideas

Reading-Related Material	Computer Activities	Art Project	Logical Thinking	Reenactment	Hands-on Learning	Listening and Viewing
• Take notes on the material. • Plot the information on a graphic organizer. • Create a fact sheet about the passage. • Identify vocabulary words and meanings. • Create a sequence board with the information. • Design a poster with the new information.	• Gather research on the Web. • Create a PowerPoint presentation. • Create a Word document about the topic. • Solve a crossword or other word puzzle. • Play an educational game. • Use a computer program related to the facts. • Design a graphic. • Use a word processor to add the facts in another genre.	• Create a collage or mobile. • Design a mural. • Make a diorama. • Develop a poster. • Sculpt a character. • Build a setting. • Illustrate the information or procedure. • Develop an editorial cartoon. • Draw the scene of the event. • Illustrate the meanings of a vocabulary word or concept.	• Write what you learned. • Develop a time line. • Write the step-by-step procedure. • Solve a puzzle or problem. • Answer questions on the topic. • Adapt the information for a practical experience.	• Create a simulation, example, or demonstration. • Write an interview for a story character. • Role-play a character or a scene. • Write a play about the reading. • Act out the meaning of vocabulary words or concepts.	• Use a manipulative. • Design an experiment. • Follow an assembly line. • Play a game. • Create an exhibit. • Work in a center. • Create a puppet show. • Build a replica. • Make cutouts of people and places to record facts.	• Listen to a tape, CD, or recording. • Study video clips. • Read with a partner. • Write and share with a partner. • Participate in a discussion of the text. • Create a literary circle for related reading. • View a reenactment.

Figure 1.10 Reading Stations and Centers

Reading Stations	Writing Stations	Manipulative Stations	Conversation Stations	Comprehension Stations
• Reference • Research • Book nook • Book reviews • Critic centers • Newspaper reviews	• Create a book • Writing response • Author's journal • Reflection • Pen pal postings • Composing • Mailbox • Poetry corner • Foldables • Character diaries	• Scrapbooking • Creative arts • Vocabulary sort • Item tubs • Puzzle place • Folder activities • Assembly line • Book making • Skill games • Stick picks	• Character debuts • Interviews • Learn a word • Vocab gab • Novel study • Listening • Reenactments • Simulations • Games • Stomp romp • Debate duo	• Brain teasers • Graphic organizer • Game show • Sports trivia • Computer lab • Observation log • Put it to a beat • Skills gala • Processing center

Figure 1.11 Color-Coded Folders/Activities

Green *Growing*	Curriculum rewinding	Filling in a gap indicated by a lack of background knowledge vital to learn the information.
Yellow *Ray of Sunshine*	Grade-level	Practicing on the targeted standard, concept, or skill.
Red *All Fired Up!*	Curriculum fast-forwarding	Challenging at a higher level of thinking, because has proven knowledge of the upcoming information.

Materials for Reading Response Stations

Use a Variety of Paper

Shape   Texture   Size   Color   Design

Use Different Types of Paper

Construction paper   Copy paper   Sentence strips   Poster board
Notebook paper   Stationery   Sticky notes   Adding machine tape
Index cards   Cardboard   Paper bags   Plastic bags
Envelopes   Onion skin   Transparencies   Notepad

Try These Other Tools for Writing

Dry-erase board   Chalkboard   Cloth   Foldables

Use Different Writing Implements

Size: Short   Long   Chunky   Thin
Type: Pencils   Pens   Chalk   Colored pencils
            Markers   Highlighters Crayons   Clipboards with paper

Technology Equipment for Stations
Equipment

MP3 player with earbuds	DVD player	Camera
Overhead projector	Desk computer	Laptop computer
Calculator	Document reader	CD player
Handheld game	Printer	Recorder
Camcorder	SMART Board	Scanner
Fax machine	Walkie-talkie	

Internet Sources and Software

MySpace.com	Class website	Web search	Blog
PowerPoint	Word processor	Weather bug	CAD program
Web quest	Chatroom	iComic	iTunes
Print Shop	Excel	Clipart	Kidspiration

Comfortable Additions

For seating: Carpet squares, rocking chair, area rug, chair, sofa, desk
For enjoyment: Lamps, stuffed animals, plants, bookmarks, bottled water, pillows

Topic-Related Resources

Text	Graphs	Directions	Graphics	Pictures
Journals	Time lines	Scrapbook	Logs	Portfolios
Word lists	References	Magazines	Brochures	Skill charts

Cubing

Cubing is a learning strategy that provides opportunities for students to use and share their thinking in relation to a reading standard, topic, character, event, setting, vocabulary word, or main idea. Each side of the cube is labeled with a direction using the information gained from reading the text or related materials. Cubes may be color coded to reflect diverse learning abilities. For example, an orange cube could display six intervention activities for struggling readers, while a blue cube could present six challenging activities for comprehending, fluent readers. Use cubing activities to add novelty to processing information.

Cubing activities build on strengths. If a student has difficulty understanding a skill or concept, incorporate the learner's talents, abilities, or strengths to learn the skill. For example, a student with musical abilities can learn the skill by using it in a song, rap, or poem. Cubing activities can also be designed to address weaknesses. Cubing activities can also be created to be fun, interesting, and stimulating. They are intriguing tools to teach standards, problem solving, and higher-order thinking skills (see Figure 1.12).

Figure 1.12 Cubing Activities	
Reading Cube	*Thinking Cube*
<ul><li>Explain the plot.</li><li>Give the character's attributes.</li><li>Draw the setting.</li><li>Create an event time line.</li><li>Place the facts on a graphic organizer.</li><li>Summarize the passage.</li></ul>	<ul><li>List.</li><li>Describe.</li><li>Argue.</li><li>Apply.</li><li>Conclude.</li><li>Evaluate.</li></ul>
Visual/Spatial Cube	*Bodily/Kinesthetic Cube*
<ul><li>Design a poster.</li><li>Create a graphic organizer.</li><li>Color code.</li><li>Make a collage.</li><li>Create a banner.</li><li>Design an ad.</li></ul>	<ul><li>Create a motion to teach a fact.</li><li>Role-play.</li><li>Demonstrate with objects.</li><li>Build a model.</li><li>Play charades.</li><li>Create cheers with actions.</li></ul>
Multiple Intelligences Cube	*After Reading Cube*
<ul><li>Illustrate.</li><li>Plot information.</li><li>Role-play.</li><li>Create a poem.</li><li>Take a stand.</li><li>Relate it to your world.</li></ul>	<ul><li>Write a summary.</li><li>Create a game.</li><li>Use a manipulative.</li><li>Create a poster.</li><li>Develop a song.</li><li>Reflect in a journal.</li></ul>

Various Ways to Identify the Cubing Task Number

- Number the list. Roll the dice to identify the item on the list to complete.
- Write each direction on a small strip of construction paper. Place the strips in a container and ask each student to draw one strip.
- Use a spinner numbered from 1 to 6.
- Have students in the group number off from 1 to 6.
- Have students write down a mystery number from 1 to 6. They reveal and share the selected numbers. If two or more students have the same number, they complete the same assignment independently. The responses will vary.

Suggestions for Designing a Cube

- Apply various levels of questioning as outlined on Bloom's taxonomy. Here are some examples:
  - Find the word that means_____. (Knowledge level)
  - How is this information valuable to our community? (Evaluation level)
- Incorporate learning styles in the reading activities. For example, an activity for the concrete learner could be "Design a model to demonstrate the _____."

On the Flip Side

This activity engages students in creating questions about a reading assignment for the class. Divide the class into three-member teams.

1. Give each team six pieces of paper for the question cards. Use a different shape for each team.

2. Assign a section of the text to each team.

3. Encourage the team to find a comfortable place to read and work.

4. Direct the team to create six important questions with their answers.

5. Write a question on one side of each card.

6. Write the answer on the other side of one of the other questions. Note: The answer must be written on the back of another question.

7. Mix the cards together and distribute them to the class.

8. Students take turns reading the question on the cards.

9. The student with the correct answer says, "Flip side."

10. The student reads the correct answer and the question on the flip side.

11. If the answer is incorrect, repeat the initial question until the correct answer is given.

Variation

Review with the flip side card game. Use the cards later in a center, station, or folder.

Choice

Include student choice in instruction and daily routines whenever doing so is appropriate and feasible. Choice becomes an incentive for learning and creates a sense of ownership. Students can show what they know by using their learning preferences. Give students opportunities to choose the following:

Seating	Genres	Study buddy
Reading materials	Facts to explore	Interest area
Presentation style	Research sources	Writing implements
Paper type	Study aids	Web resources
Reference materials	Job role or task	Being alone or with others

Use choice boards with the reading models to offer flexible learning strategies. For example, the teacher may ask the reader to select one or more activities from the board. Students usually appreciate opportunities to play a major role in task decisions.

Remember to design the board activities to teach or reinforce content information and meet readers' needs. Figure 1.13 shows an example of a choice board.

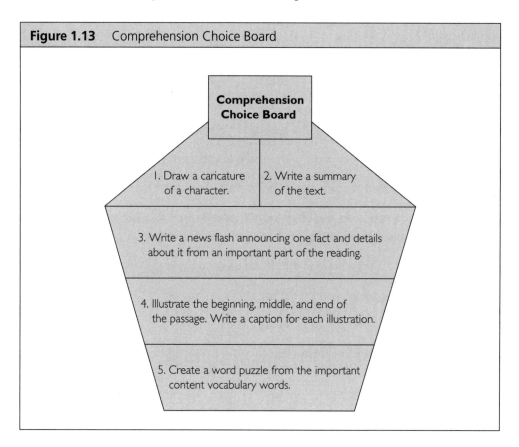

Figure 1.13   Comprehension Choice Board

Comprehension Choice Board

1. Draw a caricature of a character.

2. Write a summary of the text.

3. Write a news flash announcing one fact and details about it from an important part of the reading.

4. Illustrate the beginning, middle, and end of the passage. Write a caption for each illustration.

5. Create a word puzzle from the important content vocabulary words.

SUMMARY

The models of reading detailed in this chapter are instructional planning tools. After collecting assessment data, select the most appropriate model to coordinate the reader's needs with content standards and learning objectives. Adapt the model to customize activities for learners at all knowledge levels related to the standard.

Implement the differentiated instructional strategies to enhance the reading models. Interweave novel activities, such as agendas, cubing, and choice boards, in planning. Strategically select the model and strategies to differentiate instruction as you chart the course for each individual's reading journey.

Gradual Release to Accelerate Progress

Lois A. Lanning

Example is not the main thing in influencing others. It is the only thing.

—Albert Schweitzer (as cited in Anderson, 1975)

Think back to a complex, challenging learning experience that left you feeling proud and confident in your accomplishment. Was the experience connected to a sport? An academic class? A hobby? Think about the process you went through (the various stages of learning) and the levels of knowledge you needed to have in order to learn the complex task. Now think about how your performance improved with each phase of your learning. For example, let's think of someone learning to play golf. To play golf well, there are many components and layers of learning. A few are listed below to illustrate the point.

Factual knowledge—One needs to learn the goals, names, and use of different golf clubs, the basic rules, etiquette, and so on.

Conceptual knowledge—One needs an understanding of the key concepts that will determine how one plays the game such as the lay of the land (course), wind velocity, mental focus, motivation, and so on.

Strategies—One needs mental plans of what it takes to get the ball from here to there for various situations and conditions.

Skills—One needs an ability to adjust the golf swing and flight of the ball to effectively support the targeted strategy.

Obviously, learning golf is much more than swinging a club and hitting a ball. Like many other complex tasks, to become a good golfer, most people need quality instruction with specific feedback and many opportunities to practice on different types of golf courses. The progression from one stage of learning to the next is accelerated when closely guided by a teacher who understands the learner and the learning that needs to take place. The effective teacher is gradually releasing responsibility to the student to ensure sustainable progress and success.

How does this fit in with teaching struggling readers? Bigge and Shermis (1999) tell us that the critical question in regard to transfer (of learning) is what *conditions* engender the greatest amount of transfer. For example, teaching for transfer involves a lesson design that ensures students get explicit, focused instruction around a powerful teaching point that they will practice independently by the end of the lesson. There are several books on the market that explain how teachers in Grades 3–8 can structure and manage small group reading instruction in their classrooms. If intermediate grade teachers do make small group reading instruction a daily part of their work with struggling readers, too often the day to day teaching points are disconnected, do not follow a Gradual Release Lesson Design, and/or do not allow guided practice across a variety of types of text. As a result, many struggling readers never fully reach a deep understanding of how the comprehension process works.

Using a Gradual Release Lesson Design as a means to deliver focused comprehension instruction (around the Four Powerful Comprehension Strategies) can help deepen students' understanding and support the transfer of learning. Additionally, to help accelerate the learning of readers who lag behind, we need to provide practice with a variety of texts and appropriate scaffolding in a rich literacy community combined with a gradual release of responsibility from teacher to student.

GRADUAL RELEASE LESSON DESIGN

The teacher's role in instructing students is to maximize the likelihood that students will transfer their learning to new contexts independently. The five step *lesson procedure,* or Gradual Release Lesson Design, is patterned to scaffold the effective teaching of strategies in order to maximize transfer of students' learning. These steps are well researched (Duke & Pearson, 2002) and are used as a template for the small group reading lessons included at the end of each strategy chapter in this book. The steps are explained below.

1. **An explicit description of the strategy and how, when, where, and why to use it.** First, the teacher takes responsibility for succinctly and clearly explaining the strategy and skill that will be the teaching point of the lesson and linking it to the process of comprehension. The teacher is specifically focusing the students' attention on what they are going to do in the lesson. The teacher controls the discussion at this point but may invite students to participate by asking very explicit questions that further clarify the teaching point.

2. **Teacher and/or student modeling of the strategy in action.** The teacher is still in control at this step of the lesson. The particular teaching point of the lesson is demonstrated. The teacher makes his/her thinking public to reveal the strategic processing a good reader uses while comprehending text; "Watch how I do it."

   We don't want to assume a struggling reader will figure out what the teaching point of the lesson is about. Steps 1 and 2 may take 5 to 10 minutes of a 30-minute lesson. As subsequent lessons continue and student performance improves, these first steps are shortened to allow more time for student practice and engagement with text.

3. **Collaborative use of the strategy in action**. Students are now ready to begin putting the strategy into practice. The teacher is still leading the way but inviting students to try out the teaching point of the lesson; "You help me" or "Let's do this together."

   This small step precedes guided practice so the teacher can make sure students understand what is expected and can adjust any scaffolding that may be needed. We do not want struggling readers practicing strategies and skills incorrectly.

4. **Guided practice using the strategy with gradual release of responsibility.** Now students are ready to take over the work but still have the teacher close by with some assistance and feedback. The teacher closely observes student practice and, as needed, offers suggestions, nudging, and confirmation, but the teacher is increasingly pulling back and turning responsibility over to the students. This is a critical phase of the lesson. Decisions need to be made about how capable the students are to put the strategy into use independently. Before students are sent off to work without the teacher watching over them, they need to have enough guided practice to demonstrate their ability to be successful with the teaching point of the lesson.

   Ultimately, our goal is to help students realize what support they need to construct their own meaning of text. During this step, interaction is not limited to only one student and the teacher; rather, student to student discussion and support create a stronger sense of shared responsibility and deepens understanding.

5. **Independent use of the strategy.** Students are now ready to use the strategies and skills they have learned, often by themselves or with peers, because they have demonstrated a level of comfort and an ability to succeed independently. The type of task they are expected to perform needs to extend and reinforce the lesson. If students leave the small group only to go back to their seats and complete worksheets that are not authentic and well aligned with the lesson, the release of responsibility to the student is short-changed, the transfer of learning diminished, and the goal of accelerating progress weakened. Step 5 does not need to be a burden to lesson planning. Authentic reading and writing tasks (see Chapter 1) and peer discussion that encourage reflection on the comprehension process are highly effective activities.

The order of these steps reflects a gradual release of responsibility from teacher to students. The lesson procedures are conceptualized in Figure 2.1 below from Pearson and Gallagher's (1983) work on comprehension instruction.

Figure 2.1   Gradual Release of Responsibility Model

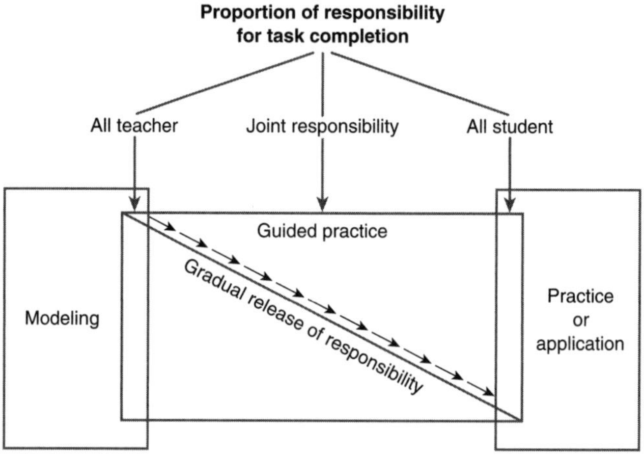

SOURCE: This figure was published in *Contemporary Educational Psychology*, Volume 8, Issue 3, P. David Pearson and Margaret C. Gallagher, "The Instruction of Reading Comprehension," Page 337, Academic Press (1983).

Using each of the five steps in every small group reading lesson is important for a few reasons: (1) The teacher is able to closely monitor students' progress in the lesson. If confusions arise, adjustments in instruction can occur quickly. (2) Students learn to know what to expect. Routines are especially important to students who are confused and lagging behind. Often the "locus of control" of struggling readers is outside of themselves, which means that rather than focusing their attention on their learning, they often spend more energy trying to figure out how to avoid looking foolish, guessing what the teacher expects from them, and what the "activity of the day" is now.

The mediated support of the Gradual Release Lesson Design offers struggling readers a chance to develop a deep understanding of the essential reading strategies that will help them make sense of text. High-road transfer of learning to other situations can be enhanced to a much greater degree for struggling readers through the bridging provided by using the five steps. "Bridging" means teaching so as to better meet the conditions for high-road transfer (Chapter 1). Rather than expecting students to achieve transfer spontaneously, the teacher "mediates the needed processes of abstraction and connection making" (Perkins & Salomon, 1988, p. 28). This involves teaching that gets students to make conscious abstractions and identify alternative applications of instructional material (James, 2006, p. 152).

Giving struggling students the opportunity to apply the lesson points across a variety of text genres that subtly increase in complexity of structure, length, vocabulary, concept load, and so on, is also important to building transfer and thus the acceleration of learning. For example, the teaching point of a lesson focusing on the strategy *creating meaningful connections* is the skill "text-to-text connections." During step 2 of her lesson (Modeling), see how the third grade teacher below helps students *bridge* the skill to a familiar text through her think-aloud:

> As I am reading this book *The Rough-Face Girl,* I am noticing that it has some things in common with the book *Cinderella.* I just learned both girls had mean sisters. Both Cinderella and the Rough-Face Girl had a hard life. They were very kindhearted people. . . . By thinking about these text-to-text connections, how the books are the same and how they are different, I now better understand both books.

In addition to the lesson procedures setting the conditions for transfer, instructional activities should be shaped so that they most closely "hug" the transfer desired. Hugging, which addresses low-road transfer, involves designing activities so they are similar to situations in which learners can apply what they have been taught (James, 2006, p. 152). For example, at the early stage of learning a new strategy, the lesson texts and activities should closely parallel (hug) the teaching point of the lesson making the skill and strategy very obvious to the struggling reader. The teaching point of the third grade lesson below is "determining and sequencing events and ideas," which is part of the strategy *summarizing.* The text closely "hugs" the teaching point by using transition words the students just discussed the previous day.

Teacher: We learned that authors often give us clue words to help us know that an event has changed. Do you remember some of the clue words we discussed?

Student: (looks at chart) First, second, next, last, finally.

Teacher: Exactly. As a warm-up, let's read this short paragraph and determine the sequence of events. Once we identify and sequence the events, we will be able to use this information to help us summarize our reading. "The New London City Zoo just received its first three animals. The first animal it received was a deer. The second animal it received was a monkey. The third animal it received was a lion. Children in New London are excited about the opening of the zoo!"

Using each of the steps of the Gradual Release Lesson Procedure balances explicit instruction with guided support to assist the transfer of learning. The steps of the lesson are used consistently yet flexibly so they follow the reader's responses thus preventing this design from being perceived as dogmatic. To accomplish this, the amount of time spent on each step is adjusted as more or less scaffolding is needed according to the reader's progress, familiarity with the text, and the learning situation.

The concept of scaffolding is grounded in the work of Lev Vygotsky (1978). Scaffolding refers to the structures that are put into place to enable a learner to carry out a task or solve a problem that is beyond his unassisted reach. If there is too much scaffolding, the opportunity to learn suffers and the inclination to defer the work to the teacher or more capable peer increases. If scaffolding is too weak, the learning becomes frustrating and exhausting as energy is overly spent on discrete parts of the task without understanding the goal.

There are six distinguishing features of scaffolding instruction (Meyer, 1993). As you read them, I think you will begin to see the rationale behind the five steps of the Gradual Release Lesson Design. Scaffolding features include

1. Teacher support that helps students relate new information to their prior knowledge

2. Transfer of responsibility from the teacher to the students

3. Dialogue that breaks from the traditional classroom discourse to more student-initiated talk

4. Nonevaluative collaboration that focuses on the student's potential for new learning rather than evaluating the student's current competencies

5. Appropriateness of the instructional level defined as what a student can do with assistance within his/her zone of proximal development

6. Coparticipation that creates opportunities for students to participate actively and cooperate in directing instruction

The process of the gradual release of responsibility from the teacher to the students (Pearson & Gallagher, 1983) is inherent in the features of scaffolding since the purpose of scaffolding instruction is to enable students to accomplish a task on their own, which initially they could not do without assistance. Mediating students' learning in this manner not only enhances their learning but also enables students to retain the learning longer and to be more flexible in transferring it to other situations (Kong, 2002).

Finally, to strengthen understanding, the Four Powerful Comprehension Strategies and skills taught through this Gradual Release Lesson Design need to be presented through multiple types of text and through "what if" problem solving. By carefully and deliberately teaching children to be mindful of their use of comprehension strategies across a broad variety of text examples, we can truly break the cycle of failure!

CONCLUSIONS AND REFLECTIONS

Teachers help students learn to comprehend well by

- explaining fully what the strategy and skill is that they are teaching and why, how, and when proficient readers use the strategy and skill while comprehending
- modeling their own thinking processes

- encouraging students to ask questions and discuss possible answers among themselves
- keeping students engaged in their reading via providing tasks that demand active involvement (RAND Reading Study Group, 2002)

Each of these actions is embedded in the lesson procedure outlined for comprehension strategy instruction. In addition, the steps of the lesson procedure support transfer theory, and when coupled with the appropriate teaching techniques, provide students—those who have difficulty comprehending—with the guidance they need to become independent, strategic readers. The lessons in this book are intended to follow a Gradual Release Lesson Design over time so that students deeply understand comprehension strategies and the transfer of learning is maximized. Recent research on how people learn shows that learning must occur with *understanding* if it is to be retained and transferred to new contexts (Bransford, Brown, & Cocking, 2000).

By honing down the list of reading strategies found in the literature and by identifying those strategies that require a reader to be mindful (to use conscious reasoning and planning while comprehending text), reading becomes a less daunting task for the reluctant, struggling reader. By identifying and teaching the "Big Four" Strategies and using them to organize and give purpose and relevance to the skills that support them, high-road transfer is promoted for the students who need it most.

Reflection Questions for the Reader

What are some of the ways your instruction currently supports the transfer of learning? How might you redesign your lessons for your struggling readers to ensure there is a gradual release of responsibility?

Which instructional activities closely "bridge" and/or "hug" the teaching points of your lesson?

How can you make sure that step 5 of the Gradual Release Lesson Design does not get dropped?

How can you encourage more student-to-student discourse in your small group lessons? How is increased student-to-student discourse an example of the gradual release of responsibility?

The next four chapters look at the instruction of each of the Four Powerful Comprehension Strategies: *summarizing, creating meaningful connections, self-regulating,* and *inferring.* Additional explanations are in the Glossary at the end of the book. Let's get started!

3

Implementing Multi-Tiered Writing Instruction

Sheila Alber-Morgan

Writing instruction has a long history of neglect in US education. This neglect is evident in the most recent report of the National Assessment of Educational Progress (NAEP), which reveals that only about 25 percent of fourth, eighth, and twelfth graders scored at the proficient level on the NAEP writing exam (Persky, Daane, & Jin, 2003). Proficient writing is necessary for successful functioning in school and community environments during childhood and throughout adulthood. Writing performance affects graduation, admission into postsecondary programs, employment options, and social opportunities (Graham & Perin, 2007). As students progress through school, they are met with increasing expectations to demonstrate their knowledge through writing. Additionally, the upsurge of computer technology in the twenty-first century has only increased the need to write (e-mail, Web-based instruction). Students who learn to write well have a powerful tool for communicating, studying, learning, creating, and increasing their quality of life. This chapter will present evidence-based practices for teaching written expression to diverse learners in inclusive classrooms using various instructional arrangements within a three-tiered response to intervention (RTI) model.

Considering the range of unique backgrounds that typify inclusive classrooms, writing instruction can provide exciting and enriching learning experiences for all students, including those who struggle. Struggling writers often have difficulty with transcription, organization, and self-regulation.

Their compositions are shorter, less focused, lacking in detail, and contain more irrelevant information and more mechanical errors (Graham & Harris, 2003; Santangelo & Quint, 2008). Struggling writers also have difficulty critically evaluating how well their writing corresponds to their intended purpose, audience, and genre (Santangelo & Quint, 2008).

In classrooms where students produce exceptional writing, teachers establish high expectations as they provide a supportive environment and frequent opportunities to produce many kinds of writing pieces (Graham, Olinghouse, & Harris, 2009). Excellent writing teachers actively involve students by implementing authentic and interesting writing activities, adapting instruction for diverse learning needs, and teaching students writing skills in whole-class, small-group, and individual teaching arrangements (Graham et al.).

EVIDENCE-BASED PRACTICES

Based on their meta-analysis of research in *Writing Next,* Graham and Perin (2007) identified the following elements as evidence-based practices for improving writing achievement: (a) teaching writing strategies for planning, revising, and editing; (b) teaching summary writing; (c) providing opportunities for collaborative writing with peers; (d) setting clear product goals; (e) using the computer to write; (f) teaching students to combine sentences; (g) teaching prewriting strategies; (h) teaching students to use inquiry skills; (i) teaching the writing process; (j) providing good writing models; and (k) writing for content learning. Additionally, teaching transcription skills (handwriting, keyboarding, and spelling) to beginning and struggling writers produces a positive effect on their writing quality (Graham et al., 2009). Throughout this chapter, the above evidence-based practices are presented within multitiered instruction in each of the following categories: handwriting, keyboarding, spelling, writing process, and using technology for writing.

HANDWRITING INSTRUCTION: TIER 1

Before children can express their ideas coherently in written form, they need to have adequate transcription skills. That is, they need to be able produce legible handwriting with correctly spelled words so their ideas can be deciphered by the reader. Teaching transcription skills can be considered Tier 1 instruction in most early elementary classrooms (K–3), with additional Tiers 2 and 3 supports for students who struggle. For older students, depending on the severity of their difficulties, basic handwriting and spelling instruction will often be needed for Tiers 2 and 3 instruction.

The use of computer technology has decreased the need for handwriting skills, but for most students, handwriting is an unavoidable and important functional skill. Handwriting requires proficient eye-hand coordination, fine motor control, and visual-kinesthetic memory. The progression of handwriting development begins with gross motor arm and wrist movements, and moves toward fine motor finger and thumb movements required for controlled handwriting. When facilitating the development of early handwriting competence, teachers should provide activities that promote fine motor skills, hand dominance, and hand strength. Examples of these activities include coloring, tracing, scribbling, drawing, cutting paper, molding clay, and doing finger plays (such as "Five Little Monkeys," "Where Is Thumbkin?").

During the elementary school years, children are expected to learn manuscript handwriting and then cursive handwriting. Some educators question the practice of teaching two different handwriting systems. Manuscript is more legible, easier to learn, less demanding of fine motor skills, and resembles print in books (Hagin, 1983). With cursive handwriting, students are less likely to reverse letters or produce spacing errors. Evidence generally supports teaching manuscript first and transitioning to cursive in second or third grade (Schlagel, 2007).

Manuscript writing instruction usually begins in kindergarten. Two common manuscript (and cursive) formats are Zaner-Bloser and D'Nealian. The Zaner-Bloser method is composed of basic strokes of circles and straight lines. The D'Nealian manuscript alphabet is designed to provide an easier transition from manuscript to cursive handwriting. It is composed of strokes that are oval and slanted with added tails or curves similar to cursive writing.

A multisensory approach is effective for teaching beginning handwriting. In this method, the teacher orally leads students through the formation of a letter, describing the strokes as the students write. Tracing letters, using color-cued lined paper, stencils, templates, and margin underlays can provide guidance for handwriting acquisition. Once students become more proficient, teachers should systematically fade out the verbal cues, colored midlines, and letter tracing guides. Cursive handwriting requires more precise and coordinated fine motor movements than manuscript handwriting. Similar to manuscript handwriting, a multisensory approach and fading model is effective.

When writing on paper, students should be seated comfortably with both forearms on the desk, grasping the pencil above the sharpened point with the writing hand and holding the top of the paper with the other hand. The paper should be parallel to the edge of the desk, not slanted. For cursive handwriting, the paper should be tilted at an angle with the top of the page pointing away from the writing hand. Teachers may want to place masking tape on the desk as a guide to the student for correct paper positioning. The following are recommendations for teaching handwriting (Graham, Harris, & Fink, 2000):

- Model the letter by writing it on the board and describing how the letter is formed (for instance, lower case *l*: "Start at the top line, pull down straight"; lower case *b*: "Start at the top line, pull down straight, push up, circle forward"). Point out the similarities and differences of the letter to other letters ("The letter *l* and the letter *b* both start off the same way.").
- Sequence guided practice by having the students trace the letter first, copy the letter from a close model (on the page), copy the letter from a distant model (the board), and then write the letter from memory.

As the students practice, they should also verbalize the steps. Written models should also include numbered arrows to show the sequence for forming the letter.

- Manuscript letters should be introduced in order of easiest to most difficult, progressing from letters with straight lines (for example l, i, t) to letters that include circles and curves (such as c, a, b). For cursive handwriting, Hanover (1983) recommends the following teaching sequence for lower-case letters: "e" family (e, l, h, f, b, k); "i" family (i, t, u); "c" family (c, a, d, o, q, g), handle family (b, o, v, w), hump family (n, m, v, y, x), tails tied in back (f, q), tails tied in front (j, g, p, y, z), and "r" and "s."
- As students are learning to write individual letters, they should progress fairly quickly to writing words, phrases, and sentences.

Effective handwriting programs provide explicit instruction, daily practice in short sessions, and application of skills to meaningful writing tasks (Schlagel, 2007). Immediate and specific feedback and praise are critical for effective writing instruction. In order to facilitate self-regulation and independence, students can practice self-evaluating the quality of their handwriting (Vaughn, Bos, & Schumm, 2006). For example, students can examine a row of letters, draw a circle around their best letters, and rewrite their less legible letters.

HANDWRITING INSTRUCTION: TIERS 2 AND 3

Handwriting difficulties are easy for teachers to identify because poor or illegible handwriting is readily apparent upon visual inspection. Teachers must examine and provide feedback on several aspects of handwriting, including position of the hand and paper, letter size, proportion of letters to each other, quality of the pencil lines, regularity and slant of the letters, letter formation and alignment, letter and word spacing, connection of cursive letters, and speed of production.

For students struggling with handwriting, the cover-copy-compare method can help them practice letter formation and self-evaluation. The student looks at a model of a letter or word, covers it with an index card, writes the letter or word from memory, uncovers the model, and compares his or her word to the model. Then the student rewrites any letters that were formed incorrectly. Self-verbalized instructions have been demonstrated to be effective for correct letter formation (Graham, 1983). The teacher models writing the letter while verbalizing instructions ("letter 'g': start at the middle line; go around; retrace down; and go half a line below the bottom line, hook to the left"), the student practices verbalizing and writing in unison with the teacher, and, finally, the student verbalizes and writes the letter independently. To increase handwriting fluency, students can practice timed repeated writing of the same brief passage, attempting to beat their previous score (Reis, 1989). Zaner-Bloser scales for letters per minute (lpm) proficiency are as follows: first grade—25 *lpm;* second grade—30 *lpm;* third grade—38 *lpm;* fourth grade—45 *lpm;* fifth grade—60 *lpm,* and sixth grade—67 *lpm.*

Students can also work with self-correcting materials such as chemical inks and templates. With chemical inks, the student uses a special pen and treated paper to practice handwriting. The ink color changes when students write outside the letter zone. Additionally, students can self-assess by comparing their letters to a template. At the secondary level, teachers can make handwriting instruction more functional for students by allowing them to write notes or letters to friends, write directions to places of interest, write the names and addresses of friends, write captions for photographs, complete a job application, or write a check.

Examples of writing programs for young children and students who struggle with handwriting include *First Strokes, Pencil Pete's Handwriting, Letterland*, and *Handwriting Without Tears*. These programs include motivating graphics and multisensory activities for improving handwriting. For example, *Handwriting Without Tears* uses multisensory play activities and materials such as Wood Pieces, Roll-A-Dough Letters, Stamp and See Screen, music CDs, and a slate chalkboard. Activities include letter stories, imaginary writing, and mystery letter games.

KEYBOARDING INSTRUCTION

Teaching keyboarding skills is a viable alternative for students who struggle with handwriting. When compared to handwriting, producing written expression at the computer is easier, faster, and more legible. Whether or not they struggle with handwriting, all students need to learn keyboarding skills in order to fully participate in our current computer age.

Keyboarding instruction usually begins at third or fourth grade. To teach keyboarding skills, model and provide feedback for correct positioning. Students should sit up straight, feet flat on the floor, fingers curved and aligned with home keys, and eyes looking straight ahead at the monitor. Keyboarding requires memorization of the letter keys and frequent practice. Ways to practice memorizing the keyboard include having students write the corresponding letters on the back of their fingers or make cut-out hand prints with the letters printed on them. Students can practice examining a keyboard and labeling the keys correctly on a work sheet. Frequent practice is the best way to help students become proficient with keyboarding Teachers can make a series of index cards with directions for different typing tasks. Pairs of students can take turns drawing index cards and performing the skill. For example, "type your name as many times as you can in a minute, blindfolded," or "type the words to your favorite song," or "type the following passage in less than three minutes: (select a brief passage from a favorite book or poem)."

There are several motivating computer programs that teach typing using video games with colorful graphics, animation, sound effects, and music. As students become more proficient, they advance to more difficult levels with different, more challenging games. An example of this kind of keyboarding program is *Jumpstart Typing*. This program simulates a series of games (such as skateboarding, snowboarding, mountain climbing) between two teams. Accurate and fast typing helps students progress through athletic events and avoid obstacles. Similarly motivating programs designed to teach typing include *Mario Teaches Typing 2, Mavis Beacon Teaches Typing for Kids, SpongeBob Squarepants Typing, Typing Tutor 7*, and *Kid Keys*.

SPELLING INSTRUCTION: TIER 1

Spelling is an essential skill for producing written expression. When children are proficient spellers, "they are more likely to focus ... on clarity, logic, and the substance of their writing, not on the orthography of spelling" (Okyere, Heron, & Goddard, 1997, p. 52). Conversely, children who have spelling difficulties may experience frustration and resistance toward writing activities.

Traditional spelling instruction uses a linguistic approach in which words in basal spelling programs are sequenced and grouped according to phonological and morphological aspects of written language production. Words within each list proceed through a series of lessons focusing on sound symbol relationships, word patterns, rhyming patterns, vowel-change patterns, syllabication, dictionary skills, synonyms, and word usage (Heron, Okyere, & Miller, 1991). In a traditional spelling program, students are given a list of 10 to 20 words on Monday, a series of practice activities using the spelling words each day, and a spelling-dictation test on Friday. Weekly activities in basal spelling programs may include completing alphabetization and syllabication exercises, finding words in the dictionary, writing sentences using the spelling words, and completing word finds or crossword puzzles. One problem with basal spelling programs is they may not provide sufficient practice for some students. For this reason, teachers using basal spelling programs should provide frequent and varied opportunities to increase active student responding (ASR). Choral responding, response cards, peer tutoring, and self-correction are evidence-based practices that should be included in Tier 1 spelling instruction.

Choral responding. Teachers can use direct instruction (model, lead, test) with choral responding to teach spelling words during brief daily practice. For example, the teacher says, "My turn—spell *envelope*, e-n-v-e-l-o-p-e, *envelope*. Together—*spell envelope* . . . Your turn—spell *envelope* . . . ." The students chorally spell the word with the teacher and then without the teacher.

Response cards. Choral responding can be combined with response cards for spelling practice. Students can write their spelling words on dry-erase boards upon teacher prompting ("Spell *watch*.") and hold their cards up for feedback when the teacher signals ("Cards up!"). Students should be encouraged to look at each other's cards and help each other. Alternately, students can be provided with preprinted response cards with "yes" and "no" printed on opposite sides of each card. The teacher can show students different words and ask them to hold up their response cards to indicate whether or not a word is spelled correctly.

Peer tutoring. Students can work in pairs and take turns prompting each other to spell words and providing immediate feedback. In this arrangement, students can practice with individualized sets of words to match their skill levels. For each word spelled correctly, the student can earn two points. If a word is spelled incorrectly, the student writes it correctly three times and earns one point (Greenwood et al., 2001). While monitoring peer tutoring, teachers can also award points for following the procedures correctly, staying on task, and providing appropriate feedback and praise.

Self-correction. With self-correction, students learn to spell by comparing their misspelled words to a model and writing the word correctly. Self-correction has been identified as the most critical element contributing to spelling achievement (Okyere et al., 1997). Teachers can dictate a list of words to students and then provide them with an answer key for self-checking. Students draw a star next to each correctly spelled word and rewrite any misspelled words correctly. Self-correction can also be individualized for struggling spellers. The teacher can audiotape individual word lists with prompts to self-correct. Students can wear headphones and work individually to practice spelling and self-correcting each word.

When making decisions about which words to teach, teachers should select words with similar spelling patterns and words most frequently used in students' writing. Graham, Harris, and Loynachan (1993) created the *Basic Spelling Vocabulary List*, composed of 850 words categorized by grade level. These words make up 80 percent of words first through fifth graders use in their written expression. This spelling list is available for free on the Reading Rockets website at the following link: http://www .readingrockets.org/article/22366.

SPELLING INSTRUCTION: TIERS 2 AND 3

Errors in spelling tend to have regular patterns that can be related to difficulties with auditory discrimination or visual memory. Students with auditory discrimination problems may use incorrect consonant substitutions and confuse vowels because they cannot distinguish subtle differences between sounds. Possible indicators of visual memory problems may include reversing letters in words (the-hte), reversing entire words (man-nam), and spelling nonphonetic words phonetically (was-wuz). Students may also have difficulty remembering spelling patterns and applying spelling rules.

Students with auditory discrimination problems can benefit from additional phonemic awareness instruction. For example, they can practice segmenting words into sounds, and forming words by adding, taking away, or substituting sounds ("This word is *wide*, what's the word if we replaced the /w/ sound with /s/?"). Students receiving instruction in Tiers 2 and 3 will benefit from a personalized word list and self-selected goals for the number of words learned per week. When providing individualized instruction, use multisensory techniques (such as saying each letter, tracing each letter, manipulating letter tiles), emphasize spelling patterns (generating and sorting words by pattern), and limit the number of words taught each week. The following are recommended methods for students with spelling difficulties: Copy-Cover-Compare, Phonovisual Method, Simultaneous Oral Spelling Method, and the Horn Method.

Copy-cover-compare (Graham & Miller, 1979). This procedure requires students to examine a word as the teacher reads it, copy the word twice while looking at it, cover the word and write it from memory, check the spelling by comparing it to the model, and make corrections if necessary.

Phonovisual Method (Schoolfield & Timberlake, 1960). This is a phonetically-based approach emphasizing an association between a familiar visual image and the auditory letter sound (a picture of a dog presented when introducing the letter *d*). Consonants and vowels are introduced in this spelling method by association with word pictures that cue the visual image of the letter sound.

Simultaneous Oral Spelling Method (Gillingham & Stillman, 1970). This method uses a multisensory approach to teach correspondence between letters and sounds. The teacher systematically makes selections based on words the student has mastered and words the student needs to learn. The simultaneous oral spelling method emphasizes sound blending, repetition, and drill. The teacher says a word and the student repeats the word. Then the student says the sounds in the word and names the letters that represent each sound. Finally, the student writes the word while naming each letter.

Horn Method (Horn, 1954). This method requires the student to proceed through a sequence of steps: pronounce the word, look at each part of the word and repeat the pronunciation, spell the word orally, visualize the word and respell it orally, write the word, and check the word for accuracy. If there are any errors made during any part of the sequence, the entire process is repeated. This method relies on visual memorization and recall.

WRITING PROCESS INSTRUCTION: TIER 1

As students work on increasing their handwriting, keyboarding, and spelling proficiency, they should be provided with opportunities to apply those essential skills to authentic writing tasks, beginning with writing words, then sentences, then paragraphs. As students get older, they will benefit most from instruction that allows them to produce varied and extended writing pieces. Producing longer writing pieces, such as narrative stories or informative essays, requires students to learn the writing process. The writing process consists of the following stages: planning, drafting, revising, editing, and publishing (Graves, 1994). In the planning stage students generate and organize their ideas. They translate their planning notes into sentences and paragraphs in the drafting stage. When revising, students make improvements to the content and flow of the writing piece not yet focusing on mechanical errors. During the editing stage, students identify and correct mechanical errors (spelling, punctuation). In the publishing stage, students focus on producing a final polished product and seeing its effects on real audiences (Alber-Morgan, Hessler, & Konrad, 2007).

Writer's workshop (Atwell, 1987). A popular Tier 1 approach for teaching the writing process, writer's workshop is ideal for inclusive classrooms because it encourages independence and critical thinking while providing a positive and supportive environment for developing writers of all ability levels. Common features of *writer's workshop* include mini-lessons (brief, explicit instruction of specific writing elements), sustained time to work on various writing tasks that are personally meaningful, frequent opportunities for collaborating and sharing with peers, and individual conferencing for guidance, performance feedback, and goal setting (Troia, Lin, Monroe,

& Cohen, 2009). During daily blocks of time devoted to writing, teachers can provide direct instruction of mechanical elements, text structures, and writing strategies to the whole class. Then students can immediately apply those skills to their own written expression. Each student should have a folder with a collection of "in progress" writing pieces at various stages of completion. After teacher-led instruction, students can work independently, with a peer, in a collaborative group, or with an adult on writing pieces of their own choosing. The following are activities for teaching the writing process and building writing skills.

Planning and Organization

During this stage, students identify topics of personal interest, generate and organize their ideas about the topic, and identify their audience and purpose. Teachers can use thought-provoking pictures, videos, literature, and discussion to help students make connections to their own background knowledge and generate writing ideas. The following activities can stimulate interest and motivate students to produce personally meaningful writing.

Pictures. Show students an interesting picture (photograph, painting, video) and lead a discussion about how the picture makes the students feel. Ask students to think and talk about how the picture reminds them of a personal experience. Have students participate in generating a list of vocabulary words related to the picture that they can use in their stories. Prompt students to make up sentences about the picture, encouraging vivid descriptions based on what they see. The sentences can be used to write a class story. After this exercise, students can come up with their own stories about the picture or select a different picture for their writing piece.

Story starters. Story starters are phrases or sentences intended to stimulate written expression. Story starters likely to produce more written expression are those that relate to the students' background knowledge and interests. For example, many students who live in coastal South Carolina probably have been to the beach, so the story starter, "One day at the beach . . ." is probably appropriate. If your students have never been to the beach, it will be difficult for them to write about it. If students are uninterested in the story starter, they should be provided with additional choices. Teachers can help students link their background knowledge to the story starter by engaging them in a discussion of their experiences related to the topic.

Visual imagery. Guiding students to think about descriptive details can be accomplished by using visual imagery. Have students close their eyes and imagine a situation they have likely encountered (such as waiting at the bus stop on a snowy day, flying a kite on a windy day, walking in the woods in autumn, going to the fair on a sweltering August day). Guide students to think about what they see, hear, smell, feel, and taste. When they open their eyes, guide them in generating descriptive sentences about their visual imagery. "The First House Memory" (Marchisan & Alber, 2001) is an example of an exercise designed to stimulate background knowledge. The teacher asks the students to close their eyes and think of a room in a house where something memorable happened. While the students' eyes are closed, the teacher verbally guides the students to think about what the room looks like, the sounds and smells in the room, and the people in the room (what they're saying, wearing, doing). After the students open their eyes, they can discuss their memories of the event, make up sentences, draw a picture of the memorable event, write planning notes, and write a story.

Literature. Literature can stimulate writing ideas and provide students with good models for various writing types, styles, and purposes (Mason & Graham, 2008). When introducing students to a different writing genre, teachers should point out the critical elements, provide guided practice for identifying those elements in other writing pieces, and have students apply those elements to their own work. For example, teachers can provide examples of how expository writing pieces are structured. The first paragraph contains an attention grabber, a rationale for the importance of the topic, and the main ideas of the essay. Each subsequent paragraph contains a main idea and supporting details that relate back to the theme of the paper. The concluding paragraph summarizes the main ideas. After having students read and/or listen to each of several expository writing pieces, teachers can explicitly point out the common structure of each piece and prompt students to imitate that structure in their own writing.

For narrative fiction, teachers can read various stories and have students identify the following critical elements: characters, setting, problem, actions, emotions, climax, and resolution. When students plan their own stories, they can be guided to think about and include each story element. Literature can also be used to inspire writing ideas. For example, after reading portions of *Tales of a Fourth Grade Nothing* (Blume, 1972), lead students to think about how their experiences with their siblings are similar to the children in the book. Students can also engage in the following writing activities in response to literature:

- Write an alternate ending to a narrative fiction story.
- Write a character analysis of the character you like or dislike the most.
- Write about a personal experience similar to that of the main character.
- Write about how two fiction stories are similar and different.
- Write an opinion piece about the meaning or message of a story.
- Write a different story using the same characters.
- Introduce students to reading passages that evoke different emotions, discuss how the authors used words to convey certain feelings, and have students practice writing paragraphs using similar techniques.

Brainstorming. After students have decided on a personally meaningful topic, the next step is to brainstorm their ideas. Explain to students that brainstorming is writing down as many things as you can about a topic, without judgment, to generate good ideas. Teachers can model brainstorming by selecting a topic (such as "Why dogs are good pets") and having students generate a list of ideas about the topic (always happy to see you, loyal, good companion, can do tricks, makes me laugh, fun to play Frisbee with, brings in the newspaper, protects the house, and so on). After the teacher and students generate a list, the teacher models and guides students in selecting the most important items, crossing out the items that do not belong, and organizing the sequence of how the information will be presented from most important to least important. After the teacher models brainstorming and organization, students can work in pairs or in small groups to practice brainstorming and organizing self-selected topics.

Graphic organizers. Students can use graphic organizers to structure their brainstorming ideas into specific categories and sequences. These tools provide a visual representation of how concepts relate to each other and are a guide for drafting the writing piece. Students can use graphic organizers as planning guides for their own narrative (Figure 3.4) or expository (Figure 3.5) writing pieces. The following are examples of other graphic organizers that can be used to plan and organize different kinds of writing: Figure 3.1 (compare/contrast), Figure 3.2 (opinion piece), and Figure 3.3 (descriptive writing).

Figure 3.1	Example of Compare/Contrast Graphic Organizer (Venn diagram)

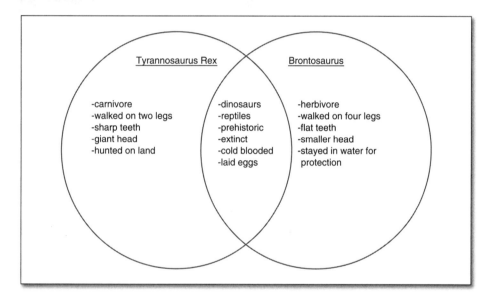

Figure 3.2	Example of Graphic Organizer for an Opinion Paper

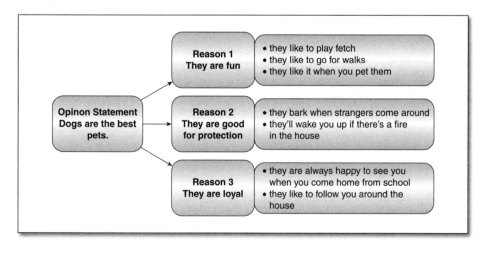

Figure 3.3   Graphic Organizer for Descriptive Writing

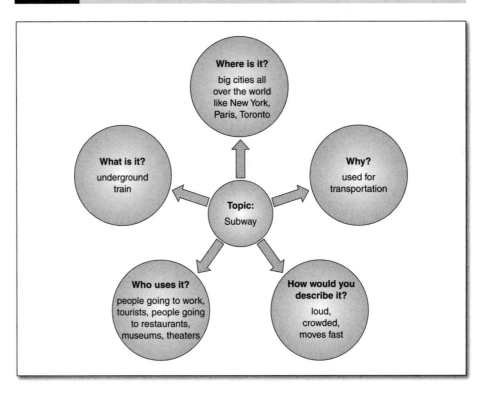

Collaborative planning. Students can work together in pairs or in small groups to select meaningful topics, brainstorm ideas, complete graphic organizers, and coauthor writing pieces. The following are two examples of how students can participate in collaborative planning for different kinds of writing. For opinion papers, Wong, Butler, Ficzere, and Kuperis (1996) had students work in pairs, each student taking a different side of an issue (for example, dress codes). Students wrote down their supporting arguments on planning sheets and discussed their arguments with their partners. During the discussion, the students asked for further explanation, clarification, and elaboration of their viewpoints. Wong, Butler, Ficzere, and Kuperis (1997) used a similar procedure to guide students in writing compare-contrast essays. Students worked in pairs to select a topic (such as concerts) and two categories of the topic to compare and contrast (like rock concerts versus school concerts). Students then brainstormed features of the topic they would discuss (goal, content, dress, demeanor). For each feature selected, the students listed details and indicated whether each detail was a similarity or difference.

Drafting

During the drafting stage of the writing process, students translate their planning notes into sequential sentences and paragraphs. Students should not worry about mechanical errors on early drafts because that may interfere with flow of ideas and writing production. Be clear that the content is the most important part of the writing piece, and that students will go back and fix all of the mistakes later. In order to teach students drafting skills, teachers should model and provide guided practice before having students work independently.

Teachers should use chart paper or an overhead projector to model translating planning notes into text. Figure 3.1 shows an example of a completed graphic organizer for a compare-contrast piece about two different dinosaurs. The teacher can use a graphic organizer like this and guide students through forming sentences. For example, "Look at the Venn diagram we made showing how the T-Rex and the Brontosaurus are alike and how they are different. Let's think of a first sentence that introduces the reader to what you are going to talk about." The teacher calls on a student who says, "The Tyrannosaurus Rex and Brontosaurus were dinosaurs that had many similarities and differences." The teacher provides feedback, writes the sentence on the chart paper, and continues guiding the students to generate additional sentences by referring to the graphic organizer ("T-Rex and Brontosaurus were both big, hungry reptiles, but T-Rex was a carnivore and Brontosaurus was an herbivore."). After this exercise, students can practice drafting sentences using their own graphic organizers. They can work individually, with a peer, or in a cooperative learning group. Just as students can engage in collaborative planning and organization, they can also participate in collaborative drafting. Pairs of students can sit together at a computer and take turns creating sentences from their planning notes. Collaborative writing has been demonstrated to improve the quality and production of written expression, especially for low-achieving students (MacArthur, 2009).

An important concern during the drafting stage is writing fluency. If students are fluent writers, they will have an easier time drafting their writing pieces. In order to increase fluency in general, students should be engaged in frequent writing activities throughout the day and across the curriculum. For example, students can write brief reactions to reading passages, summaries for different content-area reading passages, story problems for math, critiques of stories or movies, test questions for science and social studies units, directions for solving a problem or playing a game, captions for pictures, or a dialogue between two historical figures. Additionally, students can write brief daily journal entries on self-selected or teacher-selected topics. Another way to increase writing fluency is having students participate in repeated writings. This is similar to repeated readings. Students rewrite the same passage two or three times during one- to three-minute timed trials. With each successive timed trial, students attempt to increase the number of words written per minute.

A useful tool for increasing fluency during the drafting stage is the use of word banks. Teachers and students can develop various word banks to support drafting. Word banks can be individualized lists based on students' writing needs and attached to individual writing folders. Teachers can also have the whole class generate word banks on the board for specific writing activities ("Before you write your Halloween stories, let's write some Halloween words on the board.") The following are examples of word lists that may be helpful to students during drafting: adjectives and adverbs, action verbs, transition words and phrases, frequently misspelled words, and self-selected words.

Revising/Editing

During the revising stage, students critically examine their writing for clarity, completeness, and sequential flow. After the revising stage, students begin the editing stage, in which they focus on correcting mechanical errors (such as spelling or punctuation). Students need to understand that revising and editing are an integral part of the writing process and necessary for producing high-quality work. Error-monitoring checklists, peer editing, and mini-lessons are Tier 1 approaches to teaching revising and editing.

Error-monitoring checklists. Because revising and editing can be overwhelming for students, they should only focus on a few skills at a time. Students can keep individualized editing and revising checklists in their folders and use them as a guide to correct their errors. For example, a lower-performing student may have the following items on his or her checklist: (a) I wrote my name on my paper, (b) I indented the first sentence, and (c) I started each sentence with a capital letter. Additional items can be gradually added to individualized checklists as the student attains mastery of easier editing skills. For example, (a) I capitalized proper nouns, (b) I put the correct punctuation at the end of each sentence, (c) I used correct subject/verb agreement, and (d) I used correct spelling.

Peer editing. Peer editing is a particularly effective strategy for improving writing proficiency as well as motivation. Students can work together in pairs to read or listen to each other's stories, say what they liked about the writing piece, ask questions for clarification, provide suggestions, and edit for mechanical errors. Figure 3.4 shows an example of a peer revising form. Students can respond to the prompts on the form in order to provide each other with feedback. Prior to implementing a peer-editing arrangement, teachers should model, role-play, and provide practice of rules for giving and receiving feedback. For example, students should practice listening carefully, communicating in a positive way, and accepting feedback politely.

Mini-lessons. A key component of writer's workshop is using mini-lessons to teach editing skills. During mini-lessons, teachers provide direct instruction of writing elements based on an analysis of student writing errors. For example, after examining writing samples, the teacher realizes that most of the students need to learn how to punctuate direct quotes. She uses sentences from student work samples, writes them on the board, then models and demonstrates how to correct them. Students can practice several examples of the skill by writing on their response boards. Mini-lessons can be used to teach students a range of editing and revising skills. Teachers can also provide students with additional daily opportunities to practice editing and revising by writing a different sentence on the board with multiple mechanical errors. Have the students rewrite the sentence with the errors corrected, and then go over each correction. As students become more proficient with editing, more challenging errors can be gradually added to the daily sentence.

Sentence revision. Teachers can use the following practice activities to help students with sentence revision. Read several examples of interesting sentences from children's literature to the students. For example,

Figure 3.4   Example of Peer-Revising Form

Author Directions	Peer Editor Directions
Title _____	Title _____
Author _____	Author _____
Peer Editor _____	Peer Editor _____
Directions to Author: 1. Read your story aloud to your peer while he or she follows along. 2. Listen attentively to your peer's feedback. 3. Politely accept feedback and ask questions to make sure you understand. 4. Write down the suggestions you might want to use on your revision. 5. Say thank you.	Directions to Peer Editor: 1. Listen carefully and follow along while the author reads. 2. Think about what you like about the story and what might improve the story. 3. Tell your peer at least two things you liked about the story. 4. Tell your peer one thing that might improve the story. 5. Say thank you.
Author's notes:	Editor's Notes:
Possible revisions to make: _____ _____ _____ _____ _____ _____ _____ _____	What I liked: _____ _____ _____ _____ One suggestion: _____ _____ _____ _____

"Mr. Seahorse drifted gently through the sea, he passed right by a group of trumpet fish hidden in a patch of reeds" (Carle, 2004, pp. 4–5). Then guide the students to identify what makes each sentence interesting (vivid description, action verbs, rhythm, or sentence structure). Next, present a brief and uninteresting sentence ("The girl left the park."). Discuss with students that the sentence is boring because there is not enough description, then model ways to make the sentence more interesting by using adjectives, action verbs, and elaborating on details ("The nervous girl hurried away from the desolate and smelly park downtown."). Students can practice elaborating on sentences by writing on their response cards and sharing their revised sentences with the class.

Students can also practice elaborating sentences in the context of a story. Take a series of sequential uninteresting story sentences (for example: 1. I have a dog; 2. He has fleas; 3. My brother gave the dog a bath; 4. The dog tried to get away, and so on.), and read them to the class. Lead a discussion about how the story could be much more interesting. Then provide each student or pair of students with a different sentence to revise. When the students are finished, prompt them to read their sentences when you say their numbers (*Number 1:* "I have a big friendly dog who likes to roll in the mud." *Number 2:* "His itchy flea bites made him so miserable."). Discuss how the new revised story is different from the first story.

Publishing

The culminating product of the writing process is publication—sharing the writing piece with others. During this stage, students focus on polishing their work and taking pride in being an author. Publishing is an effective and motivating way to give writing an authentic purpose, and results in improvement in the quality of narrative and informative writing (MacArthur, Graham, Schwartz, & Schafer, 1995). Posting stories on bulletin boards is one popular and simple way to publish student work. Teachers can also publish student writing in classroom newspapers, newsletters, or websites. "Author's chair" is another form of publication in which students read their stories aloud to the class. Students can also create their own books—hard copy or electronic.

WRITING PROCESS INSTRUCTION: TIERS 2 AND 3

Many of the writing activities mentioned before can also be used for more intensive supplemental instruction with small groups or individuals needing extra support with planning, drafting, revising, and editing. For example, after the teacher delivers a whole-class mini-lesson of a specific skill (like using commas), she can provide additional instruction and guided practice to a small group of students who need extra help. The teacher can also provide individual assistance by conferencing and cowriting with students. During individual conferences, the teacher listens and offers support, encouragement, and constructive criticism. Conferencing should be used to foster development of ideas, planning, writing, revising, and editing (Mason & Graham, 2008). Through questioning, teachers can help students gain more insight into using the writing process to accomplish specific goals.

Cowriting can be used to support initial writing attempts and ongoing writing development. Assistance is gradually faded as the student becomes more independent, and this is called scaffolding. With cowriting, the teacher and student sit side by side at the computer. The teacher may start by typing sentences the student says, then having the student type some sentences when he or she is ready. The teacher and student can collaborate on the story, with the teacher typing the beginning and middle parts and the student typing the ending. Gradually, the student takes over writing whole stories, with reduced dependence on the teacher for support and guidance. The cowriting strategy can also be used to help students revise and edit their work. The teacher can provide guidance for determining if sentences make sense, elaborating on important details, and monitoring for mechanical errors.

For students struggling with written expression, commercial direct instruction (DI) writing programs are available (such as *Expressive Writing, Language for Learning*). DI writing programs use the same model, lead, and test sequence used in DI reading programs. For example, *Expressive Writing* (Engelmann & Silbert, 1983) provides sequenced instruction with frequent practice and review in sentence writing, paragraph writing, revising, and editing. Students build prerequisite writing skills before applying them to new tasks. Critical features of the program are systematic presentation, frequent practice, and frequent review of grammar, usage, and punctuation.

Summarizing strategy. Practice with summary writing is an evidence-based practice for increasing both reading comprehension and writing skills (Graham & Perin, 2007). The *GIST strategy* (Rhoder, 2002) is a good activity for teaching students to summarize. Students read an article and answer *who, what, when, where, why* and *how* questions. Students then compact the information down to 20 words. Teachers should encourage students to make several revisions and carefully select the most accurate 20 words for the 20-word summary.

Another activity for helping students summarize is having them create a story board (DiSpirt, 2008). Have students fold a piece of paper in half the long way and then into thirds so there are six squares. Each square represents part of a reading passage. Have students number each square from one to six. After reading a passage, have the students write a sentence in the first square that tells the beginning. Then fill in the last square to tell the ending. Students can work together or independently to figure out what goes in the squares in between. After the graphic organizer is complete, students can use it to write their summaries, and then share their summaries with small or large groups.

Writing Strategies

Explicit instruction of writing strategies enables students to self-regulate their writing to accomplish specific goals (Baker, Gersten, & Graham, 2003). Strategy instruction is comprised of implementing self-regulating procedures required to independently complete a task. A mnemonic device is usually used to prompt the student through each step of the writing task. For example, DEFENDS (Ellis & Friend, 1991) is a mnemonic strategy for writing an opinion paper. The steps are as follows: **D**ecide on your exact position, **E**xamine the reasons for your position, **F**orm a list of points that explain each reason, **E**xpose your position in the first sentence, **N**ote each reason for supporting points, **D**rive home the position in the last sentence, **S**earch for errors and correct.

Teachers can use Self-Regulated Strategy Development (SRSD; Graham & Harris, 2005) to teach students to use specific writing strategies (like DEFENDS). Decades of research on SRSD has demonstrated substantial gains for struggling writers in both elementary and secondary classrooms, including students with learning disabilities, students with intellectual disabilities, and English language learners (Graves & Rueda, 2009). Graham and Harris (2005) describe the following steps for implementing SRSD:

1. *Develop and activate background knowledge.* Students read examples of the genre they will be writing and teachers make sure students have the prerequisite skills to learn the strategy (such as knowledge of specific story elements).

2. *Discuss the strategy.* The teacher describes the strategy and its benefits, discusses how and when it should be used, and obtains the student's commitment to learn the strategy.

3. *Model the strategy.* The teacher models and describes each step of the strategy by using a "think aloud" procedure.

4. *Memorize the strategy.* The student memorizes the strategy steps and self-instructions using a cue card as an aid.

5. *Support the strategy.* The teacher and student collaboratively use the strategy to produce or edit a composition. Initially, the teacher provides more support, prompts, and guidance. As the student becomes more proficient with using the strategy, the teacher gradually withdraws support until the student can use the strategy independently.

6. *Independent performance.* The student performs the strategy independently with teacher support as needed. Programming for maintenance and generalization also occurs during this step.

There are many self-regulation strategies that can help students produce writing for different purposes. Selection of a learning strategy should be based on the needs of individual learners and the usefulness of the strategy across situations. When modeling the strategy and guiding practice, teachers should keep the wording clear and simple, adapt the strategy for individual differences, and apply the strategy to personally meaningful writing topics. Additionally, students will need frequent guided and independent practice using the strategy. Table 3.1 shows examples of writing strategies for different purposes.

Table 3.1   Writing Strategies

Strategy	Mnemonic Steps
PLEASE (Welch, 1992) *Paragraph Writing*	**P**ick the topic, audience, and paragraph type (such as compare/contrast). **L**ist information about the topic. **E**valuate whether the list is complete and determine order. **A**ctivate your writing by starting with a topic sentence. **S**upply supporting or detail sentences, using items from the list. **E**nd with a strong concluding sentence.
WWW,What-2, How-2 (Graham & Harris, 1992) *Narrative Writing*	WWW: Who? (is the main character), When? (does it take place), Where? (does it take place) What-2: What? (does the main character want to do); What? (happens when she does it) How-2: How? (does it end), How? (does the character feel?)

Strategy	Mnemonic Steps	
C-SPACE (Graham & Harris, 1992) *Narrative*	**C**haracter, **S**etting, **P**roblem, **A**ctions, **C**onclusion, **E**motion	
TREE (Graham & Harris, 1989) *Opinion Writing*	**T**opic sentence **R**easons to support premise **E**xamine soundness of each reason **E**nding	
STOP-DARE (De La Paz & Graham, 1997) *Opinion Writing*	**S**uspend judgment **T**ake a side **O**rganize ideas **P**lan more as you write	**D**evelop a topic sentence **A**dd supporting ideas **R**eject possible arguments for the other side **E**nd with a conclusion
TOWER (Schumaker, 2003) *Expository Writing*	**T**hink about the content **O**rder topics and details **W**rite the rough draft, look for **E**rrors **R**evise and **R**ewrite	
SCORE A (Korinek & Bulls, 1996) *Expository Writing*	**S**elect a topic **C**reate categories **O**btain reference tools **R**ead and take notes **E**venly organize information using note cards **A**pply writing process	
COPS (Schumaker et al., 1985) *Editing*	**C**apitalization **O**verall appearance **P**unctuation **S**pelling	
CDO (Graham, 1997) *Revising*	**C**ompare—Does my sentence match what I really wanted to say? **D**iagnose—Select problem from a diagnostic card (such as lacks detail) **O**perate—After rewriting the sentence, was the change effective? Process is repeated at paragraph level	
SEARCH (Ellis & Friend, 1991) *Revising and Editing*	**S**et goals **E**xamine paper to see if it makes sense **A**sk if you said what you meant **R**eveal picky errors **C**opy over neatly **H**ave a last look for errors	

COMPUTER TECHNOLOGY FOR WRITING: TIER 1

Research demonstrates that students produce longer and higher-quality compositions when they use computer technology for writing (Goldberg, Russell, & Cook, 2003; Graham & Perin, 2007). Additionally, using word-processing programs has resulted in increased revisions, reduced errors, and better attitudes toward writing (Sturm, Rankin, Beukelman, & Schultz-Muehling, 1997). Word-processing programs allow students to make frequent revisions without tiresome recopying, correct errors without messy erasing, and produce neatly printed work (MacArthur, 1996). The visibility of the text on the screen can be useful for facilitating collaborative writing between peers. Another benefit of visibility is that teacher can easily observe student writing processes and provide instructional feedback (MacArthur).

An excellent tool for whole-class writing instruction is an interactive whiteboard. This is a large dry-erase board on which a projector displays a computer's desktop. The whiteboard functions as a large touch screen. Text and illustrations can be manipulated on the screen using electronic pens or fingers. Any work completed on the whiteboard can be captured and modified electronically. An interactive whiteboard can be used to demonstrate how to use the computer to produce and edit written expression (keyboarding, formatting, copying, pasting, using spell check, saving text, using the thesaurus and dictionary). It can also be used to model and guide students through the writing process. For example, during planning, teachers can use the whiteboard to create brainstorming lists and complete graphic organizers. Teachers can also demonstrate how to create sentences from planning notes, revise for content, and edit for mechanical errors. The whiteboard can be used to teach students how to do an Internet search and demonstrate how to use software. For example, *REfworks* (ProQuest) and *EndNote* (Thompson ResearchSoft, 2008) are software programs that provide students with assistance with collecting and formatting references and creating bibliographies.

Whiteboards can also be used to demonstrate how to use multimedia programs that integrate drawing tools, video, and sound. These kinds of programs can be motivating for all developing writers. They can be especially useful for culturally and linguistically diverse students who may have limited background knowledge. Additionally, multimedia programs may enable culturally diverse students to select visuals and sounds that have personal significance for them.

The *Amazing Writing Machine* (Riverdeep Inc.) is an example of multimedia program that guides students through the writing process. Students begin with the "Project Picker," in which they select from five projects (essay, letter, story, poem, or journal). They can then decide to write from scratch or work on editing and customizing a prewritten outline. Other features include "Bright Ideas" (guides students in brainstorming and generating ideas), "Infosaurus" (finds words), "Reader Robot" (reads the story back to the student in one of eight voices), "Illustrating" (provides drawing, painting, rubber stamps, and clip art), and "Publishing" (prints story in various formats including fold-up books). Other examples of similar multimedia writing programs include *Kids Media Magic* and *Storybook Weaver*.

COMPUTER TECHNOLOGY FOR WRITING: TIERS 2 AND 3

Computer technology offers many levels of support for students needing more intensive instruction. Word prediction software, text-to-speech, and speech-to-text features are available in many programs to help students with planning, organization, and revising as they move through the writing process.

Planning and organization software can assist students by prompting them for specific information or presenting a series of response prompts for composing stories. *Inspiration* (for Grades 6–12) and *Kidspiration* (for Grades K–5) are examples of programs that can help students plan their compositions by helping them create semantic maps that can automatically be turned into an outline. Other examples of programs useful for planning and organization include *Kid Pix* (Riverdeep Inc.), *Storybook Weaver* (Riverdeep Inc.), and *Draft: Builder* (Don Johnston Inc.).

Programs that contain word prediction and word banks can be very helpful for struggling writers. For example, with *Co:Writer 4000* (Don Johnston Inc.), as each letter is typed, a series of words with the same beginning letters appear on the screen. The student clicks on the intended word when it appears. This program also includes speech synthesis so the student can hear whether or not he selected the intended word. Other examples of word prediction software with speech synthesis include *Word Q Writing Aid Software* (Quillsoft) and *Kid Works 2* (Riverdeep Inc.).

Text-to-speech technology allows students to hear what they have written so they can more easily evaluate the correctness of their writing (MacArthur, 1996). Discrepancies between what students have written and what they intended to express are more easily detected. Examples of text-to-speech writing programs include *Write Outloud* (Riverdeep Inc.) and *Read and Write Gold* (Brighteye Technology). Both of these programs include text-to-speech, speech-to-text, and word prediction.

Voice-recognition programs allow students to produce written expression by speaking into a microphone while the computer types what is said. These speech-to-text programs help students who have severe motor or writing production problems. Although each program must be calibrated to a specific voice, once calibrated, the software is quite reliable in recording the correct words. Examples of speech-to-text software include *Dragon NaturallySpeaking* (Nuance), *Windows Vista Speech Recognition, IBM ViaVoice 10 Standard,* and *MacSpeech Dictate.* Computer technology can provide many levels of support in inclusive classrooms.

SUMMARY

The ability to produce quality writing opens doors to many opportunities for enriching experiences. In addition to being a very important tool for learning and communicating, writing is also a highly regarded outlet for creativity. Far too many students lack motivation to write because it can be such a struggle. However, when teachers plan multitiered instruction using evidence-based practices, students with a history of failure can become successful and inspired. Authentic and personally meaningful writing tasks are more likely to motivate effortful writing. In order to focus clearly on their flow of ideas, students will need to have adequate transcription skills such as handwriting, keyboarding, and spelling. Tier 1 approaches for transcription skills include direct instruction and frequent opportunities for active responding and specific feedback. Students needing more intensive instruction can benefit from various forms of multisensory instruction, self-correction, and additional practice.

In addition to transcription skills, students also need to be able to plan, organize, and write different kinds of compositions. Teaching the writing process is an evidence-based practice for increasing writing quality and proficiency. Writer's workshop provides flexible and differentiated Tier 1 instruction for teaching the writing process. In writer's workshop, students can work independently or with peers on a variety of writing pieces. Writer's workshop encourages students to make choices, engage in personally meaningful writing, and set their own goals. Supplemental writing process instruction at Tiers 2 and 3 should include direct instruction of writing strategies because of their effectiveness for struggling writers. With strategy instruction, students memorize a mnemonic for producing a specific type of writing (such as DEFENDS for persuasive papers). Each letter in the mnemonic represents each sequential step for the writing piece. Teachers can use Self-Regulated Strategy Development (SRSD; Graham & Harris, 2005) to teach students different writing strategies. When teaching the writing process, students at all instructional tiers will benefit from the flexibility and support of computer technology. For example, teachers can use interactive white boards to provide Tier 1 instruction. Additionally, computer technology offers a wide range of support for students with physical, intellectual, or learning disabilities (voice recognition, word prediction) as well as for typically developing and gifted students (multimedia writing programs).

CARMEN

Carmen looked through her writing folder to decide which story she wanted to work on. She shuffled through the different planning notes and drafts until she found the story she started called "Honey Island Swamp." She was excited about working on this story today because her teacher was going to help her get started on the revisions.

"Did you decide which story you wanted to work on?" asked Mr. Blake.

"Yes. It's called "Honey Island Swamp.""

"Oh, I think that will be a good one to work on. Read to me what you have so far."

Carmen began reading, "Last summer I went to visit my cousin in Louisiana and we took a boat-ride tour through the swamp. We saw a lot of cool plants and animals, but this was the coolest thing that happened. The man who was driving the boat made a sound to call the alligators. Then five baby alligators came to the boat and ate marshmallows. My cousin told me that some people think Big Foot lives in Honey Island Swamp but Big Foot isn't real."

"That's a good start," said Mr. Blake, "One thing you want to do is give the reader a clear picture of what you experienced. How can you do that?"

"Describe more of what I saw and heard?" Carmen asked.

"Good, tell me what you can add to your story."

"Like, there were trees in the water that were really fat on the bottom part of the trunk and we could hear all different kinds of birds and bugs singing and chirping and," Carmen remembered something important, "it was really . . . really . . . really . . . hot!"

"Those are really important details to add, very good." Mr. Blake prompted Carmen to jot those notes down so she would remember to add those details to the story later. To provide a model, he also helped Carmen work through revising one of the sentences.

"Carmen," said Mr. Blake, "let's look at the sentence, 'Then five baby alligators came to the boat and ate marshmallows.' How did the baby alligators come to the boat?"

"They didn't splash, they just moved in a smooth way, they didn't flap their legs, they just kept them straight."

"Good, now how did they eat the marshmallows?"

By asking Carmen questions that helped her elaborate on the details, Carmen understood what she needed to do to make this story better. She proudly read the revised sentence about the alligators to Mr. Blake.

"Five baby alligators glided toward the boat with just their heads out of the water and their jaws open. When the tour guide threw marshmallows in the water, the alligators let the marshmallows float into their mouths and gently closed their jaws." After receiving positive feedback and encouragement from Mr. Blake, Carmen continued working on her revisions until the recess bell rang.

Part II

Mathematics

Differentiated Instruction and Response to Intervention in Mathematics

William N. Bender

Strategies in this chapter include the following:

- Direct Instruction Lesson Planning
- Guess, Assess, and Tear Out
- Results of Guess, Assess, and Tear Out
- Response to Intervention in Mathematics

DIFFERENTIATION AND RESPONSE TO INTERVENTION: REFOCUSING MATH INSTRUCTION

As discussed in Chapter 1, differentiated instruction involves more than mere application of effective teaching ideas that address a wider variety of multiple intelligences. In fact, differentiated instruction represents a drastic paradigm shift that fundamentally changes the way teachers teach mathematics (as well as other subjects) across the elementary school curriculum. Coupled with this refocusing in mathematics instruction is the recent national emphasis on documenting students' response to targeted interventions (Bender & Shores, 2007; Bryant et al., 2008). These two initiatives in education promise to refocus how teachers plan and deliver the mathematics lesson to the highly diverse students in today's classrooms. This chapter focuses initially on how differentiation affected lesson delivery in mathematics, and later how the response to intervention initiative across the nation tends to affect differentiated mathematics instruction.

Teachers who wish to develop a differentiated classroom for math instruction must begin in the lesson-planning phase. For the past thirty years, lesson planning has been based on a body of research that was known as the "effective schools" research of the 1970s (Bender, 1996). Other names for this research movement include "direct instruction," "mastery learning," and "effective teacher behaviors." All of these involve highly developed lesson plans designed to maximize instruction time or "engaged" time in which the student was cognitively engaged with the content (see Bender, 1996, for a discussion of effective teaching behaviors and direct instruction). In some examples of direct instruction, scripted lessons were used in which teachers literally read a prepared script while teaching (Bender, 1996).

> Such highly structured direct instruction lessons were possible in classes that involved only a small number of children and a small range of academic diversity.

For our purposes, we'll use the term *direct instruction* to represent this type of instructional approach. Today, our lesson planning and even our way of thinking about math instruction stems from this body of research, and most teacher's manuals in most math curricula are written in terms of this direct instructional approach.

Of course, to understand direct instruction we must consider the setting of the research on direct instruction. Specifically, researchers of the 1960s and 1970s based their work on the types of classrooms and the types of students who were then prevalent in the public schools. For example, if a teacher taught in Grade 5 in the early 1970s, he or she could realistically assume that most of the students in that class were working on reading and math somewhere between grade level 3 and grade level 7. In other words, while there were some differences in the children's math or reading skills, there was a fairly narrow level of academic diversity within the class. Much of the effective schools research took place in classrooms prior to the full implementation of Public Law 94-142 (the Education for All Handicapped Children Act, later recodified as the Individuals with Disabilities Education Act); thus, many students with special needs were excluded from much of this research.

In contrast, in today's fifth-grade class it is quite likely that students' achievement levels in reading and math range from grade level 1 up through grade level 10 or 11. Our nation has made a commitment to educate all students, and today's teachers face that fact daily. Thus, while there was limited academic diversity in the classes of the 1970s, the levels of academic diversity noted in the typical classroom today in the 21st century are much higher. Even with this increase in the range of academic skills present in the typical classroom, educators have not effectively reconceptualized how teachers should conduct math lessons to meet the demands of this level of diversity, in spite of the instructional recommendations that stem from the emerging brain-compatible instruction research (Sousa, 2008). In

> Because math curricula today present lesson plans in the direct instruction format, our task here will be to modify that lesson format into a set of differentiated instructional activities.

fact, the formation of the National Mathematics Advisory Panel and its subsequent report (2008) may be viewed, at least in part, as an initiative to help teachers focus on developing more effective mathematics instructional plans.

Today, modern mathematics curricula have highly developed lesson plans that employ the direct instruction teaching phases. These are almost always presented in the teacher's manual in some form. Yet, if the range of the students' mathematics skills in today's classrooms has changed, it may be time to adjust our thinking about how to structure our lessons and lesson-planning activities. Again, Tomlinson's (1999) work on the differentiated classroom represents a fairly drastic paradigm change in how teachers should lead their mathematics instruction. This chapter will explore this paradigm change to assist teachers in formulating a truly differentiated lesson plan.

Thus, the lesson-planning job in mathematics becomes an exercise in planning the activities for various groups of students in the class who do not need to follow the traditional direct instruction lesson or who need an alternative lesson format.

TEACHING PHASES IN THE DIRECT INSTRUCTION LESSON

The traditional direct instruction lesson plan would typically present a series of instructional phases that were originally referred to as the "direct instruction" steps. These phases of learning, as enumerated in the effective schools research of the 1970s, have become the steps in the typical lesson plan in schools today (Bender, 1996). Presented below are the usual steps in direct instruction, and the types of instructional activities involved in each phase of instruction. While the terms may change from one math curriculum to another (some math curricula use "activate their understanding" rather than "orientation to the lesson," for example), teachers have planned their instruction for the past thirty years around these phases of the instructional lesson.

STEPS IN A DIRECT INSTRUCTION LESSON

Orientation to the Lesson

- Gain students' attention
- Relate today's lesson to a previously related lesson
- Use essential questions to activate students' thinking

Initial Instruction

- Teacher leads completion of several sample problems
- Teacher models and has students' model problem completion
- Teacher points out difficult aspects of problem

Teacher-Guided Practice

- Students complete problems under teacher supervision
- Teacher monitors each student's success in problem completion
- Teacher assists students independently
- Students may discuss problems with each other

(Continued)

(Continued)

Independent Practice

- Students complete sample problems independently
- Students may complete homework as independent practice

Check

- Teacher checks student performance on independent work

Reteach

- Teacher identifies students with continuing difficulty and reteaches the skills

The initial and fundamental assumptions behind the direct instruction lesson format were that all students would follow this main line of instructional activities and that this sequence would facilitate learning for all students. Of course, this assumed a relatively narrow range level of academic diversity; for example, in order for this type of group instruction to work, one had to assume that students in Grade 5 were functioning somewhere around the Grade 5 level in mathematics—say between grade levels 3 and 6. It also assumed that all students could and would learn in the same fashion if the teacher presented an appropriate lesson based on high levels of engagement on the part of every student.

PROBLEMS WITH DIRECT INSTRUCTION IN A LARGE CLASS

As Tomlinson (1999) stated so succinctly, the increasing diversity of students, of learning styles, and of learning needs in the general education classroom has effectively outdated the set of assumptions on which direct instruction is based. In today's typical fifth-grade classroom, the broad range of academic diversity makes it impossible for a teacher to teach effectively using only one instructional format.

In fact, the direct instructional format has never truly worked for many students within a class (with typical classes including perhaps twenty-five or thirty students). For advanced students in those mathematics classes, this instructional sequence often leads to boredom in the early steps on any particular type of problem, since many advanced or gifted students may already have mastered the lesson prior to the teacher's initial instruction. Thus, those students would tend to be off-task by the time the teacher begins the later phases of the instructional lesson, and they might even begin to disrupt others in the class.

For students with less ability in the typical inclusive classroom, this model of instruction often failed to engage them because they may not have had the prerequisite skills necessary for the lesson. Consequently, many of those students demonstrate both off-task and disruptive behaviors, since they are bored with material that they cannot learn and are not engaged with the lesson activities. Therefore, as a result of teachers' attempting to follow this series of direct instructional steps, many students in the typical class were bored and often misbehaved, and of course managing those problems takes the teacher's time away from delivery of the lesson activity to the other students in the class.

Clearly, for today's diverse group of students, we will need to modify this direct instructional model considerably in order to differentiate the lesson and to increase the variety of activities in this class, if we wish to engage all learners in the mathematics content. While various theorists have provided such models of curriculum and lesson reorganization (e.g., Wiggins & McTighe, 1998), Tomlinson's (1999) differentiated instructional model seems to offer the most effective option.

TEACHING STRATEGY: THE GUESS, ASSESS, AND TEAR OUT TACTIC

The Guess, Assess, and Tear Out Tactic provides one way to modify the direct instructional lesson phases for increased differentiation in the class.

In using the Guess, Assess, and Tear Out idea, the teacher would begin the lesson-planning process with the first step as suggested by the direct instruction model described above—orientation to the lesson. After each instructional step in the traditional lesson, however, the teacher would do three things:

> **The Guess, Assess, and Tear Out Tactic is a lesson-planning approach that allows teachers to use the traditional direct instructional steps delineated above as the basis for instructional planning, while increasing the variety of activities offered for students who need alternative instructional approaches because of their diverse learning needs.**

1. *Guess* which students have the concept,

2. *Assess* those several students with one or two quick questions, and

3. *Tear Out* of the class a small instructional group of those students who will perform an alternative instructional activity.

In this model of instruction, the terms *guess* and *assess* are self-explanatory. The teacher is (based on his or her judgment and previous experience with the students) guessing which students may have grasped the concept. Next, the teacher will quickly "assess" them informally, perhaps with a question such as, "Do you understand this idea?"

The final term above requires a bit more explanation. I've used the term *tear out* deliberately, since forming more than one or two instructional groups in a classroom early in the lesson is quite difficult for many teachers. While teachers have been using instructional groups for many years during the independent practice phase of the lesson, in a differentiated class these instructional groups will be formed much sooner in the lesson and much more frequently. In a differentiated class, teachers will form instructional groups even before they have presented the initial instruction in the topic to the class, and will form many more instructional groups than in traditional direct instructional teaching.

Because most of today's teachers were trained in the direct instructional teaching model, the modification of this standard lesson plan in order to differentiate the math activities in the classroom may be one of the most challenging aspects of the model. In short, one of the most difficult things to encourage teachers to do is to form multiple instructional groups that will be less supervised by the teacher, since using three or four groups of students in the classroom means that teachers must assume that students can learn from each other without such instructional supervision. This idea requires some degree of faith on the part of teachers who have not been prepared for this type of teaching.

Also, students as well as teachers are generally not well prepared for this type of instruction. While learning collaboratively from one's peers during the performance of an assigned task is certainly one requirement in the modern workplace, the direct instructional teaching model is rather authoritarian and doesn't provide ample opportunity for such peer mediated learning. Thus, providing students with increased opportunities to learn content from each other in settings that are somewhat less supervised by the teacher can result in enhanced instruction for a modern world. However, both teachers and students will need some experimental learning in order to function well within this model. Perhaps a concrete example will demonstrate this concept.

A DIFFERENTIATED INSTRUCTION LESSON EXAMPLE

In order to demonstrate the Guess, Assess, and Tear Out approach, imagine the following instructional lesson in Ms. Adrian's third-grade math class. The class includes twenty-two students, five of whom are special education students, and two of those students have attention deficit disorders coupled with high levels of hyperactivity. In schools today, this would seem to be a typical class. In this scenario, Ms. Adrian is teaching a math lesson concerning the aggregation of data, the creation of a tally table, and the eventual formulation of a frequency table summarizing those data.

As an advance organizer of the Guess, Assess, and Tear Out technique, the chart below shows a comparison of the direct instruction phases of this lesson and a differentiated lesson plan for the same lesson. Note the direct instruction activities appear on the left of the chart, and the types of "tear out" activities suggested by the Guess, Assess, and Tear Out Tactic are noted on the right-hand side of the chart.

TEACHING STRATEGY
Using Guess, Assess, and Tear Out! Moving From Direct Instruction to Differentiated Instruction in Math

Direct Instruction Phases of Learning	*Differentiated Instruction Guess, Assess, and Tear Out Activities*
I. *Orientation* • Cover tally tables and frequency tables	• After the introduction, break out one group (Omega Group) to create a tally table on the floor, then rejoin main group

II. *Initial Instruction* • Teach tally tables and frequency tables	• Tear out a second group (Beta Group, using examples from the text) • Beta Group is to use the tally table on the floor for some sample problems
III. *Teacher-Guided Practice* • Have mainline group complete practice worksheet	• Have Omega and Beta groups evaluate each other's work • Tear out another group if necessary
IV. *Independent Practice* • Have students complete the independent practice	• Omega and Beta groups move into other enrichment activities
V. *Check*	• Have Omega and Beta groups describe their activities to the entire class; continue to check comprehension
VI. *Reteach* • Reteach the concepts to a smaller group of kids who haven't mastered it	• Use members of Omega and Beta groups to "buddy up" with students who need help

To begin this lesson with an attention-grabbing orientation activity, Ms. Adrian might ask students to identify their favorite type of dinosaur, since dinosaurs have become big Hollywood stars recently. She would hold up a picture of one of the five most recognizable types of dinosaurs and have a student at the dry erase board begin to tally how many students like the T-Rex, the allosaurus, the raptor, or the stegosaurus. Once she has several sets of tally marks on the dry erase board, she may then say something like, "Can we summarize these data so they make sense?" Ms. Adrian may ask for suggestions from the class, but she will eventually show a frequency table that looks something like the following.

Tally Table and Frequency Table for Dinosaur Preferences

Dinosaurs	Tally Count	Frequency

After this brief orientation activity, the traditional direct instruction lesson would suggest that Ms. Adrian begin to teach about tally tables, and ultimately frequency tables, using several similar examples. The differentiated lesson plan, however, offers another approach. For example, it is possible that, after the orientation to the lesson, and prior to initial instruction, some of the students have already mastered the concept. During the orientation phase of the lesson, several students may have looked ahead in the text and seen several examples of how to tally data in table form, and then generated a frequency table from the tally marks. In short, even before the lesson is taught some students may already have grasped the idea and may need a more challenging lesson.

> The Guess, Assess, and Tear Out Tactic offers the opportunity to provide "tiered instruction" or instruction on the same content but at slightly different cognitive levels for different groups of students. The provision of tiered lessons is one fundamental element of a differentiated instructional lesson.

At this point, the Guess, Assess, and Tear Out technique offers an alternative. After the orientation to the lesson, rather than beginning the initial instruction for everyone in the class, Ms. Adrian should use the Guess, Assess, and Tear Out Tactic. Prior to any actual teacher-led instruction, it is possible—in fact it is likely in most heterogeneous classes in today's schools—that Ms. Adrian could identify some students who have already mastered the concept. In other words, some of the more advanced students do not even need to be taught the lesson. Ms. Adrian would identify three to five students by educated guess and a quick assessment question or two directed to the group. Questions such as, "Do you think you could structure a tally table to collect data, and then transfer those data to a frequency table?" For the students who indicate they could, she should tear out these students and provide some group work as an alternative instructional activity.

Let's follow the next part of the lesson for a moment from the perspective of that tear out group, by exploring the group's tiered activity assignment.

THE OMEGA GROUP

We'll call these students the Omega Group—the first group of students torn out of the mainline instruction. Of course, you may use any terms you like to name these groups, as long as the names for the groups are nonsequential and thus do not indicate a qualitative judgment on the skills or the intellect of the group. For the first activity of the Omega Group, Ms. Adrian may hand them a preselected assignment sheet for a group work activity involving structuring such a frequency table. These five students would then be instructed to move to a separate section of the room to begin their group project.

In a differentiated lesson, the good news is that teachers usually don't have to create these alternative activities; these group project alternatives are usually described in the teacher's manual as "enrichment" activities or "reteaching" activities. Thus, Ms. Adrian does not have to create this activity—she merely selects it. She will then provide a brief set of directions for that assignment as well as any necessary materials to the Omega Group. For the directions, she may merely copy an activity out of the math text with instructions along the lines of the following:

> This activity requires some floor space (15′ by 15′), and a roll of masking tape. Students will place masking tape on the floor to develop an outline for a frequency table. The rows will represent choices of students' favorite singers (teachers should select five specific pictures of individual singers of different styles of music in advance from various popular music magazines). One column will be used for a count of individuals who like a particular singer, and another column will be used to write the digit of the number of persons who like a particular singer.

Based on a set of instructions such as this, the students in the Omega Group should be provided with a roll of masking tape, and then should do this activity in one corner of the room.

Given that the next direct instruction phase—the teacher-directed phase—typically takes approximately fifteen minutes, the group activity for Omega Group should be planned with that time frame in mind. Also, teachers should select an alternative activity that involves one or more of the multiple intelligences that have not been involved in the lesson. For example, in the activity above, the Omega Group is instructed to use masking tape and structure a "frequency table" on the floor. This grid will consist of a series of boxes in which students may stand as their preferences are noted. The Omega Group students would have to jointly plan what the tally table should look like, how big the boxes are going to be in order to hold various groups of students, and how the categories in the tally table should be organized.

In this activity, the box on the left is the "category" box, where pictures of singers may be placed in order to identify the specific category. That box need be only large enough to accommodate the pictures. In contrast, the box in the middle must be large enough for a number of students to stand in, as they stand by their preferences. The box on the right end will hold only a digit that summarizes the data in the middle box, so it can be somewhat smaller. The point is that the Omega Group has to figure all of this out—including the number of categories and the relative size of the boxes—while working as a group. The group then needs to place these boxes on the floor using the masking tape, for subsequent classroom use. Thus, this involves a variety of intelligences, including interpersonal intelligence, spatial intelligence, logical/mathematical intelligence, and bodily/kinesthetic intelligence.

Given the considerations in designing this floor grid, it is possible for the Omega Group to make a mistake in their work. For example, while the Omega Group may develop a five-by-three grid, they may forget to consider the relative size of the boxes. Specifically, rather than merely a set of tally marks—as in the earlier example on the dry erase board—the grid on the floor must include a second column of boxes that are large enough to hold a number of students. Thus, the challenge of making this grid is a more complicated activity than the example in the lesson orientation. This activity, while focusing on the lesson of data aggregation, is more intellectually demanding than the lesson activities offered to the mainline instructional group. Such tiering of instruction is characteristic of differentiated lessons.

THE MAINLINE INSTRUCTION GROUP

It is relatively easy in this classroom scenario to note the differentiation of lesson demands. After only a two- or three-minute orientation to the lesson and prior to having "taught" the lesson, Ms. Adrian has two groups of students in her class—the Omega Group and the mainline group (i.e., the group of students who were not torn out for the differentiated activity). As the Omega Group does its work, Ms. Adrian will engage in traditional teacher-led initial instruction as she normally would for the mainline students. She may use a variety of activities from the instructor's manual, but she should make certain that a variety of activities are offered, and that her instruction addresses a variety of intelligences. For example, after she models how to formulate a tally table to summarize data, and transfers those data into a frequency table, she may have students work as peer buddies to do another sample problem on data aggregation and then explain their solution of the second problem to the mainline group within the class.

In order to further understand differentiated lesson planning, we should also consider what Ms. Adrian's teaching might look like. In a math class of twenty-two students, if she selected five students for the Omega Group, only seventeen students would remain in the mainline group during the initial instruction, and they would be more homogeneously grouped. Consequently, Ms. Adrian's instruction is likely to improve. Consider the following questions:

1. Is it possible that Ms. Adrian's teaching is more focused for this mainline group?

2. Is Ms. Adrian less distracted by the gifted or advanced students who would be bored had they remained in the mainline group?

3. Is Ms. Adrian more likely to make eye contact more frequently with seventeen students as compared with twenty-two students? Is Ms. Adrian likely to have a better sense of the level of understanding of this reduced number of students?

4. Are Ms. Adrian's examples during this teaching phase more likely to be on target for these students than if she were still working with the entire class?

Based on these questions, it seems reasonable to conclude that Ms. Adrian's instruction has become more focused and responsive to students' needs in this differentiated lesson given that she is working with a smaller group of students who need her assistance. This is the strength of differentiated instruction—it is strategically targeted instruction aimed at the learning needs of individual students in the math class.

THE BETA GROUP

After fifteen minutes or so, Ms. Adrian will have completed the lesson orientation and the initial instructional phases for the mainline students. Also, the Omega Group will have completed its work in designing the grid on the floor. Again, the teacher should use the Guess, Assess, and Tear Out Tactic. With a few judicious questions, the teacher can again identify a second group of perhaps five or six other students in the mainline group that now understands the data aggregation concept and do not need the next direct instruction phase of teacher guided practice. We'll call this group the Beta Group. Again, Ms. Adrian would select this group from the mainline instructional group and provide an alternative assignment.

For example, this group may be provided the assignment to work with the Omega Group to "test out" the large frequency table grid that has been developed. The Beta Group could be given two or three frequency table assignments based on student preferences for (1) colors of tennis shoes worn in the class, (2) favorite musician, or (3) favorite national leader.

Of course at this point in the lesson, the Omega Group will also need another assignment. It would be perfectly appropriate to use them to work with the Beta Group to develop these activities for later classroom use. However, Ms. Adrian may wish to give them a separate assignment that involves writing several data aggregation problems for subsequent classroom use.

Again, we should consider what is happening in Ms. Adrian's class at this point in the lesson. First, note that Ms. Adrian's class will be quite differentiated only fifteen minutes or so into the day's lesson. Specifically, after she oriented the students to the lesson, she tore out the Omega Group, and after the initial instruction phase, she tore out the Beta Group. Thus, after fifteen minutes or so, five students in the Omega Group will be doing a second tear out assignment, the Beta Group will be testing the grid on the floor with several sample problems, and the mainline instructional group will include only eleven students who are receiving direct instruction from Ms. Adrian. Again, Ms. Adrian's instruction will be increasingly focused on these students in the mainline group who have not yet grasped the idea, and these students in turn will get the additional attention that they need from the teacher. Thus, differentiated instruction is very effective, strategically targeted teaching.

IDEAS FROM TEACHERS

Operations With Positive/Negative Integers

One interesting tiered instructional idea is to use the tear out group to create a rhythm, song, rhyme, or chant that can be used to teach some of the concepts in the lesson. This couples the use of musical intelligence with the need for differentiated group work. One teacher reported that her students created a nice little song to guide them in addition of positive and negative integers. This is sung to the tune of "Row, Row, Row Your Boat."

(Continued)

(Continued)

Same sign, add and keep,

Different sign subtract!

Take the sign of the highest number

Then you'll be exact!

Multiply and Divide,

It's an easy thought!

Same signs are positive

Different signs are not!

IS FURTHER DIFFERENTIATION NEEDED?

It is difficult to address the question concerning how much differentiation is needed in any specific class or during any specific lesson. There is no obvious rule for how many different groups should be formed in any class for any particular lesson, but there are several points we can consider that teachers may use as guidelines. First, as shown in the Guess, Assess, and Tear Out chart presented previously, the differentiated lesson format suggests that a teacher tear out a separate instructional group after each instructional phase. Thus, differentiated groups would be formed after the orientation to the lesson, after the initial instruction phase, after the teacher-guided practice phase, and so forth.

The second point involves not overdoing it! To be specific, at some point in every lesson, this process of continual group formation breaks down. For example, after the teacher completed the initial instruction and tore out the Beta Group, he or she would be working with a mainline group of students who have not grasped the concept after the initial instructional phase. According to the direct instructional model, these students would move into teacher guided practice. However, if the students still do not have the basic concept at that point, why would any teacher force them to move into the next instructional phase? In fact, for students who do not grasp a concept after initial instruction, the teacher should move directly to the "reteach" phase and present the concept in a different way. Thus, at this point, the direct instructional phases have broken down and become nonapplicable.

Also, we must realize that there may be some confusion among some of the members of the Omega and Beta groups. It is possible that some of those students, while believing that they understood the concept, did not have an adequate grasp of the idea after all. Thus, some of those students may need to rejoin the mainline instructional group. In fact, in a differentiated class, the instructional groups are quite fluid in the sense that they frequently change. Teachers should never be reluctant to tear out groups for brief specific activities or to re-include those same students in the mainline instruction should that become necessary.

Again, after the first two or three phases of instruction, the traditional direct instruction structure of the lesson breaks down. Further, by using differentiated groups the teacher is providing more focused learning and also will typically have a better grasp of where the students are in their learning. At that point, the original direct instructional model has become irrelevant for instructional purposes, since teachers will have various groups of kids at various phases of learning. This fluid differentiation is the very substance of a differentiated lesson.

ANYTHING WRONG WITH THIS SCENARIO? ENHANCING THE DIFFERENTIATED INSTRUCTION MODEL

Have you noticed several problems in the description noted above? I have learned, in workshops around the country, to initially describe the process as I first conceived it, and then to highlight several misconceptions on my part within the teaching scenario just presented. After numerous workshops on this topic, I am confident that this is a more effective teaching procedure than merely describing the total process. Thus, as a cognitive challenge, can you find the several errors that I have made? Do you see several problems in the scenario as it is described up to this point? As a guide, consider the following questions:

1. Have we used the best instructional techniques for the students who need them least?

2. Using this plan, are we using students to teach other students? Are we sure that the first group of students understands the concept?

3. Are we always tearing out the "best and brightest"?

4. Are we providing the most effective instruction to everyone?

5. Are various multiple intelligences employed in learning?

As these questions show, my first conceptualization of the Guess, Assess, and Tear Out Tactic was not completely thought out. Given the scenario, the teacher will always identify the best and brightest for the first tear out groups. Also, in the scenario, the most effective instruction—the movement-based grid development activity—is presented to the students who need that instruction least. For these reasons, we'll need to modify the scenario above a bit to see its true beauty and realize the overall efficacy of differentiated instruction.

> For tiered activities, teachers should not always tear out the same group of students after the orientation to the lesson, as this would result in the same students—the best and the brightest—always working together and always working independently of direct teacher supervision.

Rather, to form that first tear out group—the Omega Group—the teacher should identify two or three students who have firmly grasped the concept and partner them with several students who have not. This type of heterogeneous grouping will involve many more students than in the scenario I initially described. Also, such heterogeneous groups are more likely to result in student-to-student learning during the activities of the Omega Group as those students work together independently of the teacher. For example, if students working in one of the tear out groups have questions, they should be told to ask those questions first of the other group members. In that fashion, students can, and should, be learning from each other much more frequently in schools than is common in the traditional class. In this way, the differentiated instructional concept provides one alternative to facilitate such student-to-student learning. Thus, one fundamental rule in the formulation of every tear out group is to select some students who have grasped the concept and some who haven't.

Another problem can be noted in the scenario: With the Omega Group doing the instructional design of the grid on the floor, the students in the mainline group will be likely to pay attention to that group rather than to the traditional instruction being offered to the mainline students. In order to offset this problem, Ms. Adrian must make the instruction offered to the mainline group every bit as interesting, as novel, and as much fun as any of the alternative assignments offered to the tear out groups. In the scenario above, once the Omega Group is identified and given their assignment of making a grid in one corner of the classroom (which is a highly active, movement-based learning opportunity), the teacher should take the students in the mainline group to another corner of the classroom and present them with a highly active, movement-based task. In fact, it is perfectly acceptable to use the same activity. The only difference will be that the students in the mainline group will be more closely supervised by Ms. Adrian. The point is that once teachers begin to offer novel, exciting, activity-based learning in their classes, they will find it necessary to offer such activities to all students. Again, this is one of the strengths of differentiated instruction.

GUIDELINES FOR DIFFERENTIATED LESSON PLANNING

With these several modifications in mind, we can now identify the general guidelines for modifying a direct instructional lesson and transforming it into a differentiated lesson in math. I do wish to emphasize that these are merely guidelines, and that every teacher should, based on his or her understanding of the individuals in the class as well as the demands of the subject content, adapt these to the specific needs of the students. These guidelines are presented below.

TEACHING TACTICS

Guidelines for Differentiated Instruction Lessons

1. Subdivide the class early and often. The teacher in a differentiated class should provide many tear out activities. In fact, teachers employing differentiated instruction will subdivide their class much earlier in the lesson than is usual in the direct instruction model, and will do so much more frequently. For this reason, the Guess, Assess, and Tear Out Tactic offers the most effective, differentiated instructional option for students at all levels of ability in the class. When teaching within a differentiated instructional lesson, teachers should tear out a heterogeneous group of students for an alternative instructional activity after each phase in the traditional lesson plan. Teachers should select some students who have grasped the concept and some who haven't, by exercising judgment concerning who can work effectively in a group and who can or will work together.

2. Never plan just one activity when you need two or three! The academic diversity in today's elementary classes often necessitates the presentation of the same content in multiple ways, so I suggest that each time a teacher plans one activity, he or she plans at least one more and subdivides the class, with some students doing one and some doing the other. While creative teachers can always generate interesting instructional ideas, many ideas can be found in today's teacher's manuals for math curricula. These are typically included as "enrichment" or "alternative teaching" ideas. In most cases, teachers merely need to select these activities from the curriculum ideas presented.

3. Use the tear out activities more than once in the unit. In the example in Ms. Adrian's class, the Omega Group was the first to develop a frequency table on the floor. On subsequent days within that unit of instruction, other students in other groups may also be challenged with that activity. Further, it is perfectly acceptable for a particular student to be included in several groups doing the same activity. That would merely be a good example of a repetitive instructional technique!

4. Modify alternative activities to address different multiple intelligences. Ms. Adrian, in using the grid activity in her class, provided an activity that emphasized several intelligences, including spatial, logical/mathematical, and interpersonal. Can this activity be modified and subsequently used to involve other intelligences? If the assignment were to blindfold a student, and have him or her provide verbal directions for the formulation of the grid on the floor without watching the process, could linguistic intelligence be strengthened?

5. Use what you have in the local community! In math instruction, as well as many other subjects, using examples in the students' community can involve students more and motivate them to complete the math. For example, in farming communities, tying math problems to local crop sales can be quite effective. For students in urban areas, describing math problems in terms of the types of clothes or tennis shoes that are in vogue can motivate students more than simply using whatever math problems are on the page. If students live near a major historical park, teachers should consider math examples that could be tied to that local resource (e.g., How many patriots fought at the Battle of Trenton versus how many British mercenaries?).

Teachers in every field should use examples from the community whenever possible. One interesting type of assignment for some tear out groups is to rewrite each of the word problems in a particular unit using some local example. The others in the class can then use those problems for their practice work. This results in more "authentic" learning than some of the math problems presented in the standard math texts.

6. Tie students in emotionally. We now know that, prior to learning, the student must sense emotional safety in the learning environment. Further, if teachers can tie the math content to an emotional hook, students will become more involved in the content. Discussions of math in terms of the number of students who can go on a school trip might be one illustration of this idea. Here are two more examples:

> Grade 3 Problem: "We have 4 buses for the third-grade trip, and each will carry 25 students and 4 supervisory adults. If 22 adults volunteer to go on the trip, how many students can go?"

> Grade 6 Problem: "We have 4 buses, each of which will take 25 students and 4 adults. If students were selected for the class trip based on their math grades, and 96% of a total student math population of 115 students scored high enough to go, would we have to leave eligible students or adult volunteers behind?"

(Continued)

(Continued)

If students have parents in the military, a number of math problems on variable troop strength in a particular engagement might be used. I noted this personally while working in the schools in Clarkesville, Tennessee, since that city is adjacent to the military base that houses the 101st Airborne Division—a division that had recently been deployed overseas.

7. Use differentiated instruction for inclusive classes. While including students with significant disabilities in general education math classes is not new, the use of differentiated instruction as a basis for inclusion is. The overall fit between inclusion and differentiated instruction is almost perfect; again we seem to owe another tribute to Carol Tomlinson, PhD, for her groundbreaking work on this concept. Teachers should jointly plan to use differentiated lessons in inclusion classes. Moreover, with both a general educator and a special educator in the class, the monitoring of the tear out groups is much more easily managed!

8. Continue some traditional lessons. I encourage teachers not to attempt differentiated lessons each and every day. While lectures seem ineffective with many students today, other aspects of traditional instruction work wonderfully, including group project activities, whole class discussions of video- or media-based examples, student presentations, and independent student research. These instructional activities should always be an important component of learning in the elementary classroom.

One question I am frequently asked is how often should teachers differentiate? I usually tell teachers to aim for a highly differentiated lesson structure perhaps three days each week, and on the alternate days utilize more traditional instructional procedures, such as those mentioned above. I believe that this will provide an appropriate mix of activities and will create an effective classroom learning environment where the needs of all students can be met. I also find that teachers respond to this suggestion positively; while teachers have a difficult time seeing themselves teaching three or four groups of students in different tasks during each fifteen-minute segment each day of the week, they can see themselves doing this two or three days each week and using other effective whole group tactics on the other days.

9. Teachers should "test the waters" of differentiated instruction tentatively. Once a teacher decides to attempt differentiated instruction, he or she should try this approach in a successful class—a classroom that seems to be working well. The teacher should also initially do this in an area of math that students know well. This will effectively increase the teacher's comfort zone, and will be more likely to result in a pleasant teaching experience, than trying this new teaching paradigm in a challenging class. Also, testing this idea in a class that is not presenting challenges is more likely to result in initial success. After that, teachers can move into other, more challenging classes. Moreover, teachers who have moved into this slowly and have seen it work as both they and the students grow to understand this instructional system have stated that teaching is simply much more fun this way!

10. Identify practical ways to make differentiated groups work. Various teachers have suggested some simple, practical guidelines to make differentiation work in their classes. While these may not be critically important in every situation, teachers may wish to consider these additional suggestions.

   a. Be careful how heterogeneous groups are selected for differentiation. Teachers should take care not to embarrass students who may not know the content when forming the first differentiated group.
   b. Move furniture as necessary to visually monitor the tear out groups. When a differentiated group is doing a movement-based activity in the front of the room, where the extra room space might be located, the teacher should move to the opposite side of the room, and have students that will continue to work with the teacher move their desks

into a semicircle facing away from the differentiated group. Those students are thus more likely to pay attention to the teacher, and the teacher will be in a position to both teach the mainline instruction group and visually monitor the differentiated group.

c. Provide informal "coaching" to students with overt behavior problems in differentiated groups in order to include them in differentiated groups. One teacher decided that one student who often displayed anger (e.g., cursing at other students) could be included if the teacher provided that student with an "opt out" strategy. In short, she waited until the angry student asked, "Why don't I ever get to go and work over there?" The angry student was told the following. "I would love to put you working with that group, but I know that sometimes you get upset with other students and then you might call the other student stupid or something. Of course, that's never wise, since the other students don't like to be called names. Here's what we'll do. Today, I'll put you over there, but if you find yourself getting angry, just raise your hand and I'll call you back over to the group I'm working with and have you help me demonstrate that activity with them!" This informal coaching and the "opt out" strategy, conducted over a series of days, was enough to get that angry student to a place where he could be included in a less supervised, tear out group, and work in that group.

d. Empower the students in the differentiated groups that do not know the content. Experienced teachers can readily see that in differentiated groups the students who know the content might do the work, and ignore the students who do not know the content. Thus, the teacher should "empower" the students who do not know the content. In the text example involving the formation of the tear out group to develop the grid on the floor using masking tape, the teacher should give the tape to a student who does not know the content, thus facilitating group interaction. In short, the other students will need to interact with that student, and, ideally, teach him about why the grid should be formed in a certain way.

RESULTS OF DIFFERENTIATED LESSONS

Teachers who have chosen to move into differentiation for instruction in math have generally found that many of the anxieties they had about such instruction did not materialize. For example, many teachers are initially concerned about the issue of management of varied groups within the classroom. Of course, every class includes some students who, at least initially, should not be selected for tear out activities since their behavior patterns necessitate close teacher supervision. However, teachers typically find that after the class as a whole gets accustomed to this learning format, even those behaviorally challenged kids can participate meaningfully in tear out activities.

Also, because the training of most teachers in schools today was formulated on the direct instruction model, some teachers cannot bring themselves to believe that learning will take place in the tear out groups; some teachers view these unsupervised groups as disasters waiting to happen. Nevertheless, I've had teachers state repeatedly that once they moved to a differentiated instruction format, they found that students do learn from each other in the tear out groups, and that this instructional format results in increased student learning overall. All teachers are under pressure today to address the math standards mandated by every state department of education, and this learning format will result in improved instruction compared to whole class, traditional instruction. Teachers, however, must exercise some judgment in initial group formulation.

The chart below lists the typical results reported by teachers once they begin the transition to a truly differentiated classroom.

Results of Guess, Assess, and Tear Out

1. *Provision of Varied Instruction.* This offers the most effective instructional option for all students in today's classes.

2. *Increased Involvement of Advanced Students.* The advanced kids in this procedure will be more challenged and thus less likely to get bored and engage in problem behaviors.

3. *Varied Behavior Management Concerns.* Management of an increased number of instructional groups will be a concern, and the teacher should move into differentiation slowly for this reason. Students who would otherwise be bored with traditional lessons will be more engaged in this instructional model, however, and it is hoped these behavior management results will effectively even things out for the teacher in the differentiated lesson.

4. *Improved Instruction for Those Who Need It.* As the mainline group gets smaller, the instruction for that group is likely to improve, since the teacher is concentrating on a smaller group. Thus, the teacher is providing increased support for the students who really need the help on a particular lesson.

5. *Provision of the Best Instruction for Everyone.* Differentiated instruction encourages teachers to offer the most effective enrichment/instruction to kids across the ability spectrum. Teachers must make the mainline group activities as varied, as novel, and as exciting as any of the alternative assignments for the tear out groups.

6. *Effective Use as a Model for Inclusive Instruction.* Teachers can readily see the comfortable fit between the use of multiple tear out groups, formed to be heterogeneous, and the demands of the inclusive classroom. Differentiated instruction provides one of the most effective models for inclusion currently available.

7. *Teachers Become Used to Teaching This Way.* Once teachers try this instructional model, particularly if they test this model in an academic area within their comfort zone, they typically find that they enjoy this type of teaching. While all teachers differentiate to some degree, teachers who devote themselves to this approach often state that they would not like to return to teaching in a traditional fashion. In fact, teaching a differentiated lesson is simply more fun.

A DIFFERENTIATED INSTRUCTION OVERVIEW: WHAT IT IS AND WHAT IT ISN'T

With the guidelines for differentiation of instruction in mind, we can now take a broader look at the overall concept. When I first began to investigate differentiated instruction, I was somewhat confused as to what it really was. I have since learned that such confusion is quite common. Specifically, in many books I read and in many workshops I attended I found that a wide variety of great teaching ideas were presented, but I found no "central theme" on what differentiated instruction was. While I always enjoy acquiring novel teaching ideas, I left many such workshops wondering if "differentiated instruction" was merely an array of "good teaching ideas." I had not grasped the essential element or elements of the concept.

More recently, I have come to understand that differentiation is more than merely an innovative set of novel teaching tactics. Differentiated instruction is, in reality, a new way of conceptualizing learning in the classroom context. Teachers in the 21st century should no longer believe that children make up a "class" of third graders or a "class" of sixth graders.

> Rather than teachers considering students as a "class," differentiated instruction requires that they plan lessons, generate activities, and conduct assessments based on the needs of individual children rather than on groups of children who happen to be the same chronological age.

Again, differentiated instruction represents a real paradigm shift for teachers who have been trained to think of instruction as a group phenomenon—as in the direct instructional model described earlier. Teachers must now shift their thinking to lesson planning for individual children, and they must consider the emerging information on the wide variety of ways that children learn (e.g., multiple intelligences, peer learning, etc.). Only from such a perspective can teachers hope to meet the wide variety of needs in today's classrooms.

I have further come to realize that many teachers are differentiating their math classes without realizing it. Indeed, many teachers have been "differentiating" their classrooms for many years. The academic diversity found in today's classes would suggest that in order to survive as teachers, we must be about the business of novel and innovative teaching to diverse groups of students within the class. For these math teachers, the construct of the differentiated lesson plan will merely mean that they develop their different instructional activities more deliberately, more strategically. These teachers will then deliver a more diversified lesson within the math class, having initially planned to address these diverse learning needs.

RESPONSE TO INTERVENTION IN MATHEMATICS

Coupled with increased differentiation in the planning and delivery of mathematics lessons is the recent emphasis on response to intervention (RTI) in general education (Bender & Shores, 2007; Bryant et al., 2008; Fuchs & Deshler, 2007). With recent changes in federal legislation concerning options for diagnosing students with learning disabilities, teachers across the nation are now expected to deliver multiple research-based instructional interventions of increasing intensity in reading, in order to document how a child responds to those interventions. These are primarily intended as supplementary interventions designed to assist struggling students who simply need more instruction time on particular aspects of reading. According to the recent legislative changes, students who show no positive response or only a limited response to those well designed, increasingly intensive interventions may be suspected of having a learning disability (Bender & Shores, 2007). While different states have adopted slightly different RTI models, most RTI procedures emphasize the following components:

1. Universal screening for students in reading and mathematics,

2. Research-based primary and supplementary interventions for struggling students,

3. Three or more "tiered" interventions that provide progressively more intensive instruction,

4. Frequent progress monitoring in each intervention tier, and

5. Data-based decision making.

Response to intervention procedures in reading have been the basis for the shift in federal legislation, and consequently those reading interventions have been studied for a number of years. However, experts quickly recognized that many students with learning disabilities in reading likewise have difficulties in mathematics, and that resulted in recent suggestions for provision of response to intervention procedures in mathematics (Bryant et al., 2008; Fuchs, Fuchs, & Hollenbeck, 2007; Fuchs et al., 2008). In fact, in various states many school districts currently expect teachers to deliver RTI in both reading and mathematics. This is understandable when one reflects on the fact that many students display a learning disability in math as well as in reading; further, other students have a learning disability in mathematics but no similar disability in reading. Of course, these students will require diagnosis and remediation in the future, and therefore many elementary teachers should anticipate the need for implementing RTI procedures in mathematics within the next several years. Thus, RTI procedures, like differentiation, will impact the delivery of mathematics instruction for many general education teachers. Of course, in a classroom that is already differentiating instruction, delivery of RTI is not nearly as much of a burden, since students are frequently working on differentiated small group work anyway. In that sense, both differentiation and RTI initiatives mutually support each other. Here is a brief example of an RTI procedure in mathematics.

CASE STUDY: AN RTI FOR NUMBER SENSE AND EARLY MATH SKILL

Let's imagine a young girl in the first grade, Anne, who is having some difficulty with early math. Ms. Gullion, the first-grade teacher, has noted that Anne doesn't seem to "understand numbers," so she talked informally with Anne's kindergarten teacher. The kindergarten teacher reported that Anne was never terribly successful in most number exercises, but that she could count. Ms. Gullion then verified that Anne could count up to 20. However, when she was presented with pattern numbers and asked to complete the next numbers in the pattern (e.g., 3, 5, 7, 9, etc.), she could not do so. Also, Anne had great difficulty comparing sets of items (e.g., when presented with two pictures of sets of items, Anne could not ascertain which set included more items). Finally, Ms. Gullion noted that Anne, unlike many of her classmates, hadn't developed the idea of "counting on" to assist with simple addition problems.

Planning a Tier Two Intervention for Early Math

Overall, this set of math problems suggested to Ms. Gullion that Anne needed additional supplemental remedial work on early math skills. This level of additional supplemental instructional assistance typically is provided over and above the typical math lessons for the class, and thus such supplemental instruction is considered a second "tier" of instruction (i.e., the typical math lesson in the general education class may be considered the first "tier" of math instruction under most RTI models). Ms. Gullion decided to provide some additional intensive instruction on basic math skills for Anne and three other students in the first grade. She planned to work with those students three times each week for thirty minutes each time, while her paraprofessional supervised the class in other learning activities. Ms. Gullion decided to use a set of instructional activities that focused specifically on number sense and pattern recognition activities from the Grade 1 edition of the math curriculum. She also devised a set of fifteen assessment questions that featured math facts, pattern completion, counting by twos, counting by fives, and comparing sets of items to find larger and smaller sets. She intended to use that informal assessment as a repeated measure assessment, once each week to carefully monitor the performance of the students.

Next, Ms. Gullion shared a written synopsis of this intervention plan with the first-grade team leader, Mr. Westall, indicating which students would be included and when the intervention would take place. Finally, Ms. Gullion sent a letter to the parents of the four students informing them of the intervention. Ms. Gullion then began this tier two intervention with those four students.

Post Tier Two Decision Making

As Ms. Gullion progressed through this intervention over the next few weeks, she noted that the weekly assessments indicated that three students were moving toward increased success with this supplemental assistance in math. However, Anne seemed to be making little progress, and based on the weekly assessment data for Anne, Ms. Gullion decided that Anne would need more intensive instructional assistance. Therefore, after five weeks in the tier two intervention, Ms. Gullion wrote some informal notes summarizing her tier two intervention efforts for Anne. She also created a data chart to summarize Anne's performance on the weekly tier two intervention assessments (see Figure 4.1). With the summary and those data in hand, She met with the teacher/student support team in her school and recommended a tier three intervention for Anne.

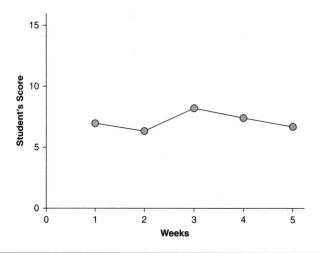

Figure 4.1 Anne's Tier Two Intervention Results

Data Review and Tier Three Intervention Planning

The teacher/student support team at the school included Ms. Gullion, Mr. Westall, Mr. Askew, the school principal, and Ms. Bullock, the instructional coach for the school. Ms. Gullion presented the data summarized in Figure 4.1 and discussed her intensive instruction with the team. She noted that while Anne seemed to be progressing somewhat, she was not moving forward quickly enough to have a realistic opportunity to "catch up" with the other first-grade students by the end of the year, since most of the other students had mastered these early number sense and early math skills.

Next, Mr. Westall told the team that he'd participated in selection of the instructional activities that Ms. Gullion had used with Anne. He indicated that the instructional activities were the correct type of activities for Anne, but that Anne would, in his estimation, need more time on those types of early math activities. Therefore, both he and Ms. Gullion recommended that the team consider a more intensive tier three intervention that would address these early math skills, and would offer a more intensive supplemental intervention program for Anne. After all team members concluded that an intervention seemed reasonable, Ms. Bullock suggested a possibility for such an intensive tier three intervention program.

Because she was the instructional coach, Ms. Bullock was typically given the responsibility for the tier three interventions in both reading and math in this particular school. She worked in a room called the instructional lab, and was provided with a paraprofessional to assist in those responsibilities. With that support, she could conduct very intensive interventions for various students in small instructional groups. She was currently teaching such a group of four students for forty-five minutes daily in a computerized curriculum that focused on early number skills, and Ms. Bullock suggested the possibility of having Anne join that group. On that basis, Anne would receive math instruction with Ms. Gullion daily, as well as forty-five minutes of intensive supplementary

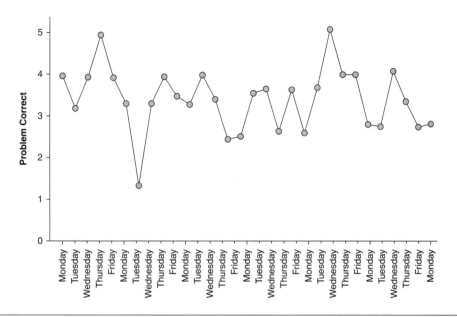

Figure 4.2   Anne's Tier Three Intervention Results

instruction on the specific skills she needed with Ms. Bullock. The team decided to go with that recommendation. They also agreed to meet at the end of the next grading period in six weeks to consider Anne's progress. Ms. Gullion and Ms. Bullock then worked out the time that Anne could go into Ms. Bullock's lab daily.

Figure 4.2 presents the performance data on Anne's performance in the tier three intervention. After five weeks of the next grading period, the team reviewed the tier three intervention data and determined that Anne was still not making sufficient progress in early math. On that basis, the team believed that Anne might have a learning disability. They decided to recommend that the child study team consider Anne's learning performance, based on these intervention data, and other psychological assessments to make a determination.

Because the RTI process is new, many educators may have never had the experience of participating in an RTI process in math. Figure 4.3 presents a completed summary form for this process that may serve as a guide. This summary form, coupled with the data presented in Figures 4.1 and 4.2, describes an acceptable math RTI.

Important Points for Tier Two and Tier Three Interventions

There are several important points to consider when implementing a tier two or tier three intervention. First, note that in describing the interventions above, the teachers attended to the RTI expectation that higher tiers provide more intensive instruction in mathematics. The indicators of increased intensity were described in the various notes and documented within the decision-making

Pupil Name: *Anne Scenscench*   Age: _6_   Date: *9/24/08*

Initiating Teacher: *Ms. Diane Gullion*   School: *Toccoa Primary*   Grade: _1_

Statement of Academic/Behavioral Problem: (and supporting evidence)

   Anne is having difficulty in mathematics at the first-grade level. Her work indicates that, while she can count up to twenty, she does not know number patterns, or basic math facts. She has no strategy for basic number combinations (i.e., adding simple digits by counting on, etc.). This leads to problems in every aspect of math. An informal math assessment at the end of kindergarten last year indicated she was struggling in math readiness. I have shared a written synopsis of these concerns and the intervention plan below with first-grade team leader Mr. Westall.

Signature: *Ms. Diane Gullion*   Date: *9/24/08*

Tier Two Supplemental Intervention Plan

   I will provide Anne with some additional intensive instruction on basic math facts and number patterns, along with three other students with similar needs, as a tier two supplemental math intervention. I will work with this group of four students three times each week for thirty minutes each time, while my paraprofessional supervises the class in other learning activities. I will use a set of timed instructional activities that focus on automaticity in addition facts and number patterns. Once per week, I will use an informal assessment of these skills, and chart those data. Finally, I will send a letter to the parents of the students informing them of the intervention. We plan to begin the intervention on next Monday, 9/27/08.

Signature: *Ms. Diane Gullion*   Date: *9/24/08*

Observation of Student in Tier Two Intervention

   I observed Ms. Gullion on 10/5/08, as she delivered the tier two supplemental math instruction on number patterns and math facts for Anne, along with several other students. Ms. Gullion used several practice worksheets, and then did 3 one-minute timings using a worksheet that included addition math facts and number pattern problems. This procedure is consistent with best practices instruction, as demonstrated in research articles in mathematics journals, for the early grades. The data from these assessments were used as Anne's score. She completed six problems correctly on the day of this observation.

Signature: *Mr. Thomas Westall, Grade 1 Team Leader*   Date: *10/5/08*

Tier Two Intervention Summary

   The data from the five-week tier two intervention, conducted by Ms. Gullion, indicated that while other students were moving toward increased math facts and number pattern skill, Anne did not seem to be making progress. Based on these weekly assessment data, we believe she will need more intensive instruction in mathematics. On 11/15/08, the Student Assistance Team (often called the SAT Team) met, including Ms. Gullion, Mr. Westall, and Ms. Bullock at Toccoa Primary School. We jointly decided that the tier two intervention had not been successful overall, and was not likely to have enough impact to help Anne begin to catch up in mathematics achievement. Therefore, we discussed a third tier of intervention for Anne.

Signature: *Ms. Sandra Bullock, Instructional Coach*   Date: *11/15/08*

Tier Three Intervention Plan

   As the instructional coach at Toccoa Primary School, I, Ms. Sandra Bullock, typically take responsibility for tier three interventions. In my instructional lab, I have the services of a paraprofessional, and various computer-based instructional programs designed to provide remedial intervention support at various math readiness and early math levels. We conduct very intensive interventions for various students working individually using this technology.

For Anne, the SAT recommended an intensive intervention of forty-five minutes daily that focuses on math facts and number pattern recognition, and subsequent number combination problems. Therefore, Anne will receive math instruction with Ms. Gullion each day, as well as forty-five minutes of intensive, computer-based, supplementary instruction on the specific skills she needs in the instructional lab. The student support team will meet at the end of the next grading period in six weeks to reconsider Anne's progress, and Ms. Gullion and I will work out a time that Anne can come to the lab each day.

Signature: *Ms. Sandra Bullock*   Date: *11/15/08*

Observation of Student in Tier Three Intervention

I observed Anne on 1/6/09 while she worked on a computerized math program in the instructional lab, led by Ms. Bullock. This computer-based instructional program was utilized correctly by Ms. Bullock (she has received intensive professional development on use of this program). As a result, Anne was very engaged, and completed most of the problems successfully. The program stressed math facts and early number combination strategies, such as counting representations of numbers and counting on strategies.

Signature: *Mr. Thomas Westall*   Date: *1/6/09*

Tier Three Intervention Summary and Recommendations

The SAT team met and reviewed Anne's progress in math after five weeks in the intensive tier three intervention. Based on the daily performance-monitoring data generated by the computerized program, Anne still does not seem to be making good progress in mathematics, and she is clearly not functioning at grade level. However, she has actively participated in this math instructional program.

The SAT team recommends that Anne's performance be considered by the child eligibility team for inclusion in the program for students with learning disabilities at Toccoa Primary.

Signature: *Mr. Jackson Dean Askew, Principal, Toccoa Primary*   Date: *1/10/09*

Figure 4.3   Summary Form for a Math RTI

process, as noted above. These included such things as documenting the pupil-teacher ratio for each intervention, noting the duration and frequency of the intervention (how many minutes per day and days per week, over how many weeks, etc.), and noting the frequency of performance monitoring in each intervention tier. This level of detail should be included in every RTI documentation summary.

Next, note in the RTI procedure above that the general education teacher was responsible for the tier one intervention in the general education class, and also implemented the tier two supplemental intervention. In many cases, the general education teacher may have to handle these activities without extensive support, and for that reason, finding the time for such interventions may be one of the largest challenges to RTI. In this case, the tier two intervention that Ms. Gullion could offer, while seemingly appropriate, could not be provided to Anne as intensively as she needed as demonstrated by the progress-monitoring data in Figure 4.1. Therefore, in this instance, a tier three intervention was necessary.

In most states, general education teachers will be responsible for both the tier one and tier two interventions for students struggling with reading and math (Bender & Shores, 2007). Further, while the third intervention is typically considered a general education intervention, it does not necessarily mean that general education teachers must implement those tier three interventions alone. In fact, the time pressures in the typical general education classroom would become unbearable in most cases, and it is unrealistic to expect general education teachers to teach math for an entire class, implement a tier two intervention in math for a small subgroup of struggling students within the class, and also implement a more intensive tier three math intervention for other class members with no additional help. It was possible in this example for Ms. Gullion to do the tier two intervention only because she had the services of a paraprofessional in the class. Thus, in most cases, general education teachers will probably not implement the third intervention tier. In this example, that was undertaken by Ms. Bullock, the instructional coach of the school.

Next, note that the data demonstrated that neither the tier two nor the tier three intervention succeeded. Thus, there is some reason to suspect a learning disability in this case. However, the RTI process does not, in and of itself, document a learning disability. Eligibility for learning disabilities services requires a decision of a qualified child study team, and while the RTI procedures may be considered strong evidence for a learning disability, other factors (attention skills, working memory skills or other mental processes, medical conditions) must also be considered. To be specific, after a student has not succeeded in two supplemental interventions (i.e., tier two and tier three), a learning disability may be suspected, but at that point the learning disability has not been demonstrated. The determination of the existence of a learning disability is the responsibility of the eligibility team's evaluation of the data from tier one, two, and three, coupled with their interpretation of the underlying psychological processes, along with other relevant data.

Research in reading and literacy suggests that approximately 40% to 60% of students who begin a tier two intervention have their needs met by either the tier two or tier three intervention, and thus are not considered for learning disability services; to date, there is not a similar body of research on RTI procedures in math. However, some students for whom a tier two or tier three intervention is working should be maintained in either the tier two or tier three intervention in mathematics until he or she has reached the benchmarks for his or her grade level in mathematics. Thus, provision of interventions for students who are having their needs met in tier two or tier three should also be considered when allocating time and resources for RTI.

Next, note that many students struggling in math may be participating in the general education curriculum and a supplemental tier two intervention at one point, and at a later point may participate in the general education curriculum and a supplemental tier three intervention. Struggling students should not be pulled out of math instruction in the general education classroom to do the tier two or tier three interventions. Further, while tier one intervention is maintained for all students in the general education class, no student should be participating in more than one supplemental intervention at any one time.

Finally, we should note the serious responsibility that general education teachers now have in the eligibility process when documenting a learning disability in mathematics. Of course, general education teachers have always participated in determining the eligibility of students for services in learning disabilities (LD). Historically, general education math teachers have participated in eligibility meetings, brought in math work samples, and reported on error analysis and/or task analysis of the student's math skills. Still, general education teachers completing an RTI procedure will have more responsibility, because these teachers will be responsible for providing one of the two most critical pieces of data in that LD determination—the performance-monitoring assessment data chart for the tier two intervention. General education teachers should be made aware of that increased responsibility, and the need to understand the intricacies of RTI, and in particular monitoring a child's performance repeatedly in tier two interventions.

Again, both differentiation and RTI impact how the teacher plans and conducts lessons, and these two initiatives are mutually supporting. In differentiated classes, having students work in small groups is not an infrequent occurrence, and this sets the stage through which tier two RTI procedures may be completed.

WHAT'S NEXT?

At this point, we have investigated the brain research as well as the practical concerns in formulating a differentiated lesson in math. We've also described how RTI might impact general education teachers in mathematics. The next chapter presents techniques that will assist in learning early math skills in kindergarten and the lower grades. In the next chapter, and all subsequent chapters, a variety of instructional ideas are presented, but these must be placed in the context of both a strategically developed, differentiated lesson plan and the emerging requirements for documenting response to intervention in mathematics, as described in this chapter.

5

Supporting Students Who Are Low Achieving

Leslie Laud

Each student who enters our classroom is a mystery with a uniquely varied learning profile. Uncovering how each child thinks and feels about mathematics is one of the most fulfilling and rewarding opportunities we have as teachers. Among those students with identified learning challenges, no two are ever the same, though some may share certain similar learning patterns such as difficulty with efficient and organized thinking or trouble retrieving what they know (Swanson & Deshler, 2003). However, two students diagnosed with attentional and memory difficulties may have entirely different readiness skills in different areas of math. Although familiarity with each child's learning profile is valuable, it is equally important to know simply what each child can and cannot do for each specific math unit because our preconceptions about their diagnosed difficulties may bias us, and students often surprise us in wonderful and unexpected ways.

Since the varying units, such as algebra versus geometry, draw on diverse underlying capabilities (symbolic thinking, language skill, or visual reasoning), students need opportunities, such as diagnostic preassessments and continuous formative assessments, to show what they have and have not yet mastered before and during each separate unit. Then based on what teachers learn from these assessments, differentiated content supports can be offered to address students' learning needs and to help them be more strategic in how they learn overall. However, some students with more severe gaps or learning challenges will require more than the kinds of adjustments recommended so far. In a sense, we may need to intensify our efforts to differentiate how we teach them. Although differentiation is intensified in this chapter, the emphasis remains on promoting self-direction and having students participate in directing the next steps needed for their learning as much as they can. One caveat to keep in mind throughout this chapter and book is that not all students may fully master all unit essential learnings with the same depth, but attaining a level of proficiency on each of these should always be the goal.

Beyond addressing differences in readiness levels for each specific unit, as discussed in the previous chapters, teachers can intensify how they differentiate support for the underlying, more serious difficulties students may have in three areas:

- Basic facts
- Concepts
- Procedures

Response to Intervention Tier II Interventions Described in This Chapter

Basic Facts:

- Preassess facts to develop a systematic list to address.
- If facts are known but recalled slowly, use speeded retrieval interventions.
- To build basic fact conceptual knowledge, use decomposition and arrays interventions.
- Use explicit and systematic instruction.

Conceptual Knowledge:

- Clarify difficulty first to pinpoint precise breakdown to address.
- Manipulatives: Concrete-representational-abstract learning sequence (CRA).
- Present information in graphic organizers.
- Directly teach diagramming techniques.
- Coresearch alternative explanations.

Procedures:

- Preassess procedures to develop systematic list to address.
- Use distributed practice over time rather than massed practice at once.
- Have students create checklists of procedural steps.
- Teach heuristics.
- Design strategies.

DIFFERENTIATING INSTRUCTION IN BASIC FACTS

Beverly knows her basic facts but recalls them slowly. She dreads being asked in front of the class to work out problems because she's even slower to recall them when anxious. Steven, on the other hand, never quite mastered the basic facts. Solving 6 × 7 can take a few minutes as he laboriously adds up seven 6s. Both of them have trouble with longer calculations because they cannot pull up their basic facts quickly.

By middle school, students particularly dislike drilling basic facts. However, research suggests it is critical that they know and do these effortlessly, to free up their mental resources, organize and monitor their thinking, and focus on the higher order aspects of middle school math (Delazar et al., 2003). This may also be important if students are not given certain kinds of accommodations. Teachers do need to advocate for the small percentage of students who simply cannot master the basic facts because that is part of their disability and they should be allowed to use calculators, in line with the National Council of Teachers of Mathematics (NCTM) guidelines. For those who can learn basic facts yet use calculators, the research is mixed on whether accommodations such as calculator usage increase the performance of these students (Tindal & Ketterlin-Geller, 2004). As students want to be independent at this age and research shows fostering self-directness enhances achievement (Montague, 2007), they respond well to support that allows them to take charge of their learning of these facts, in the following ways.

To determine which students need support with basic facts, students can take the preassessment shown in Figure 5.1, and teachers can note when it is turned in. The timing should be discrete—for example, use a timer on a small computer screen—or it might heighten anxiety. Teachers should have the entire class do this, and note time needed on each. Then class norms can be used to determine which students perform these most slowly and so would need practice to increase their speed.

Data-Informed Instruction **6**

To differentiate which students know the facts, but are slow, from those who lack conceptual strategies for solving them, the last question asks them to explain strategies for solving various problems. Students can self-score these preassessments with blue ink ("all pencils away") and then create a plan for how they will learn the strategies and increase their speed (see Figure 5.2). Students should be given the opportunity to retake alternate versions of the test every 2 weeks before or after school or during a lab or free period. When they ask to set up an appointment to retake the quiz, they must bring a log of how and when they practiced (see Figure 5.3). Some teachers have difficulty getting students to make an effort to improve and retake the quiz every 2 weeks, so they mark down a student's homework grade.

Figure 5.1

Basic Facts

1.	9×8	$96 \div 12$	$17 - 9$	$3 + 8$
2.	$9 + 7$	7×8	$42 \div 6$	6×4
3.	$5 + 8$	$12 - 4$	6×7	$7 + 8$
4.	$3 + 6$	12×7	$7 + 4$	$12 - 5$
5.	$6 + 8$	$11 - 5$	$13 - 7$	$14 - 8$
6.	$4 + 7$	$15 - 8$	$16 - 9$	7×6
7.	$48 \div 6$	$21 \div 3$	3×6	8×6
8.	7×4	$14 - 8$	$8 + 4$	$14 - 9$

Explain how a person who can't recall a fact can solve:

6×7 $84 \div 12$

$8 + 7$ $17 - 9$

Figure 5.2

My Plan to Improve My Basic Calculations

Based on my preassessment, I'd like to improve: speed   or   accuracy (circle one).

The kinds of errors I made were:

_____

_____

_____

_____

_____

_____

_____

_____

_____

The problems I figured out most slowly or couldn't recall were:

$+$

$-$

$\times$

$\div$

My plan to improve is:

Resources:

Websites:

Distributed times I'll practice:

Figure 5.3

My Practice Log

Date	What I Did	Adult Signature
_____	_____	_____
_____	_____	_____
_____	_____	_____
_____	_____	_____
_____	_____	_____
_____	_____	_____
_____	_____	_____
_____	_____	_____
_____	_____	_____
_____	_____	_____

My Graph (Goal: Number per minute)

5

4

3

2

1

(Min)

Dates ___ ___ ___ ___ ___ ___ ___ ___ ___ ___

Knows Facts but Slow Recall—Use Speeded Retrieval Strategies

For students like Beverly who know their facts but recall them slowly, they can use varied practice options such as using timers as they take timed fact tests. They can chart their time and accuracy on graphs (refer to Figure 5.3) and set goals for each successive practice. In addition, they can use cover, copy, compare types of strategies in which they do the following:

1. Copy a fact reading it aloud.

2. Cover it up.

3. Write it from memory.

4. Compare it to the original problem (adapted from Stading, Williams, & McLaughlin, 1996).

Teachers can have students who need to strengthen these skills work in pairs quizzing each other or have students bring in signed evidence that they worked on these at home. In addition, students can also use motivating practices such as games at www.multiplication.com, particularly "The Magician," or http://www.tomsnyder.com/fasttmath/index.html. The Magician gives a certificate when students master a certain number of problems in a given time, and fast-t charts progress, but it is a pay site. FASTT tracks students usage and provides progress monitoring quizzes every set times of practices, such as every hour. Many more sites exist, as typing "multiplication games" into a search engine shows. When selecting websites (or having students select them), keep the following in mind:

Factors to Consider in Selecting Online Practice

- Does the game have a quick pace? (time on task)
- How many problems are solved per minute?
- Is it a timed practice?
- Does the game offer immediate feedback and corrections?
- Does the game chart progress?
- Is there a competitive element, that is, a high scorer's list?
- Can it be set up so only unknown facts are practiced?

One site has students navigate through a cave to find facts to practice. Most time is spent on navigating and little on practicing facts. Charting progress and moving up on high scorer lists can be super engaging and motivating, as on www.iknowthat.com. The website www.coolmath-games .com can be set up so students practice only those facts that they need to learn, as does FASTT. Other websites such as www.algebrahelp.com and www .mathscore.com provide personalized feedback and differentiated tips on how to improve.

Needs Conceptual Understanding of Basic Facts

In addition to drill, those students like Steven who have not mastered their basic facts because of conceptual problems benefit from learning strategies for figuring out the answers. It is essential that students practice responding correctly when practicing these facts so that if they do not know the correct responses, they can best learn them using strategies described below. In fact, research has found that when both drill and the kind of strategy instruction described in this section are integrated, the two approaches result in the greatest gains and transfer (Woodward, 2006), and so this makes the argument that both should be taught to all students.

Strategy instruction enables students to understand the relationships between basic facts so that they can use these to better understand them and remember them more efficiently. Students decompose numbers in the following ways. For example, if a student knows $3 \times 7 = 21$, then 6×7 can be decomposed and figured out by doubling 21 to get 42. Or if they know $6 + 6$, they can use this to solve $6 + 7$. The following are excellent resources for reinforcing such a strategic approach to learning basic facts:

- Dale Seymour's *Mental Math* series (addition and subtraction)
- Sopris West's *Fact Fluency and More!* (addition and subtraction)
- http://www.mathscore.com (addition, subtraction, multiplication, and division)

Students should monitor their own progress with weekly quizzes and should be sure to graph their progress (refer to Figure 5.3) so they can monitor the effectiveness of the approaches they are using. Fuchs and Fuchs (1986) have found that such progress monitoring is highly effective, particularly when graphed and used with data-based decision rules such as: If after seven attempts, students' graphed scores are not increasing, encourage them to practice with an alternative strategy, or in a more distributed way (over time, rather than all at once). Possible sequences for teaching these calculation strategies are shown in Figure 5.4.

To further deepen students' understandings of basic facts, mathematical representations can be used to model concepts. As an example, Fosnot and Dolk (2001) demonstrate how arrays of numbers can be used to help students construct understandings of basic facts through seeing pictorial number arrays, a research-based practice recommended by The What Works Clearing House's Math Practice Guide (Gersten et al., 2009). In this approach, students see how four rows of six can transform into an arrangement of three rows of eight, with the number of chips or dots representing the total of 24 remaining constant.

Explicit and Systematic Instruction

Teaching basic skills can be introduced in a constructivist, discovery-oriented approach, but some students will require explicit and systematic instruction. These need not be opposing approaches. The teachers in the

Figure 5.4

Basic Facts Calculation Strategies

Addition Facts

	I have mastered:
Count on (Use when adding 1 or 2. Start with larger number, then count up 1 or 2)	_____
Doubles and Neighbors (i.e., 4 + 4, so 4 + 5)	
Neighbors (8 + 7 ≈ double 7 plus 1 more)	_____
Five-Bars (5 + 1; 5 + 7 ≈ 5 + 5 + 2)	_____
Ten-Frames (2 + 8; 4 + 6; 7 + 3)	
Nearly 10: All 9 facts (5 + 4, 7 + 2) and 11 facts (3 + 8; 4 + 7)	_____
Decomposing numbers—10 facts with 8 or 9	_____
8 + 6 = (decompose 6 into 2 + 4) 8 + 2 which is 10, then +4, so a total of 14	
Remaining 8 facts: 8 + 4, 6 + 8	_____

Multiplication Facts

	I have mastered:
0, 1, 10, 11—Instant patterns	_____
2, 5—Double the number or count by 5s	_____
Doubles (2 × 2, 3 × 3 . . .)	_____
Double the doubles: 3 × 7 = 21; so 6 × 7—double 21 is 42	_____
The 9-times quickie (think of 10 fact, subtract a 9)	_____
Use a related fact, i.e., add one more (6 × 8 + 8 = 7 × 8)	_____
6s—Think-of-5 fact, add one more (5 × 8 + 8 = 6 × 8)	_____
3s—Think of 2, add one more	_____

focus groups I led were deeply committed to a constructivist, discovery-oriented approach, yet when students needed additional supports, they had a wide array of explicit and systematic options to use to offer this, often as a backup, which included providing written models of proficient problem solving, encouraging students to verbalize thought processes, having students engage in guided practice with corrective feedback offered, and frequent cumulative review, all of which are strongly supported by research according to The What Works Clearing House's Middle School Math Practice Guide (Gersten et al., 2009).

DIFFERENTIATING FOR CONCEPTUAL UNDERSTANDING

> *Elizabeth shrank back when she heard that the next unit would be on geometry. She knows her learning style well, and she knows that she has difficulty interpreting visual images. When her teacher had recently tried to explain fractions through visual images, she noticed that Elizabeth actually looked away. Elizabeth is a cooperative student and eager to learn, but it was an epiphany for them both when they realized that she did this because she just cannot make sense of images. Elizabeth has a mild nonverbal learning disability, which often means that she struggles with making sense of nonverbal images, and she prefers to learn through words.*
>
> *Teddy usually performs well on math tasks, though not extraordinarily well. However, on a recent probability task, he had real difficulty understanding the idea of independent events. His teacher drew a diagram for him, but he still did not seem to get the concept. Teddy has no diagnosed disability; he just often requires more time, exposures, and practice to master certain conceptual understandings.*

Students who struggle with conceptual understanding can pose some of the toughest challenges for teachers. Often teachers feel most of the class is ready to move on but recognize some need more time. The following approaches are designed to be used as homework or tiers built into full class lessons so the whole class is not held up while a few students get extra help with a concept. It is recommended that teachers focus on developing and solidifying conceptual understandings before procedures, as recommended in NCTM's (2000) Learning Principle that cautions against teaching procedures without fully addressing conceptual understanding as well. A continued emphasis on solidifying conceptual understandings is prominent in the new core standards for mathematics as well (http://www.corestandards.org).

Clarify a Concept and Assess It

Before attempting to use a more intensive strategy to help strengthen a student's grasp of a concept, teachers should ensure they themselves have a clear sense of the specifics of the concept that they would like to develop as well as precisely where the student falls on a continuum of understanding the concept. Teachers can ask themselves questions such as:

- What are the specifics of the concept I want the student to grasp?
- What is already grasped?
- What else can I try to develop it?

To determine what the student already does understand, the teacher can sit with the student and ask him or her to verbalize their thought processes or explain their thinking, with prompts such as, "Tell me all you do understand." However, teachers often don't have the luxury of this time, and so they can have students fill in a form such as Figure 5.5. Often just having students complete this form, which requires them to focus on what they do know, crystallizes their questions. After the teacher has these data, alternative approaches for clarifying the concept can be chosen from the following list of strategies. Research supporting each is given in the following sections:

- Manipulatives: Concrete-representational-abstract learning sequence (CRA)
- Graphic organizers
- Diagramming
- Coresearching alternative explanations

These strategies are described in more detail in the following sections.

Manipulatives: Concrete-Representational-Abstract Learning Sequence

Students can also gain conceptual understandings through working with manipulatives, though teachers need to tread cautiously to ensure these are novel, small, and not perceived as childish (though some teachers disagree that manipulatives would be perceived this way). If many students need this support, manipulatives can be used with the entire class regularly and approached with a mature attitude. Otherwise, a manipulative center can be set up in one area of the classroom, and students who need that practice can spend time there. In this way, a lesson can be easily differentiated. (See Chapter 6 for more on using centers to tier instruction.)

Research has found certain manipulatives used in a CRA learning sequence (CRA—concrete objects, representational or pictorial, then abstract or written symbols) uplifts algebra achievement (Witzel, 2005; Witzel, Mercer, & Miller, 2003). For a resource on this approach, see Riccomini and Witzel (2010). Among the manipulatives available for middle school content that I and teachers in the focus groups I ran have found helpful are the following:

Differentiation of Student Work 7

- Algebra tiles (linear and quadratic equation solving)
- Didax Geofix (nets)
- Models of shapes (surface area and volume)
- Soft 1 cm squares (available from (http://www.etacuisenaire.com)

For example, in a unit on exponents, manipulatives can be used to teach a concept through a tiered lesson. By having students build multiplicative growth models of 4×3 with small cubes and exponential growth models of 4^3, they can actually see the striking difference in

Figure 5.5

Concept Questions

A concept we are learning is:

_____

_____

_____

A diagram for understanding this is:

```
┌───────────────────────────────────────────────┐
│                                                 │
│                                                 │
│                                                 │
│                                                 │
│                                                 │
│                                                 │
└───────────────────────────────────────────────┘
```

The parts I understand are:

_____

_____

_____

The questions I have are:

_____

_____

_____

how quickly the models grow in contrast to each other. This lesson can be instantly and easily differentiated in that students who immediately show that they already know exponents can move on to challenging activities, such as researching and writing an explanation for why a number raised to the power of zero is one. Again, these manipulatives should differ from those used in elementary school or they may be rejected as immature by middle school students. It is important to keep in mind that some students can gain abstract understandings without needing the concrete instructional phase and so they should be allowed to skip ahead.

As noted earlier, if only very few students need manipulatives, they should be offered as a station in a learning center, rather than a full class activity. After building models, students should then sketch diagrams of these kinds of models to move through the representational phase of this learning sequence. Finally, they can work with only the number symbols on paper. In general, when using manipulatives, researchers have found three exposures to manipulatives followed by three exposures to representations has ensured that many students with mathematics disabilities understand the concept (Miller & Hudson, 2007).

Graphic Organizers

Another key way to accommodate diverse learners that can be easily used at any time and during any unit of study is graphic organizers. Students who can grasp information when presented in a compact way with relationships among the pieces of information expressed symbolically benefit from graphic organizers. These can be presented in varied formats to help different kinds of learners all make sense of information. Excellent graphic organizers that have actually been tested and research has found to be effective are available at www.graphicorganizers.com. Note the

Polynomials		
Monomial (one term)	Binomial (polynomial of two terms)	Trinomial (polynomial of three terms)
5	$5a + 5b$	$5a + 6c + 12d$
X	$10h + 10i$	$x^2 + 2 \times 2 + 4 \times 3 + x$
$5b$	$10 + 12i$	$4 \times 2 + 3 \times 2 + 6x$ (nonexample)
$\frac{1}{5}$	$7y - 2x$	$3 + 4x + x^2$
$\frac{10}{2}$	$3x - 4x$ (nonexample)	

sample graphic organizer that shows how monomials, binomials, and trinomials fall under the umbrella category of polynomials.

Research has found that using graphic organizers results in improved performance in areas such as solving linear equations (Ives, 2007). Lessons can be differentiated in that some students can be asked to create graphic organizers on their own, while others are given support for creating them with models or templates, such as that in Figure 5.6.

Diagramming

Most textbooks recommend students make diagrams but give little direct instruction for how to do so. With diagrams, students learn how to map relationships within common word problems visually into diagrams. Since students with learning needs often have difficulty understanding visual and numerical relationships, diagramming may be one of the most important and potentially widely used strategies worth teaching. Diagramming can enable students to understand concepts or problems through designing solution plans that keep track of their thinking while solving word problems (Marshall, 1995). As the brain is hard wired to create and use schemas that can be represented in diagrams, this facilitates how students naturally organize their interpretation and solution for word problems.

Research has found that using schematic images is positively related to success in mathematical problem-solving, whereas the use of pictorial images (irrelevant to the math, e.g., coloring petals on flowers along a road in a distance problem) is negatively related to success (Van Garderen, 2006). Schematic representations were used to *correctly* solve problems most of the time, whereas pictorial representations were used most of the time for *incorrect* solutions. Pictorial representations include drawings that focus on irrelevant aspects of the problem while schematic images use codes or symbols to show relationships.

Students should use the most time-efficient strategies for drawing diagrams. They should be told that diagrams should not be realistic pictures, but just quick symbols or codes to show relationships between mathematical models. Students could even practice drawing inefficient diagrams (with trees and leaves along a road between two boys' homes) and then more efficient ones like those in Figure 5.7.

A diagram can be used as a tool to show initial understanding of a problem, to show how it tracks what is happening in the problem, and to justify the solution (Van Gardener, 2006). When using it to track thinking, marks such as arrows that show flow should be outside the diagram to avoid confusion. Teachers should repeatedly emphasize that diagrams are not products, but just tools to model thinking. Furthermore, some diagrams that model relationships have been found to be more effective than those that are set up in a way that less clearly

Figure 5.6

Designing a Graphic Organizer

A concept we are learning now is:

Different categories of this concept are:

Differences among the pieces of the categories are:

List each category in the box.

List distinguishing factors below.

Figure 5.7

Diagram Types

The following are four categories of diagram types:

1. Networks or line diagrams

Peter and Tom live 1,000 feet apart. Tom walks twice as fast as Peter. If they planned to meet and leave at the same time, how many feet will each walk?

This type works best for problems that can be presented in a line.

2. Matrices or tables

3. Tree diagram

Sprinkle	Caramel	Fruit
^	^	^
Vanilla or Chocolate	Vanilla or Chocolate	Vanilla or Chocolate

4. Part to whole

Near a pond, there were 22 sets of footprints from each animal. The two types of animals were ducks and rabbits. How many were there of each type?

Sources: Van Gardener, 2006; Xin, 2007.

models relationships between quantities; an example of this is ******—ooo to show a decrease by a factor of 2 (Xin, Jitendra, & Deatline-Buchman, 2005).

Xin and Jitendra (2006) offer research validated strategies for teaching students to diagram such rate and ratio in proportion problems. A full curriculum for teaching this strategy is available from Pro Ed (Jitendra, 2007).

Figure 5.8

Creating My Own Diagram

My diagram:

_____

_____

_____

_____

_____

_____

This diagram shows:

_____

_____

_____

_____

_____

_____

Diagram Checklists

1. Does it show all relevant parts of the math problem? (not necessarily everything)
2. Does it show how these parts are related? (how they belong together)
3. Does it lead into a solution?
4. Is there any extra information or details that can be deleted?
5. Did I draw it as quickly but accurately as possible? (does not need to be realistic)
6. Did I use codes? (teacher to demonstrate)
7. Can I show how I track my understanding of the problem with it?
8. Can I use it to explain how I justify my solution?

Students should first determine whether the given word problem fits into the structure of the "vary" type of problem diagram. "Vary" problems are those in which two amounts vary in relation to one another. These are common types of problems that students encounter in middle school such as ratio, rates and proportion, making this a useful strategy to learn.

In addition, Xin and Jitendra (2006) recommend that when readiness levels show a need, teachers can begin by presenting all available information to students at first so that there is nothing to solve for while the process is being introduced and modeled. Students merely gain practice in how to set up the diagrams, as in the following example:

A car travels 25 miles on a gallon of gas. It can travel 75 miles on 3 gallons of gas. (Jitendra, 2002)

After students are comfortable with diagramming, then problems with missing information can be diagrammed.

Coresearching Alternative Explanations

When students are having difficulty mastering a topic, teachers and students should explore multiple explanations in alternative textbooks or on the Internet. *Transitional Mathematics Program* (Woodward & Stroh, 2004) published by Sopris West is an alternative text with clear direct instruction and explanations, designed for students who struggle.

As an example of research on a topic, students might be invited to find three definitions of what a transversal is and how this can be used to calculate angle measures in parallel lines crossed by a transversal. The different websites might offer varied verbal descriptions, visuals, and examples. Using a guide like Figure 5.9, students could then select which they prefer and explain why. ❹ To structure this type of task, teachers can create hotlists or webquests of diverse and high-quality websites that students can access to find such comparisons, such as www.kn.sbc.com/wired/fil/pages/listallthinli.html.

This site presents links to varied geometry Web pages. Additional good sites include:

http://www.eduplace.com/kids/hmm (concept review, math glossary, games)

http://www.sadlier-oxford.com/math (concept review, math minutes)

As a word of caution, be sure to check all links and ensure they are active before using an existing hotlist. Also, if teachers do not have sufficient Internet access for the entire class to be online at once, students can work in groups or could use alternative texts to do similar activities as one group uses the Internet. Free sample math texts are often available from most publishers.

Figure 5.9

Alternative Sources Project

Concept I explored:

_____

_____

_____

_____

Sources I used:

_____

_____

_____

_____

Summary of explanations:

_____

_____

_____

_____

The best one was _____ because _____

_____

_____

_____

_____

Teach Students Time Management

One of the realities of having a learning challenge is that schoolwork inevitably takes more time, even when students are using top notch learning strategies. Once students grasp a concept, it is not *learned*. To hang on to it, they must do distributed practice until it is internalized. How much practice varies and so needs to be differentiated, as I have found over-drill once a concept is mastered can actually decrease learning. Some students will simply require more time, particularly when teachers give students the option to work on their homework in class while helping students who need extra help. The students who receive the extra help in class will not get the time to work on their homework. If available, teachers can refer these students to a counselor or another specialist who can help them with time management. Such students could be asked to fill out a time management form. As time management is a great topic for all students, the form could be offered to all. To avoid losing class teaching time, it could be given as a homework assignment. To strengthen the value that students get from it, they could be asked to work on it with an adult.

DIFFERENTIATING PROCEDURAL SUPPORT

Leo's eyes light up whenever he is given a challenging math problem that he can really sink his teeth into and think about deeply. However, Leo becomes frustrated whenever he needs to perform basic mathematical procedural calculations such as long division or multiplying decimals because he has long-term memory difficulties that cause him to forget the simple steps needed to perform these and so he constantly makes accidental miscalculations. Nevertheless, he enjoys toying with mathematical problems that intrigue him.

Jason, on the other hand, has a solid long-term memory of how to perform these kinds of calculations because he has over practiced them over the years. However, Jason struggles with attentional and working memory problems that cause him to forget steps or do steps out of order when he is working on learning new algorithms such as how to solve linear equations. When calculating, he needs support with organizing how to approach solving a problem, then with monitoring his thinking as he carries out the steps.

This section addresses difficulties students have with following procedures: taking the right steps in the right order to perform calculations, after conceptual understandings have been built and students merely need support with recalling steps, or the order of steps. First, strategies are recommended for students like Leo who need backfilling; practicing basic calculations such as long division or multiplying fractions and decimals, skills needed for middle school math. Next, general and content-based strategies are presented for students like Jason who have difficulty with mastering procedures, even after understanding concepts behind them. Again, as a caveat—some students will have inordinate difficulty mastering basic facts because of the nature of their disability. Others will be so put off by the practice that teachers need to weigh how important it is to teach these against potentially fostering a dislike of mathematics globally because these have been over-taught. I have attempted to cite the most motivating and enjoyable ways to learn these. However, if a student is just not making progress and is not receiving the kind of innate satisfaction that comes from mastering these, then placing too much emphasis on them needs to be reconsidered and options such as calculator use explored.

As students self-score their basic fact preassessments (refer to Figure 5.1), they should also take and self-score the basic calculations preassessment (see Figure 5.10). Then in Figure 5.11, they are given an array of options for how they can take steps to improve.❹ It is important they keep track of these efforts, graph improvements on each subsequent retaking of the preassessment, and determine if their chosen strategy is helping them improve. Teachers should tread cautiously in recommending strategies, or students might groan and complain at strategies such as "checklists," feeling that it is being imposed rather than embrace it as valuable. Students are more likely to appreciate the value of strategies when they self-direct which they choose and how they use them.

Student Self-Direction ④

Figure 5.10

Basic Calculations Preassessment

$2\frac{1}{3} + 4\frac{5}{8}$ $\qquad\qquad$ $6\frac{1}{5} \div 1\frac{2}{3}$

$482.01 \div 9.6$ $\qquad\qquad$ 5.82×63.09

$\frac{3}{8} \times 4\frac{1}{4}$ $\qquad\qquad$ $33.6 \div 9.807$

$2\frac{1}{5} - 1\frac{4}{7}$ $\qquad\qquad$ $99 - 3.08$

$3 \div 8$ $\qquad\qquad$ $3.6 \div 0.006$

Backfilling Basic Calculations

Students like Leo show up with gaps in their ability to perform basic calculations. Basic calculations are distinguished from basic skills in that calculations involve longer procedures (long division) in contrast to a simple fact (7 + 8). As noted earlier, teachers can give a brief pretest to the entire class in the beginning of the year to find which students need to strengthen their ability to perform basic calculations (refer to Figure 5.10). Students who cannot complete all the calculations accurately within a reasonable timeframe can be expected to design a practice plan (refer to Figure 5.11) and to retake the test every 2–4 weeks until they are able to pass it. Before taking it, they should submit the same practice log recommended in the basic facts section (see refer to Figure 5.3) with a graph of improvements. Ideally, they should be able to make their own, or at least research and find ones that appeal to them on the Internet. For example, the following is a sample mnemonic to help students recall the steps of long division:

Figure 5.11

My Practice Plan for Basic Calculations

My preassessment shows I need to practice:

Circle each:

Addition of fractions/decimals

Subtraction of fractions/decimals

Multiplication of fractions/decimals

Division of fractions/decimals

List where I had difficulty (which step) for each:

_____

_____

_____

_____

_____

_____

_____

My plan for practicing this is (be specific—list websites/resources):

_____

_____

_____

_____

_____

_____

_____

DMSB—Divide Multiply Subtract Bring Down
Dracula must suck blood.

A major key with such mnemonics is that they provide cues and help students organize themselves, two facets of successful instruction with students with learning challenges, according to the research (Swanson & Deshler, 2003). Again, it should be stressed that these tricks should only be used with students who fully understand the concept. More of this type exists, including whole rap songs.

Distributed Practice

Distributed (spread out over time) rather than massed (done all at once) practice should be recommended. Students can do distributed practice at many websites, and with self-correcting worksheet puzzles such as Math With Pizzazz (Marcy & Marcy, 1989). These puzzles have students solve problems, then use the answers to solve a puzzle. If a wrong answer is calculated, the answer will not appear in the puzzle and the student will get instant feedback that the answer needs to be reworked.

Checklists

Checklists are an effective way to help students understand and mentally organize procedural routines that can be used in many versatile ways. Research has found that even in isolation, when used alone rather than as part of a comprehensive strategy, checklists can significantly support low achieving, bringing their performance level close to their peers and that all students reporting enjoying using them (Zrebiec Uberti, Mastropieri, & Scruggs, 2004).

Checklists provide an instant tier in a lesson plan. When teaching the area of triangles, for example, teachers can have some students move on to challenge problems in class, while giving students who show they are having difficulty with recalling the necessary steps scaffolded support in creating step checklists (see Figure 5.12). See also the example of a student-created checklist that was designed to address the specific kinds of errors this student made most frequently in finding the area of a triangle. Students should be expected to fade using this scaffold as they become comfortable with the needed steps.

Sample Student-Created Checklist

☐ Did I identify the type of triangle? If it is not a right triangle, do I know what to do?
☐ Did I recall the formula for the triangle? Did I divide by 2 (or multiply by $\frac{1}{2}$)? If not, where can I find the formula?
☐ Did I identify base and height?
☐ Did I identify a height that is perpendicular to the base?
☐ Did I diagram it? (Can I see this in relation to a square/rectangle?)
☐ Did I label it?
☐ Can I justify the reasonableness of my response?

Figure 5.12

Making a Checklist of Procedural Steps

List all steps I need to do (number them and read them to someone who can do the procedure):

_____

_____

_____

_____

_____

_____

_____

_____

Write the steps as questions to ask yourself to self-direct you through the process.

_____

_____

_____

_____

_____

_____

_____

_____

When/How will you practice these?

_____

_____

_____

Heuristics—Specific Strategies for Remembering a Sequence of Steps

In addition to checklists, students can be helped to design and use strategies for remembering sequences of steps needed for procedures through heuristics. Recent research has found that among those strategies that significantly uplift achievement among students with learning disabilities in mathematics, those that apply heuristics are by far the most powerful (Gersten, Chard, Jayanthi, Baker, Morphy, & Flojo, 2009). Students with some learning needs have difficulty with monitoring and directing their thinking while they engage in solving math problems (Montague, 2007), particularly following procedural steps. The following strategies, which are examples of heuristics, can be offered to all students, to assist them with following procedural steps if checklists are not enough support.

Look-Ask-Pick

Look-Ask-Pick (LAP) is an example of a procedural strategy that is somewhat of a heuristic, in that it is used to teach students the specific steps for solving one type of math problem. LAP was developed and validated by Test and Ellis (2005) to help students understand the necessary steps for adding and subtracting fractions.

LAP: Adding and Subtracting Fractions

Look at the denominators ($\frac{1}{2} + \frac{1}{3}$)

Ask yourself the questions: Are they the same/Will the smaller denominator divide into the larger denominator an even number of times? (No.)

Pick your fraction type. (They fit into sixths.)

The steps for teaching LAP include:

☐ Teacher modeling of the strategy.
☐ Guided practice of the steps with the teacher and students restating the steps.
☐ Individual practice of the strategy steps.
☐ Pair practice using games and flash cards to recall the strategy steps and types of fractions.

Source: Test & Ellis, 2005.

A strategy like this can be posted in the classroom or placed on small laminated cards and given to students to hold at their desks. After addressing any prerequisite skill gaps and gaining buy-in from students through discussing when and how it will be useful to them, the teacher can model the strategy with a think-aloud and ensure students learn it through activities such as reciting or writing each step before entering or leaving the classroom.

Students can initially use checklists they have developed to ask themselves whether they have correctly carried out each step as a means of evaluating how they implemented the strategy. These can then be faded. As students continue to practice LAP, they too can draft think-alouds (based on their checklist) so that the teacher can observe how each step is applied and offer feedback. Having students write think-alouds is also important so that they practice instructing themselves because this maximizes the potential that students will internalize the strategy and use it when not directly reminded to do so.

All students may not need to learn this strategy and so they won't need to complete the self-directed learning plan. Instead, they can work on independent projects, self-correcting materials (exercises with answers available), or other types of activities. To reinforce instruction, students could also then teach these types of strategies to the larger class. Offering them to the larger class can also remove any stigma that these students might feel when they see their peers choose to use them as well.

Parentheses, Exponents, Multiplication and Division, and Addition and Subtraction

Another sample heuristic, also called a mnemonic, for recalling the order of steps needed when performing multiple operations is PEMDAS, which stands for Parentheses, Exponents, Multiplication and Division, and Addition and Subtraction. When solving multiple-step computation problems, PEMDAS (or Please Excuse My Dear Aunt Sally) tells you the ranks of the operations: Parentheses outrank exponents, which outrank multiplication and division (but multiplication and division are at the *same* rank), and these two outrank addition and subtraction (which again are together on the bottom rank). The meaning of why PEMDAS works can be conveyed through having students solve word problems such as Jonah receives $25 from Sefu and $5 from each one of his three other friends. Students will immediately see that if they solve $25 + $5 × 3 without using PEMDAS, they will not be able to justify the reasonableness of the solution (see Sanjay, 2002, for a fuller explanation).

Read-Identify-Diagram-Evaluate

An additional heuristic students can use to carry out a more generic sequence of procedures that can be applied to variety of types of problems (such as any type of word problem) is the following modification of RIDE (Read Identify Diagram Evaluate),which was developed by Mercer and Mercer (1993). This strategy can be used to teach students how to approach solving a word problem. For students who require more support, a single step of RIDE, such as diagram relationships, can be expanded to include substeps as needed. This strategy can be taught in the same way as described for LAP.

RIDE

- *R*ead problem carefully, slowly and entirely.
- *I*dentify relevant information and highlight it.
- *D*iagram relationships in a way that leads to a solution.

  Create simple symbols for each piece of critical information.

- *E*valuate your answer with computation and justify its reasonableness.

Source: Mercer & Mercer, 1993.

To gain buy-in to any strategy, students can complete the debriefing sheet shown in Figure 5.13.

Designing Strategies

Students can be encouraged to design their own strategies and to tailor those aspects of the routines that they find most helpful to meet their own individual needs. Teachers often make the mistake of moving on too quickly and teaching a new strategy before the first is fully internalized. As a rule of thumb, my experience has shown that students should learn no more than two to three strategies per year in their first years of learning these.

A few guidelines are cited in Ellis and Lenz (1996), who identified a number of critical features for creating successful mnemonics for these kinds of strategies. These have been summarized in Hudson and Miller (2006), who write that the strategy should contain steps that lead to the problem solution, the steps should be generalizable to other similar problems, each step in the strategy should begin with an action word, and each step should be as brief as possible. The first letter of each action word for each step should be a mnemonic, as in the example RIDE.

Essentially, according to Ellis and Lenz (1996), the steps should use research-validated principles of learning such as setting goals, activating background knowledge, or self-monitoring one's own work. They should not be just a loose collection of suggestions for separate tasks. They should use the minimal number of steps needed and be organized in the most efficient and comprehensive way. Each step must be essential, not "Open your book." Steps need to be thorough, and the entire process broken down fully. Although this may seem inefficient, adults often forget all the small substeps we had to take when initially learning a procedure. Ellis and Lenz (1996) present a valuable checklist that can be used to evaluate the potential effectiveness of any strategy.

In the next chapter, strategies suited for differentiating for math talented students are presented.

Figure 5.13

Strategy Debriefing Sheet

The strategy I used was:

_____

_____

_____

_____

_____

I used it in the following way:

_____

_____

_____

_____

_____

It helped me improve by:

_____

_____

_____

_____

_____

6

Challenging Students Who Are High Achieving

Leslie Laud

Students who are regularly high achieving in mathematics often crave intellectual stimulation. Finding or designing just the right level of challenge that is neither too easy, nor beyond their grasp can be challenging for teachers. These students often react emotionally when they are bored with easy work, or they disengage when work is too much of a reach. When the work is right at their challenge level, they exhibit an almost perceptible sense of enjoyment in their engagement. Their body language or comments offer valuable feedback that teachers can use to make instructional changes and inform future planning decisions. Essentially, students' responses to the work they are given provide valuable guidance, which is important to use as a gauge since less empirical research on teaching this population exists than for others. The research that does exist (Tieso, 2005) suggests that two broad factors should be kept in mind when planning for the students: exemptions and higher order thinking.

One caveat to bear in mind that I often hear from practitioners that is true for this chapter, as well as for the previous chapter, is that the strategies mentioned in both of these chapters are often good for all students.

EXEMPTIONS BASED ON PRIOR KNOWLEDGE OR PACE OF LEARNING

Two major reasons exist as to why students should be allowed to be exempt from completing all of the regular work assigned to the entire class. First, when formative assessments reveal a student has already mastered certain information, then that student should be exempt from having to complete some or all of the practice material. Second, although some students may not have been exposed to certain math content before and so will not recognize it on preassessments, they learn at an accelerated pace. They master new material far more quickly than do their peers and require fewer repetitions of practice problems to achieve this. Therefore, they should also be exempt from regular amounts of practice.

Yet, meeting the needs of the second group requires greater flexibility on the part of the teacher because it requires shifting gears, often mid-lesson, when it becomes apparent that some have mastered the topic and so are ready to move ahead more quickly than others. Ideally, teachers will have predicted this and will have alternate activities prepared. However, at times this can happen unexpectedly. For that reason it can be helpful to keep emergency spare folder of challenges on hand to be used rarely. These challenges should never be extra work but should instead *replace* work that is unnecessary. When students clearly master a concept after doing half the required practice, they can do the challenges in place of the unnecessary practice. Challenges should always be viewed as replacements and not as extra work.

Dale Seymour publishes excellent mathematical challenge materials that can be used for this purpose. The journal *Mathematics Teaching in the Middle School* also often publishes excellent challenges that can be copied and saved. In addition, these students may participate in math competitions, and so making challenge problems from resources such as "Math Counts" or "Math Olympiads" available to them can be helpful as well. However, programs for math talented students are often criticized for merely offering such types of ancillary enrichment. More substantial enrichment with a scope and sequence that is tied more closely to the curricular topic being taught to the full class is preferable and will be described later in this chapter. The above suggestions are merely for those unanticipated times when students appear disengaged while having to wait for peers to master material that they have already mastered.

Strategies for Instant Enrichment

As mentioned, teachers can keep folders with enriching activities on hand for unexpected times when some students are ready to move on and others are not. In addition, and more strongly recommended, teachers can offer instant enrichment through asking students who have completed their work early the following kinds of questions related to the current work:

- Can you solve this problem in another way?
- Design and explain an alternative new algorithm for solving this problem.
- Describe several ways to solve this, then defend which is the most efficient and why.

These types of immediate extensions can be posted in a classroom. When students announce, "I'm done," teachers can merely point to these options so that the classroom culture shifts from students looking to the teacher for enrichment to students knowing where and how they can find it for themselves.

Curriculum Compacting

One strategy for exempting students from regular practice is called curriculum compacting (Winebrenner, 2001). In this strategy, the assignment is literally compacted. Based on preassessments, teachers can determine in advance to allow some students to only complete alternate problems or just the final problems on a page, as these usually provide practice but are also often the most difficult problems as well. It is a constant judgment call to determine the exact amount of practice each student requires, because these students do require some practice, just not as much as their peers. The amount they need differs, as students who are math talented are a heterogeneous group. Teachers need to beware that students can sometimes appear to understand the concept, yet may not have mastered it until they receive some amount of drill. Alternatively, when teachers realize mid-lesson that some students should move more quickly, they can compact *on the fly* and allow students to do fewer problems. From experience, it is wise to make notes on students' papers and in one's grade book when doing this, because it can be easy to forget which students were told to do what.

Codesigned Learning Contracts

When preassessments reveal that a student has already mastered the majority of a new unit, it may sometimes be helpful to design learning contracts with that student (see Figure 6.1). These work well with students who are exceptionally well directed. Students can complete these at home, after taking a preassessment. They can then come in and see the teacher before or after school, or at another convenient time set to discuss the plan. The teacher may attach a list of challenges and projects that coordinate with the unit topic for the student to reference when proposing alternative work to do.

Figure 6.1

Math Learning Contract

Summary of what the preassessment shows I have mastered:

_____

_____

_____

_____

_____

I still need to learn:

_____

_____

_____

_____

My plan for learning this is:

_____

_____

_____

_____

In place of the work that I have already mastered, I will:

Parallel-Related Curriculum

Another option for students who have already mastered unit concepts is for them to work on a parallel, related curricular topic during the unit. This option works better for students who benefit from more structure. On the preassessment, items from this parallel curriculum can also be assessed to ensure that students don't already know the parallel curricular topic as well. For example, the following absolute value questions were placed at the end of integers preassessment. Several of the students who performed well on the preassessment missed these questions, so they worked on these types of problems in place of the regular class material that their preassessments had shown they had already mastered (see Figure 6.2).

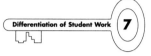

Differentiation of Student Work 7

Figure 6.2

Integers Parallel Curriculum

Determine whether each statement is true.

Justify the reasonableness of your opinion for each.

1. If $x < 0$ and $y > 0$, then $x - y > 0$
2. If $x > 0$ and $y > 0$, then $x + y < 0$
3. If $x < 0$ and $y < 0$, then $x - y > 0$
4. If $x < 0$ and $y < 0$, then $x + y > 0$
5. If $x < y$, then $x - y > 0$
6. If $x > y$, then $x - y > 0$
7. If $x > 0$ and $y < 0$, then $x - y > 0$
8. If $x < 0$ and $y < 0$, and $x - y > 0$, then $|x + y| > 0$
9. If $x < 0$, then $-(-x)$ is positive
10. If x and y are negative integers, then $x + y$ is negative
11. If x and y are positive integers, then $|x + y| = |x| + |y|$
12. If x and y are integers, and $x + 2 > y + 2$, then $|x| > |y|$
13. If x and y are integers and $5 - x < 5 - y$, then $|x| < |y|$
14. If $(x) + (-y) =$ a positive integer, then $|x| > |y|$

OPPORTUNITIES FOR HIGHER ORDER MATH

Students who complete work early because preassessments show they already know the material or because they master it more quickly than their peers should use their freed up time to engage in higher order math challenges that are not viewed as extra work, but as replacement or enrichment work. Various enrichment options have been described in prior chapters. Yet, some students need more than these types of enrichment. They learn in qualitatively different ways from their peers. They do not just need harder or more advanced work. They need opportunities to engage in higher order thinking. Although each child is unique, certain patterns or common traits exist that these students share. These patterns or traits can be helpful to bear in mind when planning for these students.

Researchers of mathematically gifted middle school students have proposed various models for categorizing how these students think mathematically. For example, Sak (2009) has proposed that three major categories of gifted mathematical minds exist: knowledge expert, creative, and analytical. The knowledge expert shows an extraordinary ability for memory recall and routine problem-solving. The creative mind excels at intuition/induction and using novel ways to produce new knowledge. Finally, the analytical mind excels at logical deduction/proof and reproducing knowledge.

This framework can be helpful in guiding the kind of enrichment that will best suit the type of mathematical strengths that different students show. For example, knowledge experts would probably thrive from being given opportunities to tackle accelerated math challenges. Creatively minded students might enjoy an opportunity to design a new algorithm. Alternatively, if a student shows a strength in one area, the teacher might want to give the child an opportunity to develop strengths in other areas.

Another, less analytical, model for understanding students who are high achieving in mathematics is to consider the abilities that are common to students who have been identified as math talented or gifted (Greenes, 1981). These include the following:

- Spontaneous formation of problems
- Flexibility in handling data
- Fluency of ideas
- Data organization abilities
- Originality of interpretation
- Ability to transfer ideas
- Ability to generalize

Carol Tieso's (2005) research on math talented students provides concrete examples of exactly how higher order thinking skills can be taught. In this research, students taught in small homogenous groups, with repetitive and unchallenging material replaced with the following kinds of real-life complex dilemmas, far outperformed ability-matched peers who were taught in the full class with the regular curriculum. Specifically, during a unit on data analysis, this study used a newspaper article that revealed how baseball statistics can be manipulated to further certain private agendas. This idea, of relating a unit topic to real-world complexities can be replicated, as shown in Figure 6.3. This activity is designed to serve as an extension for an integers unit. It shows how accountants' balance sheets, which one might think should simply list gains and losses, instead can also be manipulated in complex ways. This final *dilemma* type of task is not designed for most math-talented students, just those at the end of the continuum who seek out intensely challenging tasks.

Figure 6.3

Integers Extensions

Find the greatest distance among: 5, −2, −9, 11, 15

_____

Are the following statements sometimes, always or never true? Justify your reasoning.

$|X| + X = X$ doubled

$|X| + -X =$ a negative number

If you graph a point X anywhere on a number line, the numbers to the left will always be smaller than X.

_____

Write an equation for:
 A snail climbs 3 feet up a tree, then slips back 2 feet every day. How many days will it take this snail to climb the tree?

_____

Choose among these three:

1. What does 5 look like? Do not use any kind of physical model to explain your answer. What does negative 5 look like? Using physical objects to model your answer, which of these is easier to model?

2. In area problems, if you have a negative measure, you cannot solve the problem. What if you could? What would a rectangle with sides measuring 8 × −2 look like? What would a shoebox with two negative sides look like? Make a drawing and explain your answer.

3. Right now two categories of integers exist: positive and negative. Can you invent a third type of integer? Explain your invention and gives examples of out this new system would work.

_____

Complete the following dilemma on integers in accounting.

Integers in Real Life: Murky Waters

Businesses use integers to show gains and losses and report these to investors who have given their own money to these businesses in order to share in their profits. Obviously it is in the company's interest to show that they are profitable and making money so that they will attract investors.

(Continued)

(Continued)

Unfortunately, in the recent past companies have been able to use complex reporting regulations that allow them to appear more profitable than they actually are.

In the early 2000s, these reporting tricks had allowed companies to claim acquisitions (items they have purchased, so technically losses) as having less value so the losses appear to be less. Similarly, another trick used in the past involved "so-called 'pro-forma' numbers, which strip out negative numbers from a statement." In addition, while tangible costs such as materials must be reported, *intangible* costs can be hidden such as stock options (giving employees the opportunity to purchase company stock in the future at reduced prices) or costs associated with internally developing software computer programs that can increase a company's efficiency. These are more complex to report and can be easily hidden.

Sample Balance Sheet			
Date	Transaction	Price	Net Balance
March 5, 2002	400 air-conditioners*	−$4,000*	$96,000
March 12, 2002	Stock options to employees**	0**	$96,000
March 20, 2002	Marketing research funding (off balance sheet)	−$1,000	$96,000
March 28, 2002	Received 500 air-conditioner filters	−$5,000	$96,000
March 29, 2002	Dorbin to buy air-conditioners*** (to be paid next month)	$10,000***	$106,000
March 30, 2002	Losses we expect to recover	−$20,000	$106,000

*Market value if we resold them—actual price was $250 per air-conditioner.

**This may cost up to $20,000 2 years from now when we actually pay.

***The sale may not actually happen.

Companies report straightforward gains and losses on the main balance sheets, but many of these less tangible type of items could be hidden in footnotes or *off balance sheets*, then suddenly appear on the balance sheets when it suited the company's interests. For example, one off-balance-sheet option, called *special purpose entities*, could be used to fund research and development, or used to hide risks that a company takes. Another trick companies used was to commit to a purchase, but not note that as a debt on their balance sheets, even when they have already taken the material they commit to purchase. Companies could also record gains when they booked a sale, even if the sale never even actually happened.

Hundreds of pages of such loopholes existed that were overly detailed and easy to circumvent, or get around. Formerly, before the 1960s, these rules were simpler, based on broad principles. Yet with the advent of so many lawsuits, accounting firms demanded more detailed, laws to help them in court.

These laws had been designed by organizations that are privately run and staffed by accountants, unlike in Europe where these standards have been set by the government, and the principle of providing a true and fair end balance sheet overrides nitty-gritty rule application. When new regulations are proposed, in the past companies have lobbied and offered cash indirectly to the regulators to force them to act in their favor. The regulators may give in if they need that funding.

Some recommended improvements included having alternate sources, such as the U.S. Treasury, fund the organizations that make these accounting rules so that they won't be so susceptible to donations from companies that want them to make rules in their favor. Other efforts tried internationally have been aimed at preventing off-balance-sheet tricks and forcing companies to disclose more of their less tangible gains or losses, such as forcing companies to write up losses even if they expect to recover them soon, which they previously had not had to do. Such efforts might help, but to avoid the kind of problems of the past, it was argued that companies must "reveal far more economic reality in their accounts than they do at present."

This summary is based on the article "Badly in Need of Repair," which appeared in *The Economist* on May 2, 2002, when accounting problems were popular news items. Since then, further improvements have been made to protect investors from scans. What steps would you have recommended to ensure that businesses balance sheet reporting be more fair and accurate? Respond to the specific obstacles described in this article. Provide at least three recommendations and prioritize which among the three you most recommend and explain why you would prioritize that one.

When designing and evaluating enrichment resources, it can be helpful to keep the following factors in mind:

- Does this activity open out the task and/or allow for multiple-solution possibilities?
- Does it tap abstract thinking capabilities?
- Does it enable students to invent or design novel ways to approach problem-solving?
- Does it allow for flexibility in reasoning?
- Does it allow students to think in greater depth about how and why, not how to?
- Is it inquiry-based?

STRATEGIES TO AVOID

Two strategies that I have frequently seen used, yet that have little research support, are ad hoc peer tutoring and requiring that students master basic skills before tackling higher order thinking challenges. Although carefully planned and well-supported peer-tutoring models, used for limited time and in specific circumstances, have value, regularly asking students to explain topics to peers when they finish early does not offer them the kind of intellectual challenge they need. Also, some students who show extraordinary math talent with higher order thinking can sometimes have difficulty mastering basic facts. As described earlier in this chapter, math talents can manifest in different ways. Students should not be precluded from engaging with higher order math until they have mastered the basic facts. Instead, they should be allowed to master these outside of class through strategies described in the first section of Chapter 3.

IMPORTANCE OF CHALLENGE

It is sometimes believed that students who are high achieving will excel whether or not teachers put much effort into challenging them. This may be true in some cases. Yet research (Tieso, 2005) shows the vast difference good teaching and curriculum can make with these students. This research (Tieso) underscores that if students are not taught at their instructional level, achievement can actually decrease due possibly to the boredom and disengagement that result. Furthermore, often because math has always come so easily to them, they don't develop the strength of perseverance unless they are challenged. They need frequent opportunities to really sink their teeth into solid math challenges so that when they reach higher levels, they will have the inner resources to persevere.

Teachers often find that when they give these students challenges, they frequently, and surprisingly, require teacher assistance, such as scaffolding hints (see www.nrich.org for excellent scaffolding hints provided for each challenge problem). Also, it cannot be assumed that they will always choose the most challenging problems when given the option. Often, they need to be compelled to do so and held to higher standards. To scaffold helping these students persevere more challenging material, they can also be given solutions and taught how to work backward from the answer in these cases. Yet, fundamentally a climate needs to be built over time in which the students are regularly challenged, with coaching and support being given initially. For students who show math talents and are accustomed to coasting easily in math class, it cannot be assumed that they will immediately and easily take to being challenged. Building the skills and how to approach challenges independently with perseverance is a gift we can give them that will have enormous long-term value.

Mathematics Interventions Overview

7

Paul J. Riccomini and Bradley S. Witzel

Mathematics interventions delivered in an RTI framework can have a positive effect on student learning. It is important to choose appropriate interventions and deliver the interventions wisely in order to have the desired effect. If math interventions are developed and the time is used inappropriately, then RTI will be the failure, not the student. It is our belief that if Tier 2 or 3 intervention time is used for homework or extra independent practice only, then RTI is a waste of time. Moreover, if an ineffective curriculum is selected and/or is taught by an ill-informed or unprepared teacher, then RTI is a waste of time. More accurately, instruction and intervention are not possible.

> The NMAP recommends that those responsible for math education have strong math skills.

Mathematics interventions should be taught daily using systematic, explicit, and research-supported instruction and curriculum that includes ongoing assessment and progress monitoring tailored to the specific areas of weakness of each student. By placing students in small groups for Tiers 2 and 3, the instructional delivery options increase. As students are placed into increasing tiers, group size must decrease in order to best meet the individual needs of each student. In small groups, students may be peer grouped and called on individually more often to increase interactions, individualized feedback, and informal assessment. Additionally, decreasing the size of the group allows for easier adaptation of curricular content.

For example, in a class of 25 students, the teacher may spend a great deal of effort and time making certain that everyone is on the same page and accomplishing the same task. When a small group of students are not keeping up or are unable to keep up, it is more difficult to recognize the errors being made and make immediate adjustments for those select few students, all the while keeping the rest of the class at their same pace. In a Tier 2 class of six students, the teacher is more likely to notice the difficulty of a particular student and make immediate adjustments to the instruction so that the student can acquire the skill. In Tier 3, class and group size are even smaller, and thus curriculum, instruction, and assessment are individualized to the specific and immediate need of each student.

Math intervention research has grown in recent years since RTI was first endorsed in government white papers and then with the Individuals with Disabilities Education Act (IDEA) of 2004. As such, some research projects have made claims of being an effective Tier 2 intervention while others have claimed effectiveness for *all* students in Tier 1. Because of the various claims, research reported in this book will use research that supports whole-class curriculum and instruction for struggling students to constitute Tier 1 instruction and research that focuses on small-group curriculum and instruction to constitute intervention research. The focus of this book is to prevent a learning disabilities diagnosis by using highly effective intervention methods. As such, Tier 3 modifications are looked at as more intense renditions of the interventions. Because the focus of RTI is on prevention of disabilities, alternative graduation curriculum, nondiploma track, and work study interventions are not the focus of the interventions explored in this document.

WHO NEEDS INTERVENTION?

We must consider a number of factors when concerning ourselves with who requires intervention in math. Many people focus on struggling groups such as those with a low socioeconomic status (SES), females, those with memory issues, or those who are hyperactive. In reality, it is highly unlikely that any person will never struggle in mathematics. Mathematics, unlike other content areas, is very complex and ever increasing in difficulty and demand. So it is important to look at screening data and make individual recommendations accordingly. Extra attention should be given to the grade level of the struggling student. If a kindergartner or second-grade student is struggling in math early on in their academic career, then the need for intervention is urgent. Weaknesses in early learning concepts can interfere with future math performance. Students who struggle early require immediate and effective interventions to prepare for future success. While the need for early intervention is important, it does not negate the need for intervention of students in upper elementary to secondary levels. In fact, as students progress in grade level, mathematics difficulties become more complex, which requires more complex and intensive interventions.

WHAT DO I TEACH FOR THE INTERVENTION?

Some assessment batteries will help pinpoint specific areas of weakness for students. Knowing exactly in what to intervene is a key to successful intervention. While some assessment batteries provide a detailed picture, other assessment batteries do not. Assessment batteries that provide a percentile or rating only do not provide guidance as to what to intervene in but rather to whom the intervention should occur.

Typical areas of mathematics intervention research, as identified in preassessments, cover the topics of number sense, computation, fractions/decimals/proportions, algebraic equations, and problem solving. Students who exhibit math difficulties early struggle in understanding and task performance with number sense concepts such as counting, quantification or magnitude of number, number-to-numeral identification, base 10 and place value, and fluent arithmetic strategies. Students who continue to struggle in mathematics require intervention in fractions, computation, and problem solving. If problems persist into middle school, interventions with algebraic concepts, such as solving equations; continued work on fractions, decimals, and proportions; along with computation involving negatives are important.

WHO SHOULD INTERVENE?

At any school, the person who is intervening with the students may be a general or special education teacher, a mathematics coach, a mathematic supervisor, or even an instructional assistant (Gersten et al., 2009). No matter who is delivering the intervention, that person requires training in the intervention curriculum, the instructional delivery most effective for the student, and the assessment procedures to best ensure informed instruction for the student. Additionally, the interventionist must possess curricular and content knowledge of the grade level of at least the year before and after the student's current grade and curricular placement so as to make proper goals for the student and work with the material to which the student already has been introduced.

> "Substantial differences in mathematics achievement of students are attributable to differences in teachers. Teachers are crucial to students' opportunities to learn and to their learning of mathematics."
>
> —*NMAP (2008)*

WHERE?

An area free of distractions is required for the intervention. Students with attention or peer pressure concerns require the ability to be allowed to focus on the work and not on others' behavior. For example, a former recess closet accessible only to the outside with one wall conveniently used for ball play by a couple hundred children every afternoon is not appropriate. Special education has come a long way in the past two decades to move special education classes to classes that, at the least, appear like those in the rest of the school. It is conceivable that broom closets would be reopened to provide interventions. Instead of looking for a convenient location, it is better to find the most effective place for students to learn. Although six students and a teacher could fit in a former book room, it is not always conducive to learning. The best place for interventions to take place is an area that is free of distractions, capable of handling and displaying technology appropriate for the selected interventions, and large enough to allow necessary instructional groupings, movement, and interactions. Some example seating arrangements taken from the IRIS Center (n.d.) are displayed in Figure 7.1.

Figure 7.1 Example Seating Arrangements for Class Instruction and Small-Group Intervention

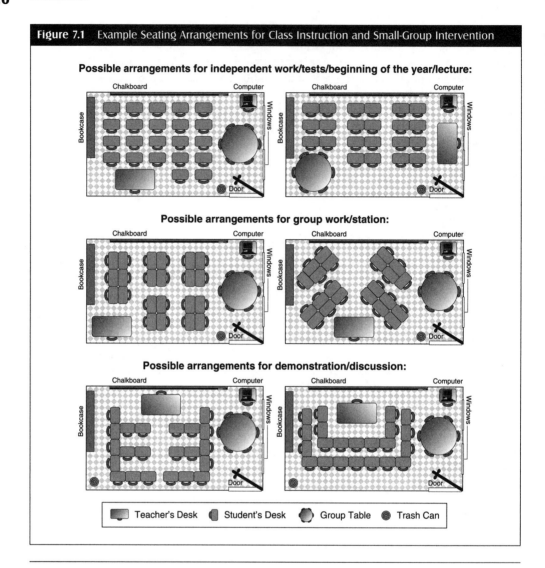

Source: Courtesy of the IRIS Center, Peabody College.

HOW LONG?

Interventions should happen 4–5 days per week for a minimum of 20 minutes. Considerable research conducted across many years has consistently demonstrated improved student achievement through the increase of instructional time (Ellis, Worthington, & Larkin, 1994). Although no absolute time recommendations exist, the recommendations that we put forth should be considered starting points and should only increase. Student attention span and instructional delivery will cause fluctuations in the actual time for intervention. Some interventions are preset to last up to 50 minutes for middle school classes. This is fine, but make certain that the delivery varies the activities quickly and maintains frequent interactions to help keep the students focused. The intervention set should occur until the students meet grade-level expectations or the students are assessed to need more intensive instruction.

What kinds of instructional delivery work best with interventions?

> Instructional practice should be informed by high-quality research, when available, and by the best professional judgment and experience of accomplished classroom teachers. High-quality research does not support the contention that instruction should be either entirely "student-centered" or "teacher-directed." Research indicates that some forms of particular instructional practices can have a positive impact under specified conditions. (NMAP, 2008, p. 11)

Students who struggle in mathematics require explicit and systematic instruction (Gersten et al., 2009). Such instruction should be provided in all tiers for struggling students. However, while there are many similarities between tiered instructional deliveries, the extra time allotted in each successive tier provides additional classroom opportunities. Gersten and his colleagues suggest that educators use the time opportunities to provide extra practice and more interactions through the use of clear examples and models, more detailed feedback, and extra and different use of think alouds. The think alouds that are recommended for the teacher to use in Tier 1 can be used more extensively in Tier 2. Not only should teachers use think alouds, but the students should as well. Verbalizations of thought process and understanding have a history of research effectiveness, particularly for students with learning disabilities (Baker, Gersten, & Scanlon, 2002).

Using teacher think alouds can be an awkward means of teaching for someone who is unfamiliar with the process and the research. However, it is highly effective, particularly for students who have not established a means to approach a problem. Thus, it is important for teachers to learn this skill. There are a couple of things to keep in mind when implementing think alouds. The first is that you need to have developed a clear and simple set of sequenced procedures that solves the problem (and hopefully several problems like it). Next, when implementing, it is good to go through at least one whole problem aloud first without student interaction. The students need to see the problem solving in its entirety. Also, depending on the students, you will have to scaffold the steps individually or in groups so that they can be repeated. Finally, provide practice so that the students can name the steps and think aloud accurately and independently.

In Figure 7.2, the teacher is at an intermediate step in showing an integer method for subtraction without regrouping. It is important to verbalize the reasoning rather than simply reading the problem as it would be written on a board. Once a teacher models a problem using a think aloud, he should ask the students to repeat the thought process. This extra step adds instructional time, but the additional interactions are valuable when teaching students who have a history of memorization difficulties.

Figure 7.2 A Stepwise Example of Teacher and Student Think Alouds to Solve a Problem Using an Integer Method

A

$$253$$
$$- 75$$

$$200 + 50 + 3$$
$$- 70 - 5$$

Example of step one of teacher and student shared think aloud

T: "253 is the same as 2 hundreds plus 5 tens plus 3 ones."
S: "253 is the same as 2 hundreds plus 5 tens plus 3 ones."
T: "Negative 75 is the same as negative 7 tens and negative 5 ones."
S: "Negative 75 is the same as negative 7 tens and negative 5 ones."

B

$$200 - 20 - 2$$

Example of step two of teacher and student shared think aloud

T: "I work from left to right."
S: "I work from left to right."
T: "I find that 200 is not computed."
S: "I find that 200 is not computed."
T: "Since the negative also acts as a minus, 5 tens minus 7 tens is negative 2 tens."
S: "Since the negative also acts as a minus, 5 tens minus 7 tens is negative 2 tens."
T: "Since the negative also acts as a minus, 3 ones minus 5 ones is negative 2 ones."
S: "Since the negative also acts as a minus, 3 ones minus 5 ones is negative 2 ones."

C

$$200$$
$$- 20$$
$$- 2$$

$$178$$

Example of step three of teacher and student shared think aloud

T: "Now, 200 minus 20 is 180."
S: "200 minus 20 is 180."
T: "180 minus 2 is 178."
S: "180 minus 2 is 178."
T: "The answer is 178."
S: "The answer is 178."

Along the line of increasing frequency of interactions, teachers can use several forms of simple and advanced technology to increase student participation in class. One of the more recent technologies to make it to the classroom is an interactive whiteboard. The SMART Board and other interactive board technologies have options for student input in a couple of formats. Students can answer multiguess questions from a portable keypad, or they can write directly on a portable notepad allowing their original work to be displayed. Contrary to the belief that open discussions can hurt a student's feelings thus causing their work effort to disintegrate, when handled correctly, discussing a student's work can provide the student with clear explanations from other students. In many cases, students are more resistant to teacher feedback than they are to peer feedback. Students need to be taught how to provide constructive and supportive feedback in order to make this work.

Along the lines of increasing peer interactions and appropriate peer feedback, the use of peer-assisted learning strategies (PALS) has had great success in mathematics and reading. Specific to the mathematics, Fuchs, Fuchs, and Karns (2001) found success across achievement levels in kindergartners when PALS was implemented. PALS is enacted by pairing two students of slightly different achievement for 30 minutes three to four times a week. If there are an uneven number of students, then flexible groups of three are a possibility. The intervention is focused on practice of ideas already taught to the students. Each intervention is individually arranged according to the student's needs. Each member of the pair plays the role of coach and student in a reciprocal role play. Additionally, each member of the team is involved in progress monitoring. To learn more about PALS mathematics research, visit the site http://kc.vanderbilt.edu/pals/library/mathres.html.

HOW DO I ORGANIZE MY CURRICULUM?

Information from assessments should provide the teacher/interventionist with a focused outcome on what the student is lacking that may be preventing success in the general education curriculum. With this focused outcome in mind, the teacher can design curricular steps to help the student reach that goal. One such way to break down instruction is through task analysis. Task analysis has long been recognized as a means for taking large and difficult tasks and breaking them down into reasonable, sequential, and learnable chunks (Witzel & Riccomini, 2007). In special education, task analysis has been used for low-incidence special education populations to teach life and work skills. The teacher would start by teaching a small first step of the sequence of things someone must learn. For grade-level mathematics, the approach is similar. With a typical second-grade standard of two-digit addition and subtraction, students must not only know addition and subtraction facts but also know the reasoning behind addition and subtraction and place value in preparation for regrouping and borrowing. To best instruct a standard like two-digit addition and subtraction, teachers need to task analyze the standard to ensure that students are prepared for success and to appropriately teach *all* precursor skills. Some teachers in Tier 1 elect not to task analyze their curriculum to minute steps because of reasons such as concern with instructional time or demands made by preset pacing guides. However, because Tiers 2 and 3 provide more instructional time and many of the intervention curricula available do not incorporate a rigid pacing guide, teachers are more able to task analyze curriculum into "baby steps" to best meet the learning needs of struggling students.

One strategy to help teachers and curricular analysts task analyze a curriculum to more accurately reach a desired outcome and best meet the needs of students is through the use of OPTIMIZE (Riccomini, Witzel, & Riccomini, in press; Witzel & Riccomini, 2007). The eight steps of OPTIMIZE help teachers examine and revise their current curriculum to fill in gaps or reduce unnecessarily spiraled activities. The steps of OPTIMIZE are:

1. O—Organize the math skills of a textbook chapter before teaching.

2. P—Pair your sequence with that of the textbook.

3. T—Take note of the commonalities and differences.

4. I—Inspect earlier chapters and later chapters to see if they cover the differences.

5. M—Match supplemental guides to see if they cover the differences.

6. I—Identify additional instruction to complement the current text/ curriculum.

7. Z—Zero in on the optimal sequence with your new knowledge.

8. E—Evaluate and improve the sequence every year.

See the example in Table 7.1 that demonstrates how to enact OPTIMIZE with your curriculum. In this example, a Tier 2 interventionist, Mrs. Hunt, tackles the demand of intervening with a group of students to learn the above-mentioned skill, two-digit addition and subtraction. Reviewing the textbook,

Table 7.1   Example Application of OPTIMIZE to Instructional Sequence for an Algebra Chapter

Textbook Chapter Sequence	Alternative Textbook	New Instructional Sequence
1. Comparing real numbers on a number line	1. Ordering real numbers on a number line	1. Pretest for knowledge of integers
2. Adding integers on a number line	2. Adding integers with positive addends	2. Ordering integers
3. Subtracting integers on a number line	3. Adding and subtracting integers with negative and positive addends	3. Adding integers on a number line
4. Adding and subtracting in a matrix	4. Multiplying and dividing integers with one positive product or quotient	4. Adding and subtracting integers on a number line
5. Multiplying integers	5. Multiplying and dividing integers with two negative or positive addends or quotients	5. Rules for positive and negative terms
6. Using the distributive property to simplify expressions		6. Multiplying and dividing integers
7. Dividing real numbers to simplify expressions	6. Application of integers in real-life scenarios	7. Application with distributive property and expressions
8. Solving the probability of an event		*Note:* Include real-life scenarios throughout unit and include maintenance of each successive skill per chapter.

Note: This is just one example sequence and should not be interpreted as the only or correct sequence. The instructional sequence is dependent on state standards, access to curriculum and materials, and, most important, the students' instructional needs. OPTIMIZE was developed by Witzel & Riccomini (2007).

Mrs. Hunt observes several extraneous skills like spatial relations and telling time. Since these are important topics, they can be used as tools to teach this skill rather than as separate lessons. Additionally, this textbook alternated addition and subtraction several times. While examining the alternate textbook, she finds fewer extraneous math skills, but that textbook did not include some ideas, such as fact families. Instead of choosing one textbook or the other, Mrs. Hunt task analyzes a sequence of math skills that leads directly to two-digit addition and subtraction. Her delivery of this task analysis in a Tier 2 setting requires Mrs. Hunt to assess where students are along the task analysis to better know where to start in the sequence.

WHAT TYPES OF CURRICULAR STRATEGIES SHOULD BE USED FOR TIER 2 AND TIER 3 INTERVENTIONS?

There are several instructional approaches that can be used to present curriculum at the Tier 2 or 3 level. Research is in its infancy, but sufficient evidence is emerging to preliminarily endorse certain intervention strategies. Among the research-supported and evidence-supported approaches are explicit instruction for word problems (Wilson & Sindelar, 1991) and computation (Tournaki, 2003), use of visual representations for word problems (Owen & Fuchs, 2002), schema-based problem solving for word problems (Xin, Jitendra, & Deatline-Buchman, 2005), the concrete to representational to abstract (CRA) sequence of instruction for fractions (Butler, Miller, Crehan, Babbitt, & Pierce, 2003), algebra (Witzel, 2005; Witzel, Mercer, & Miller, 2003) and computation (Miller & Mercer, 1993), and meta-cognitive strategy instruction for fraction computation (Hutchinson, 1993). Moreover, in meta-analyses of research findings from studies during the past three decades, Baker, Gersten, and Lee (2002) as well as the National Mathematics Advisory Panel (2008) and RTI Math Practice Guide Panel (Gersten et al., 2009) support these instructional and curriculum interventions.

The repeated conclusion that visual and concrete representations should be incorporated in instruction should not be overlooked. CRA and visual representations are very important strategies for teaching students to learn complex tasks. The NMAP (2008) and RTI Math Practice Guide Panel (Gersten et al., 2009) both supported the use of CRA based on its significant effect size. CRA is a three-stage process of learning whereby students first learn by interacting with concrete objects (see Figure 7.3). Then they use the same steps to solve the problem using pictorial representations. Finally, the students use the same steps again to solve the problem using the abstract or Arabic symbols. It is important to use the same steps for each stage of learning so that students learn the procedures to solving problems.

Some teachers may find it difficult to locate manipulatives that can be used in the manner in which CRA is founded. If so, the National Library of Virtual Manipulatives (NLVM) can be used as a resource to help the teacher peruse the

Figure 7.3 The CRA Sequence of Instruction

Example 8. A set of matched concrete, visual, and abstract representations to teach solving single-variable equations

	3 + x = 7	

Solving the Equation With Concrete Manipulatives (Cups and Sticks)	Solving the Equation With Visual Representations of Cups and Sticks	Solving the Equation With Abstract Symbols

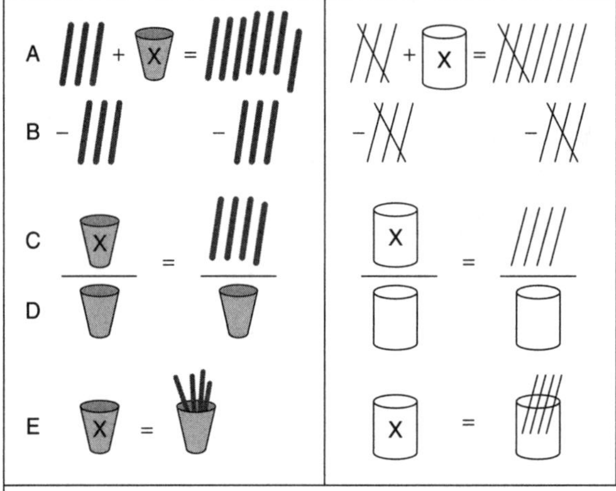

Concrete Steps
A. 3 sticks plus one group of X equals 7 sticks.
B. Subtract 3 sticks from each side of the equation.
C. The equation now reads as one group of X equals 4 sticks.
D. Divide each side of the equation by one group.
E. One group of X is equal to four sticks (i.e., 1X/group = 4 sticks/group; 1X = 4 sticks).

Source: Gersten, R., Beckmann, S., Clarke, B., Foegen, A., Marsh, L., Star, J. R., & Witzel, B. (2009). *Assisting students struggling with mathematics: Response to Intervention (RTI) for elementary and middle schools* (NCEE 2009-4060). Washington, DC: National Center for Education Evaluation and Regional Assistance, Institute of Education Sciences, U.S. Department of Education. Retrieved from http://ies.ed.gov/ncee/wwc/publications/practiceguides.

use of manipulatives (see Figure 7.4). In each math strand and grade-level band, teachers can review several manipulatives designed to help students learn concretely. Once found, the teacher can obtain the manipulatives and use them in a CRA sequence.

The interventions in Chapters 6 through 9 will depict how to enact these curricular strategies with the specific areas of math weakness that are found to be most prevalent with students at risk for learning disabilities in mathematics: number sense, fact computation, fractions and decimals, and problem solving.

Figure 7.4 Sample Manipulative View From the National Library of Virtual Manipulatives (NLVM)

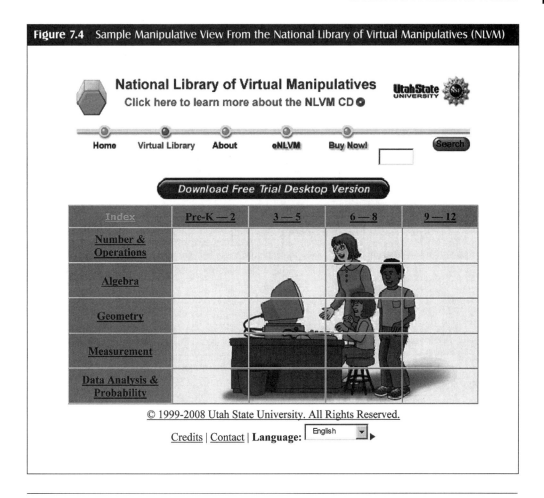

SUMMARY

Students who exhibit repeated difficulties in math require a different mode of
instruction. A knowledgeable interventionist using evidence-supported curricula should explicitly teach deficit skills to mastery in hopes of curbing each
student's poor performance. The intervention should cease when assessment
data show that the student has begun to succeed in mathematics or when the
assessment data show that it is time for more intensive intervention. There are
several interventions from which interventionists may choose. It is important to
choose interventions for their curriculum support and necessary instructional
delivery. The next four chapters will focus on key areas frequently requiring
interventions: number sense, computational fluency, fractions and decimals,
and problem solving.

List of Mathematics Interventions and Programs

Peer-Assisted Learning Strategies: http://kc.vanderbilt.edu/pals

PALS Reading and PALS Math were developed to help teachers accommodate diverse learners and to promote their academic success. PALS is listed among the best evidence-supported math programs on the Johns Hopkins University website, Best Evidence Encyclopedia (BEE). The What Works Clearinghouse found "The Peer-Assisted Learning Strategies© instructional program to have potentially positive effects on reading achievement" for elementary-age ELL children. For information specifically about Hot Math and other Tier 1 and 2 interventions, contact flora .murray@vanderbilt.edu.

Hot Math: Problem-Solving Program

Hot Math is available in a manual that includes teaching scripts for implementing all five units and provides all necessary materials (e.g., posters, overheads, worked problems, classroom exercises, scoring keys, homework assignments, personal charts, class charts). For information specifically about Hot Math and other Tier 1 and Tier 2 interventions, contact flora.murray@vanderbilt.edu.

Otter Creek Institute: http://www.oci-sems.com

A leading provider in high-quality training and resources, Otter Creek is dedicated to the success of our nation's teachers and students. Specific instructional interventions for Writing Numerals, Mastering Math Facts, and Problem-Solving Strategy Instruction.

Voyageur Learning-VMath: http://www.voyagerlearning.com/vmath/index.jsp

Many students need extra support to succeed in math and pass high-stakes tests. VMath fills critical learning gaps with a balanced, systematic approach, combining print materials, robust assessment, and online technology to create confident, independent learners in math.

Computation of Fractions: Math Intervention for Elementary and Middle Grades Students: http://www.pearsonhighered.com/educator

This intervention is based on the CRA instructional sequence and contains 30 instructional lessons, pretest, and posttest to determine effectiveness. The effectiveness of this instructional sequence is supported by research in which certified teachers provided daily whole-class and/or small-group instruction using concrete manipulative objects, then pictorial representations, and finally abstract representations of fractions.

Computation of Integers: Math Intervention for Elementary and Middle Grades Students: http://www.pearsonhighered.com/educator

This intervention is based on the CRA instructional sequence and contains 30 instructional lessons, pretest, and posttest to determine effectiveness. The effectiveness of this instructional sequence is supported by research in which certified teachers provided daily whole-class and/or small-group instruction using concrete manipulative objects, then pictorial representations, and finally abstract representations of positive and negative integers.

Computation of Simple Equations: Math Intervention for Middle Grade Students: http://www.pearsonhighered.com/educator

This intervention is based on the CRA instructional sequence and contains 30 instructional lessons, pretest, and posttest to determine effectiveness. The effectiveness of this instructional sequence is supported by research in which certified teachers provided daily whole-class and/or small-group instruction using concrete manipulative objects, then pictorial representations, and finally abstract representations of simple algebraic equations.

Core Program: Algebra Readiness: https://www.sraonline.com

SRA Algebra Readiness teaches concepts introduced as early as Grade 2 through Algebra I to ensure that students are brought to mastery of pre-Algebra skills and concepts. SRA Algebra Readiness spirals development needed for success in an Algebra I program.

Core Math Program: Saxon Mathematics Program: www.harcourtachieve.com

Saxon Math, published by Harcourt Achieve, is a scripted curriculum that blends teacher-directed instruction of new material with daily distributed practice of previously learned concepts and procedures. Students hear the correct answers and are explicitly taught procedures and strategies. Other key factors of the program include frequent monitoring of student achievement and extensive daily routines that emphasize practice of number concepts and procedures and use of representations.

Core Math Program: Math Expressions: http://www.hmco.com/indexf.html

Math Expressions, published by Houghton Mifflin Company, blends student-centered and teacher-directed approaches. Students question and discuss mathematics, but are explicitly taught effective procedures. There is an emphasis on using multiple specified objects, drawings, and language to represent concepts, and an emphasis on learning through the use of real-world situations. Students are expected to explain and justify their solutions.

Solving Math Word Problems: Teaching Students With Learning Disabilities Using Schema-Based Instruction: www.proedinc.com

This intervention, developed by Dr. Asha Jitendra, is a teacher-directed program designed to teach critical word problem–solving skills to students with disabilities in the elementary and middle grades. The program is carefully designed to promote conceptual understanding using schema-based instruction (SBI) and provides the necessary scaffolding to support learners who struggle with math word problems.

Solve It! A Practical Approach to Teaching Mathematical Problem-Solving Skills: http://www.exinn.net/solve-it.html

Solve It! is a curriculum designed to improve the mathematical problem-solving skills of students in the upper elementary, middle, and secondary school grades—including students with disabilities who are having difficulties solving mathematical

(Continued)

(Continued)

problems. This program helps teachers help students develop the processes and strategies used by good problem solvers. Explicit instruction in mathematical problem solving is provided in lessons that teach critical cognitive and metacognitive processes. This research-based program is designed for easy inclusion in a standard mathematics curriculum. Solve It! was validated and refined in intervention studies with students with mathematical learning disabilities between 12 and 18 years of age.

Note: This list in not intended to be comprehensive, just a sample selection of programs and interventions to consider for use within your school's RTI math model.

Part III

Science

Differentiated Science Inquiry

Douglas Llewellyn

WHAT IS DIFFERENTIATED SCIENCE INQUIRY?

Chapter 1, "Pathways to Inquiry," implied a whole-class approach to inquiry. That means the teacher usually selects *one* inquiry approach for *all* the students in the class for a particular topic. In this chapter, we will be introduced to Differentiated Science Inquiry (DSI) and the various possibilities that combine a mixture of approaches to inquiry within the same lesson, thus offering different methods of inquiry for different student learning needs. Using a differentiated inquiry approach, the teacher constructs a science investigation with multiple or tired levels of guidance and structure so that each learner has an opportunity to choose a level that is developmentally appropriate for his or her particular learning style. Although the lesson offers various process-oriented pathways, in the end, all students arrive at the common understanding of the concept and standard being studied.

Although many of us are familiar with the various approaches to inquiry, DSI takes a slightly different twist. When used judiciously, DSI is an instructional practice that enhances classroom learning by matching the individual student's needs and learning style to the level of structured and guidance inherent in an inquiry lesson. In DSI, teachers recognize and value a student's particular learning style (or styles) as well as the student's need for guided instruction and structure versus less structured, open-ended learning opportunities. Teachers additionally provide need-satisfying environments on top of various levels of learning experiences and investigations based on student choice and tailored toward students' personal requisites. When teachers differentiate the approach or level of science inquiry, they do so in response to the child's readiness and preferred learning style—whether it is visual, auditory, tactile, or kinesthetic. Readiness and learning styles will be addressed in more detail later in Chapter 4.

ONE SIZE DOES NOT FIT ALL

Imagine a coach ordering jerseys for a middle school basketball team. The coach orders all medium-size jerseys, and when the jerseys arrive, passes them out during a practice session the day before the first game of the season. For most players, the jerseys fit fine. For others, the jerseys are either too big or too small. Mike plays the guard position on the team and is quite small in stature. His jersey reaches almost down to his knees. Mike expresses his embarrassment to the coach. The brusque coach replies, "Just tuck in your jersey. It will be fine. Quit complaining." Rudy, the center of the team, is five foot ten inches tall and can hardly pull the shirt up over his head. He too voices his disapproval to the coach, but the coach responds, "That's too bad. Wear it. I ordered only one size." The other players quietly giggle in ridicule.

Unfortunately, the jersey story is a lot like many classrooms where we see teachers teach by the "one size fits all" preponderate method—lecture to preteach vocabulary, followed by a discussion period to reinforce the content, followed by a verification lab to confirm the fitness of the content presented earlier. DSI teachers take a dissimilar tactic. They know that students respond best to a variety of instructional methods, so they adapt their approaches by selecting the appropriate level of instruction based on the topic being presented and needs of the class. That's not to say inquiry-based teachers don't lecture. They do. For inquiry-based teachers, lectures and formal presentations are designed to apply and reinforce experiences, not introduce them. Using the Invitation to Inquiry Grid, DSI teachers design their yearlong science plans to include an array of demonstrated inquiries, structured inquiries, guided inquiries, and self-directed inquiries, generally moving from more structured to less structured opportunities as the school year goes on. For many teachers, offering various modes of learning is a skillful and impressive instructional leap—especially when the offerings include a range from structured activities to true inquiry-based investigations where students formulate their own questions from an open-ended exploration, plan their own procedures, and choose the means to collect and organize their data.

In many ways, DSI is analogous to a golf bag full of clubs. You wouldn't expect an experienced golfer to have just one driver or, say, one putter in his bag. The golfer carries a variety of golf clubs, each suited for a different situation. Sometimes, he needs a driver for hitting the ball long distances, while other times he needs a sand wedge for lofting the ball out of a sand trap. Teaching with differentiated instructional tools is just the same. There's a saying that "when the only tool you have in your toolbox is a hammer, every problem looks like a nail."

As challenging as this venture is, differentiating science instruction takes inquiry-based instruction one step further. As you will now read, Balls and Ramps is presented in four different approaches: as a demonstrated inquiry, as a structured inquiry, as a guided inquiry, and as a self-directed inquiry. The four approaches offer students the opportunity to choose a mode that best fits their interest, preferred learning style, and individual comfort level with inquiry-based learning.

BALLS AND RAMPS: A DIFFERENTIATED SCIENCE INQUIRY LESSON

The inspiration for differentiated science inquiry originated, in part, from an e-mail I received from a sixth-grade science teacher at Williams Middle School. Ms. Soto (the names of the teacher and the school have been changed) participated in a summer collegial book study using *Inquire Within* and became intrigued by the notion of offering different modifications to the marble activity described in Chapter 6 (Llewellyn, 2007). Since she observed a broad span of inquiry skills and abilities in her students, the interest of differentiating the levels of inquiry instruction as well as moving from a single-approach methodology to a self-selecting, "multiple-choice" methodology appealed to Ms. Soto. We continued to communicate over the summer to refine the concept of differentiated science inquiry and planned the initial DSI lesson for Balls and Ramps in the fall of the upcoming school year. Since Ms. Soto was unfamiliar with many of the underlying principles with forces and motion, she took the next several months to read up on several National Science Teachers Association (NSTA) print resources, including *Forces and Motion: Stop Faking It!* (Robertson, 2002).

The purpose of the Balls and Ramps activity is to have students explore the concept of motion energy and investigate variables that affect the momentum of rolling objects. The inquiry aligns to the *National Science Education Standards* (NRC, 1996) for Grades 5 through 8. During this activity, students will do the following:

- Design and conduct a scientific investigation (p. 145).
- Develop descriptions, explanations, predictions, and models using explanations (p. 145).
- Think critically and logically to make the relationship between evidence and explanations (p. 145).
- In addition, as a result of this activity students will understand the following:
  - The motion of an object can be described by its position, direction, and speed (p. 154).
  - Unbalanced forces will cause changes in the speed of direction of an object's motion (p. 154).

Note: Although the activity was originally conceived as a middle school level, Balls and Ramps can easily be adapted for elementary and high school classes.

Let's now imagine you were invited to observe Ms. Soto's Balls and Ramps lesson and have just entered her sixth-grade science classroom at Williams Middle School. There are 24 students in the class; one teacher, Ms. Soto; and one student teacher, Mr. Balfour. Mr. Balfour is from a local university completing his coursework for teacher certification.

Prior to your arrival, Ms. Soto and Mr. Balfour set up the room to accommodate three learning stations, with a fourth station across the hall in a vacant room. Materials for each of the four stations were preplaced in clear plastic baggies. Materials include assorted small wooden blocks, several 12-inch grooved plastic rulers, assorted-size marbles and balls, several golf balls, measuring tapes, and plastic protractors. A full description and explanation of the Balls and Ramps lesson plan can be found in Resources A and B.

"Today, students," Ms. Soto commences the lesson, "we will begin to understand the concept of motion energy and investigate variables that affect the momentum of rolling objects. To do this, you can join any one of four groups to learn about these topics." She then describes to the class the procedure and the level of structure for each station, emphasizing that students have a choice in selecting a particular station. Ms. Soto knows that at first, students may choose a station based on which friends choose the same station. She knows that as she continues to provide further opportunities for choice, students will begin to select approaches that best fit their learning style rather than by their friends' choices.

Before students go to their chosen stations, Mr. Balfour explores students' prior conceptions about motion energy. He begins by saying to the students, "Being good scientists, tell me what you already know about rolling balls. Take out your science journals, open to the next clean page, and write down five things you know about rolling balls. After you are done, pair and share your statements with a partner. Compare and contrast your statements. See what similarities and differences you had with your partner. You will have five minutes to complete this portion of the lesson. Is everyone ready?" Seeing that everyone is eager to start, he says, "Okay, begin!"

While the students are busy writing their responses, Ms. Soto and Mr. Balfour walk around the room making themselves available for any questions that might arise. They frequently scan students' written responses for the possibility of identifying any prior naive conceptions students may have about motion or friction. After the students have had a chance to compare and contract their responses, Mr. Balfour passes out several yellow 3-inch by 3-inch Post-it Notes to each student and asks them to write their favorite response from the assignment on the Post-it Note. He then asks the students to come up to the front of the class, one at a time, and tape the Post-it Notes to the whiteboard (see Figure 8.1). The class reads each response and discusses the 24 responses.

Mr. Balfour uses the Post-it Notes to pre-assess students' previously held notions and understandings about motion energy. As he reads them silently to himself, he scans the statements for possible incomplete or misconceptions held by students. He makes a mental note of any conceptions that will need further attention later in the lesson. Next, he, with the assistance of the class members, organizes the notes into patterns and relationships to make meaning of their prior conception. Mr. Balfour constructs a concept map from the students' Post-it Notes and adds linking verbs to connect one idea to another. The end product results in a semantic web of interrelated words that represent the class's present understanding on motion and momentum.

Once the preassessment is complete, Ms. Soto and Mr. Balfour are ready to move on to describe the four stations in the lesson. Since Ms. Soto's science room is carpeted, most of the small groups will work on the floor rather than at table tops. The carpeted surface gives extra room for students to move about and limits the balls from rolling too far. The carpeted hallway can provide an overflow if the classroom becomes too crowded.

With all the stations properly identified, Ms. Soto invites the students to individually choose a station to go to. She explains that each station

Figure 8.1   Post-It Notes Preassessment

has a different learning approach and that each student can choose which station he or she prefers. Once the students assemble at their chosen stations, they are ready to explore the forces of motion.

THE FOUR STATIONS

Station A: As a Demonstrated Inquiry

Station A is set up in a separate room across the hall. At Station A, there is a demonstration table. Student desks are arranged in rows and columns. At Station A, Mr. Balfour will follow the procedures identified in Station B but present them via a teacher-led demonstrated inquiry. Mr. Balfour will present to the group the question to be investigated and the procedure to answer the question. But before he begins, Mr. Balfour will post the question on the front board and ask students to clarify the meaning of the question. He will also ask students to suggest how they might go about answering the question and propose a procedure to follow. He will then lead students into deciding what data need to be collected and how might we expect the outcome to be.

While conducting the demonstrated inquiry, he will call upon several students to assist him in the presentation but will provide a structure in guiding the students in recording and interpreting the data. The students will then use the results for the presentation to construct additional meaning to their already held conceptions of momentum.

The demonstrated inquiry, by design, is very teacher led. Mr. Balfour also has several "going further" questions and investigations he will pose to the group who chose Station A. These questions will serve as a springboard to engage the students in additional inquiries after the initial presentation is modeled. Several of Mr. Balfour's follow-up investigations include the following:

- What would happen if we used different-size marbles (small = 1/4", medium = 1/2", large = 3/4") in the investigation?
- How does the release point on the ruler affect the distance the marble will travel?
- How will the distance the marble travels be affected if the ramp (ruler) is shortened from 12 inches to 6 inches?

Station B: As a Structured Inquiry

In one corner of Ms. Soto's classroom, Station B is set up as a structured inquiry (see Figure 8.2). At this station, the question and the procedure will be provided by the teacher, but collecting the data and examining the results will be the responsibility of the students (see Resource B).

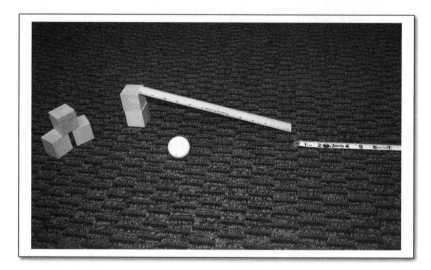

Figure 8.2   Station B

At Station B, along with the bag of materials, are several copies of directions available for the students who choose this approach. At Station B, students will write a statement or hypothesis to test, follow a given procedure, collect the data, but will determine on their own how to record and organize the data. Ms. Soto knows that some of her students may have trouble designing their own data table and explaining the results. For that reason, she has copies of a suggested data table (see Figure 8.3) to distribute if necessary. She knows that by giving the data table, she is providing more structure to the students who need it.

Balls and Ramps
Data Table for Station B

Title: _____

Height	Distance marble traveled			
	Trial 1	Trial 2	Trial 3	Average
1"				
2"				
3"				
4"				
5"				

Figure 8.3

Problem:

How does the height of an inclined plane affect the distance a marble will travel?

Materials:

One 12-inch ruler with groove

Five blocks (or books), each one inch high

Several marbles

One measuring tape

Graph paper

Procedure:

1. Place the 12-inch end of the ruler on the edge of a one-inch block.

2. Place the marble in the ruler's groove as far up the ruler as possible.

3. Release the marble.

4. Using that observation, make a prediction or hypothesis as to how the height of an inclined plane will affect the distance the marble travels. Record that statement in your science journal.

   My hypothesis: As the height of the ramp increases, the distance the marble travels will _____.

5. Repeat Steps 1 through 3 of the procedure for three separate trials. Using the measuring tape, measure the distance (in inches) the marble traveled for each trial.

6. In your journal, design a data table to record and organize the results.

7. Repeat the same procedure for two inches by placing a second block on top of the first. Place the ruler on the top of the second block so the height of the ruler is now at two inches. Release the marble and record your results in the data table.

8. Repeat the same procedure for three inches, four inches, and five inches, and again, record your results in the data table.

9. Calculate the average for each height. Show your work.

10. Use the graph paper to make a graph of your results. Be sure to provide a title to the graph and label the horizontal axis and vertical axes.

Conclusion:

Using the data collected, decide if the prediction you made was correct or not and explain why. Place your explanation on the lines below.

_____

_____

_____

Follow-Up Investigation:

In your science journal, design an investigation that will determine how the surface the marble rolls on affects the distance it will travel. Include a diagram to illustrate your design. Place the question being investigated on a sentence strip and post it above the area where you complete your investigation. Carry out your investigation and record all important data. Be prepared to provide an explanation as to whether or not your prediction or hypothesis was correct. Or you may choose to investigate any of the following questions:

- What would happen if we used different-size marbles (small = 1/4", medium = 1/2", large = 3/4") in the investigation?
- How does the release point on the ruler affect the distance the marble will travel?
- How will the distance the marble travels be affected if the ramp (ruler) is shortened from 12 inches to 6?

Similar to what students experience during the demonstrated inquiry, those who choose Station B will also be analyzing the data and evidence to seek patterns and relationship among the variables tested. Ms. Soto will be sure to question students about their drawn conclusion and what evidence they have to support their claims and conclusions. She will also ask students to form explanations and think about how they would communicate their new finding to others who did not do the inquiry.

Station C: As a Guided Inquiry

Station C is set up in another corner of the classroom. Station C is designed as a problem-solving activity or guided inquiry where the problem

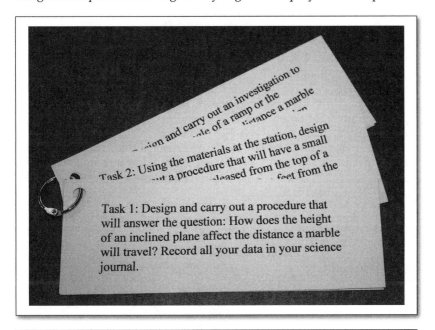

Figure 8.4   Station C Task Cards

task is provided by the teacher, but the procedure and collecting the results are left to the students. This station provides students with five laminated task cards and the materials to complete each task, although not all students will complete all five tasks (see Figure 8.4). There are assorted balls and marbles in the bag of materials that act as both distracters and enablers. In this case, rather than being told, students will have to determine which items they need (and which items they don't need) to complete the task. The additional materials may also spur other questions and tasks to investigate. On each card is a separate numbered task to complete.

Choose any one or more of the following tasks:

- Task 1: Design and carry out a procedure that will answer the question: How does the height of an inclined plane affect the distance a marble will travel? Record all your data in your science journal.
- Task 2: Using the materials at the station, design and carry out a procedure that will have a small ball or marble, when released from the top of a ramp, stop precisely at a point five feet from the end of the ramp. Draw an illustration of the design in your science journal.
- Task 3: Repeat Task 2, this time using a golf ball instead of a small ball or marble. Answer the question: How did you change the design of the procedure for Task 3? Record all your data in your science journal.
- Task 4: Design and carry out a procedure that will answer the question: How does the composition, diameter, or mass of a ball affect the distance it will travel? Record all your data in your science journal.
- Task 5: Design and carry out an investigation to determine how the angle of a ramp or the surface of the floor affects the distance a marble will travel. Draw an illustration of the design and record all your data in your science journal.

Include a diagram to illustrate your design. Place the question being investigated on a sentence strip and post it above the area where you complete your investigation. Carry out your investigation and record all important data. Be prepared to provide an explanation as to whether or not your prediction or hypothesis was correct.

At Station C, Ms. Soto will help students focus on a particular task and record a question pertaining to that specific task. She may ask these students to explain what data they expect to collect and how they will organize their data. At Station C, as students mark the end of their inquiries, she will prompt students into explaining the meaning of their results and their newly acquired knowledge.

Station D: As a Self-Directed Inquiry

Station D is set up as a self-directed inquiry. Here, students devise their own questions, design and carry out the procedures to solve the questions, and collect evidence to support or refute the claim or hypothesis made from the initial question posed. Like at Station C, there are assorted balls and marbles in the bag of materials that act as both distracters and enablers to complete the task (see Figure 8.5). Not all the supplies in the bag need to be used. Again, like Station C, students will have to determine

Figure 8.5   Station D Materials

which items they need to complete the task. The additional materials are expected to stimulate added questions to investigate.

The process for Station D mirrors the segments of inquiry identified in the Introduction. Students at Station D will first be directed to set up an exploration similar to the first two steps in Station B. From this initial observation, students will consider possible questions to investigate.

After reading all the possible questions, students will choose their first questions to investigate. Ms. Soto encourages students to record their question on sentence strips and post them on the wall above their work

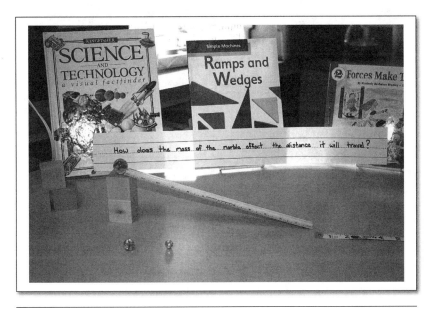

Figure 8.6   Question on a Sentence Strip

area at Station D (see Figure 8.6). This way, every member of the group will be able to see what questions other students are considering.

If the group is large, several questions can be investigated at the same time. Each smaller group at Station D will seek additional evidence to propose a hypothesis or preliminary explanation. The groups then design their investigations to determine the variables and controls needed and design appropriate data tables to collect the evidence from their investigations.

Available at the teacher's desk are additional materials students might need in their investigations (see Figure 8.7). Materials include the following:

- Various-size groove ruler ramps (18", 12", and 6" lengths)
- Various-size wooden balls (1", 2", 3", and 4" diameters)
- Various one-inch-size balls (glass, wood, steel, plastic)
- Various-size marbles (small = 1/4", medium = 1/2", large = 3/4", extra large = 1")

Although each of the approaches has its own identity, all the stations demonstrate varying degrees of the seven segments of scientific inquiry introduced earlier. You can see as the approach become less teacher directed, the responsibility for the segments becomes more student owned. However, all four approaches will involve some aspect of analyzing the data and evidence, connecting new knowledge to preexisting knowledge, and communicating the results through whole-class discussion and reflection time.

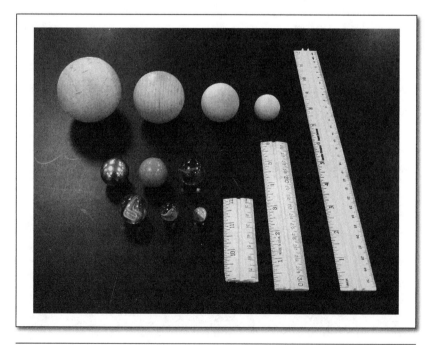

Figure 8.7   Materials Photo

VARIATIONS OF THE DSI MODEL

Balls and Ramps is just one example of how a teacher provided a way to differentiate the methodology for a lesson on motion energy. The example is provided with the understanding that most teachers may not have an additional teacher, adult, volunteer, or parent to present the demonstrated inquiry station. For many teachers, offering just three stations—B, C, and D—may be more suitable. Or for other teachers, only two stations are offered. Sometimes, based on the nature of the content, it is possible to present all four approaches. Other times, all four may not be applicable. The concept being introduced may lend itself to only two or three approaches. We will now identify six additional variations to this model and offer alternatives that may fit your class's needs.

The assignments or source for questions can fall into two categories: (a) those questions assigned by the teacher to all students and (b) those where the students have individual choice and self-assignment opportunities for the question. Usually, it is the teacher (or the textbook) who provides the assignment of the question and the method, not the students. Now, DSI can offer multiple options for both teachers *and* students. We will now look at several alternatives in assigning the question and method for the investigation, keeping in mind that different situations require different instructional responses.

Same Method Assigned for All Students

In this category, let's think of two teachers, Allen and Bruce, who use somewhat similar routines for teaching. Allen first provides an introductory lecture to preteach vocabulary didactically and then incorporates a conventional demonstration to illustrate the concepts made during the introductory presentation. In this case, Allen shows *all* the students in the class the *same* teacher-led demonstration. Later, Allen has *all* students carry out the *same* teacher-assigned, step-by-step, cookbook lab to reinforce what was presented earlier (see Figure 8.8).

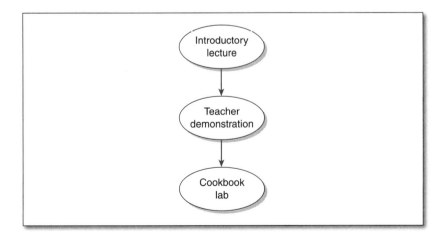

Figure 8.8   Allen offers the same assignment to all students.

Bruce also begins a lesson first with a lecture and then has *all* the students view the *same* demonstration. Following the demonstration, Bruce has students carry out the *same* structured inquiry or complete the *same* teacher-initiated, problem-solving challenge, or guided inquiry (see Figure 8.9).

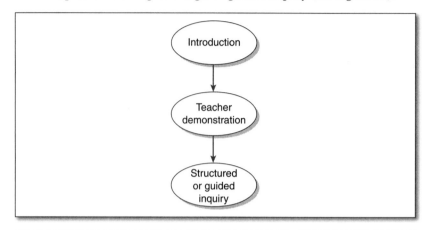

Figure 8.9   Like Allen, Bruce offers the same assignment to all students.

Due to preservice preparation and/or limited availability of resources, many science teachers fall into the "one-size-fits-all" style similar to Allen and Bruce. You may even have colleagues who are reminiscent of Allen and Bruce. And although these teachers may be highly qualified, successful educators, and their methodology may have a notable purpose, their teaching bears little or no sign of opportunities for student choice.

Methods With Opportunities for Choice

Now let's consider the next category of assignments. In this case, our third teacher, Charlie, provides both prescribed as well as nonprescribed methods, together with opportunities for choice. Charlie has *all* his students witness the *same* demonstrated inquiry but then makes an effort to offer students a *choice* of different follow-up structured activities and labs at least two or three times a semester (see Figure 8.10).

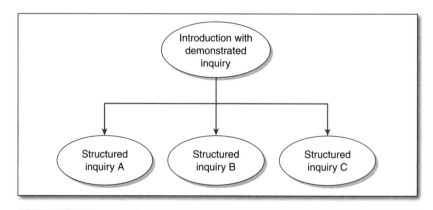

Figure 8.10   Charlie offers a choice of structured-inquiry assignments.

As an example, Charlie is presenting a lesson on the growing cycle of plants. To present this concept, he has his students grow bean plants under different lighting conditions: full light, partial light, and in full darkness. His students make daily measurements as to the effect of light on the growing bean plants. After the light experiment is completed and students make meaning of their results, he has students choose other variables to test as a follow-up investigation. Some students choose to investigate how the amount of water affects growing conditions. Others choose the effect of fertilizer or the type of light (white, blue, green, yellow, and red) in plant growth. Still other students design ways to determine if music affects plant growth, and if so, what kind of music promotes the most growth? In the follow-up investigations, the emphasis is on the self-selection of variables to investigate.

Our fourth teacher, Dave, is somewhat similar to Charlie. Dave has *all* students observe the *same* demonstrated inquiry followed by all completing the *same* structured activity but then offers students a *choice* in completing *different* follow-up guided inquiries and problem-solving challenges (see Figure 8.11).

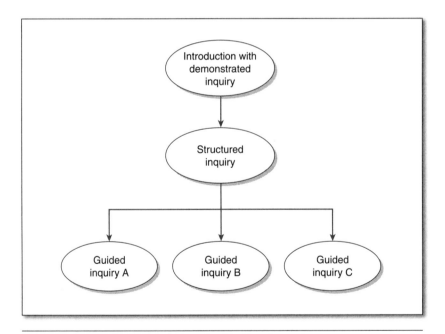

Figure 8.11   Dave offers a choice of guided-inquiry assignments.

Evan, our fifth teacher, is like Ms. Soto in the Balls and Ramps activity. He gives a brief introduction but then offers students a choice in selecting one of four different approaches that best fits their interests and learning styles. When differentiating science inquiry, Evan provides a bouillabaisse of activities—with each approach adding a taste of diversity, yet keeping it own distinct instructional flavor (see Figure 8.12).

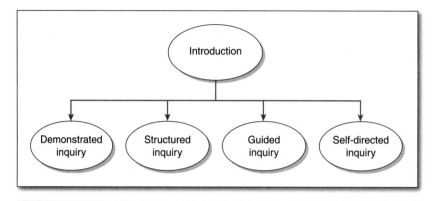

Figure 8.12 Evan offers a choice of four types of inquiry assignments in this instance, when he has another adult in the room.

If Evan did not have an extra adult in the room (like Ms. Soto had with Mr. Balfour), he might not have been able to offer the demonstrated inquiry option and therefore could provide only three stations: a structured inquiry station, a guided inquiry station, and a self-directed inquiry station (see Figure 8.13), making the analogy of this situation to a three-ring circus!

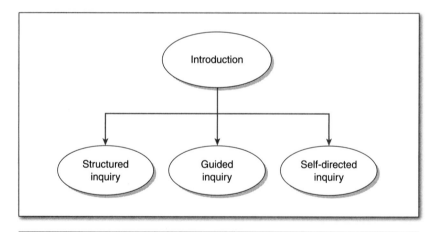

Figure 8.13 Evan offers a choice of three types of inquiry assigments in this instance, when he does not have another adult in the room.

As you can now see, there are many variations and possibilities for DSI. The range of approaches that best fits a situation depends on the teacher's tolerance for instructional diversity as well as the desire to attend to a variety of learning styles. It also depends on the nature of the topic, the sophistication and level of experience students have with science inquiry, as well as the teacher's professional goals and vision for science education. In actuality, teachers switch from one option to another when it is most appropriate. As you begin to implement DSI, you will come to acknowledge that distinctive instructional goals and objectives necessitate atypical approaches. A methodology for one concept may not work for another. Knowing what approach to use takes time and practice. Be patient and allow the appropriateness of methodology to germinate slowly.

THREE AREAS OF DIFFERENTIATION

According to Tomlinson (1999), there are three principal areas where teachers can differentiate in heterogeneous classrooms: content, process, and product. When differentiating content, the teacher considers *what* students are expected to learn. In this case, teachers may extend or further elaborate the subject matter for gifted and talented science students and for those needing an additional challenge, or on the other hand, provide academic intervention support in the form of corrective assistance where the content is complex or foreign to the student. When differentiating process, teachers modify *how* students will learn a new concept.

Using the Invitation to Inquiry Grid, the four modes of instruction provide the foundation for DSI. In appropriate and relevant situations, teachers can modify their favorite prescribed activities to provide varied levels of collaboration, challenge, and complexity. And finally, when differentiating products, teachers modify *ways* students can demonstrate what and how they learned. Students can exhibit their proficiency through standard assessment measures including multiple-choice and extended response questions, or through alternative or authentic means, including portfolios, journal entries, oral or PowerPoint presentations, performance assessments, tri-fold poster boards, and self-evaluations. Of the three areas just mentioned, this book will spotlight the *process* aspect of differentiation and provide instances when it is and isn't appropriate. If you would like to learn more about differentiating content, process, and products, there are a host of excellent books from Corwin. Two recommended resources are Gregory and Chapman's (2002) *Differentiated Instruction Strategies* and Gregory and Hammerman's (2008) *Differentiated Instructional Strategies for Science, Grades K–8.*

OTHER METHODS FOR DSI

Besides the variations you just read about, there are three other familiar instructional methods that support DSI: the K-W-L approach, the use of individual stations, and the 5E Learning Cycle. If you are already familiar with these three approaches, it's probably best to move on to the next section, Three Student Needs. If you are new or want to refresh your memory about K-W-L, individual learning stations, and the 5E's, this section is for you.

The K-W-L technique (Ogle, 1986) provides opportunities where students (1) assess their present knowledge of a topic, (2) raise and carry out their individual inquiries, and (3) elaborate on new knowledge gained. With K-W-L, the teacher begins a new unit of study by asking the class, "What do you already *know* about the topic?" During the K phase, students write their prior experiences on Post-it Notes or on a prepared K-W-L worksheet (see Figure 8.14). The teacher can collectively record the students' prior

K-W-L Chart

What do you *Know?*	What do you *Want* to know?	What have you *Learned?*

Figure 8.14

knowledge by listing the responses on the chalkboard or a large poster sheet under the "What I Know?" column. The teacher can also construct a concept map of the students' previously held knowledge and experiences and assess and uncover misconceptions students hold as they share what they already know about the topic.

Next, the students raise "I Wonder" questions and inquiries about the topic. At this time, the teacher or the students would record the questions in the "What I Want to Know" column of the K-W-L chart. If, however, students have difficulty writing questions to wonder about, the teacher can provide a nondirected experience in which students engage in an exploration about the topic of study. Exploring and observing an initiating engagement often acts as a prompt to stimulate questioning. The questions can now be listed in the "W" column and be discussed and reworded if necessary. The second part of the "What I Want to Know" stage involves students brainstorming ways to answer their questions. The teacher may decide to investigate one question for the entire class or allow two or three students to investigate their own question. As the students devise ways to solve their questions and go about carrying out their plans, the teacher rotates from group to group and encourages the groups to write down other questions that come up during the course of their investigations. Sufficient materials should be readily available at a supply center for groups to carry out their investigations.

At the conclusion of the "I Wonder" inquiries, the teacher and students record what they learned in the "What I Learned" column of the K-W-L chart. During this stage, the teacher helps students make meaning of their inquiries and make concluding claims and support and defend the claims based on the evidence collected. If a concept map was constructed during the initial "K" stage, the teacher and students can return to the concept map and add newly acquired knowledge to the map.

In many ways, teachers who implement the K-W-L strategy with small groups of students investigating their own question make accommodations for individual academic growth during the "I Wonder" portion of the strategy. Having six or seven individual inquiries going on in one classroom all at once takes years of practice and patience. It also takes flexibility and tolerance, but it can be done. Readers who want to know more about the K-W-L method will find a wealth of resources and strategies online and in academic libraries.

Likewise, learning stations provide occasions where students choose varying topics set up around the classroom in the form of individual discovery places. Learning stations can take many forms. They can be set up as individual exploratory centers for enrichment work or sequential stations where students choose a topic within a specified unit of study. Stations can also provide a means to assess students' understandings, skills, and abilities. "Measurement Stations" (Llewellyn, 2005), an article from *Science Scope,* provides 12 stations where students work in pairs to collect data from an initial exploratory task on the science process skill of measurement. Each station introduces the pair to a measurement skill with a step-by-step activity followed by "Inquiring Further" questions and tasks. When teachers allow students to choose the questions to investigate or choose the stations to explore, they make strides toward differentiating science instruction and enhancing self-directed learners.

The third method is the 5E Learning Cycle that was introduced earlier in the Introduction section of the book. Using the 5E's, Emily, a seventh-grade physical science teacher, integrates differentiated inquiry into her lesson as an adaptation of the Balls and Ramps activity. The first E, Engagement, commences the lesson with Emily assessing students' prior knowledge about rolling objects (much like Mr. Balfour did in the previous example). She then shows a quick demonstration of the ramp apparatus and how to release the marble at the desired height. For the second E, the Exploration phase, students complete a structured inquiry as prescribed in Station B. Following the Exploration, Emily leads a full-class discussion on potential and kinetic energy and lays the foundation for the district content standards for forces and motion during the third E, the Explanation phase. Then for the Elaboration or Extension phase, students choose one of the guided inquiry tasks as a follow-up investigation. Later, Emily provides time for students to communicate their findings and explanation for the investigations to the entire class during a "Momentum Convention." During this time, students engage in sharing their claims and supportive evidence. This phase of the lesson helps student to understand and appreciate the role of scientific argumentation as a critical means to how scientists enhance their knowledge about the natural world. For the final E, Evaluation, Emily prepares an appropriate unit test to assess students' understanding of motion energy as well as the elements in designing a scientific investigation.

THREE "STUDENT NEEDS" FOR DIFFERENTIATED INSTRUCTION

Like good teaching, effective differentiation centers on the needs of students. Tomlinson and Kalhfleisch (1998) remind us that if quality learning is to take place, regardless of the subject matter or method of presentation, three essential conditions need to occur. First, students need to feel emotionally safe, meaning free of intimidation regardless of their abilities or behaviors. Second, students need to experience an appropriate level of challenge, preferably just slightly beyond their ability and readiness. And third, students need time to reflect as *meaning-seekers* in constructing meaning from inside and outside of classroom environments and experiences.

In DSI, elementary, middle, and high school teachers meet the three criteria by valuing and recognizing a student's particular learning style (or styles) as well as the student's need for guided instruction and structure versus open-ended learning opportunities. The DSI-based teacher accomplishes this by providing various levels of opportunities and investigations that are built on student choice and tailored to students' personal needs by offering options and learning modes at different levels of challenge and difficulty. By providing a menu of choice and options, the student experiences what I call the "Goldilocks Effect"—choosing an activity that is not too structured or too open-ended—it's just right!

When a teacher differentiates the approach or level of science inquiry, she piques a student's interest in response to the learner's readiness, skill level, and preferred learning style—whether it is visual, auditory, tactile, or kinesthetic. Most of all, in DSI lessons, the teacher differentiates the instructional approach based on the student's attention span or need for structure, whether it is providing explicit versus ill-defined directions to a procedure or a traditional seating arrangement (rows and columns) versus a small-group setting. Furthermore, when a teacher differentiates the approach or level of science inquiry, she offers a variety of instructional practices that leads to students becoming more engaged and motivated in science classes. Creating opportunities for students to be appropriately challenged is predicated on designing activities focusing on choice, which leads to engagement, which leads to motivation, which leads to academic success.

With classrooms becoming increasingly academically and culturally diverse, teachers are challenged to meet these needs in all subject areas—but especially science, which lends itself to hands-on and manipulative learning opportunities. Differentiated inquiry can become the catalyst for flexible instruction and assessment, varied student groupings, variability in directive and supporting assistance, and acceptance for various routes for students to demonstrate what they now know and are able to do.

Although the reality of "teaching to the middle" and hoping to "reach as many students as possible" seems to be the predominate course of instruction in many classrooms, we now see there are instances where science teachers can differentiate an existing time-honored, favorite lesson and modify it to accommodate a range of learner needs.

The process of differentiation usually commences when teachers acknowledge the reality that classrooms are changing and that they need to reassess and recalibrate their instructional plans based on the varying prior knowledge, experiences, skill levels, and abilities of their students. In essence, there are two ways to deal with the changing climate of school classrooms: one is to ignore it and continue to teach to the "middle," knowing full well that many of our students will be either "lost" or bored, while the alternative is to make a resilient and passionate effort to adjust teaching to accommodate the various strengths and interests of the children and young adolescents entering into today's mixed-ability classrooms.

The naysayer may ask if the required planning is worth the time, while the risk-taking teacher unhesitatingly knows that best practices and various orientations to inquiry, when strategically employed, will maximize student engagement and achievement at every turn. In the end, DSI is not a panacea, and it's not the method "du jour." Understanding that all learning environments have their distinct physical and psychological obstacles, DSI is, however, an alternative means that teachers can employ once a month to shake up the ordinary routine of instruction. DSI can be an additional strategy teachers have in their instructional toolboxes to reposition learners from complacency to creativity.

WRITING QUESTIONS
FOR REFLECTION AND DISCUSSION

Write three questions that concern you at this point. Share and discuss your questions and responses with a colleague.

1.

2.

3.

If you are having difficulty writing three questions, consider the following guided questions for discussion and reflection:

1. Differentiating an inquiry lesson requires a substantial background in science content knowledge. What suggestions could you make to a third-year elementary school teacher who lacks a deep understanding in science but wants to attempt a DSI lesson?

2. What would you do if you planned three stations for an inquiry and the choices students made ended up in an unbalanced number at each station? For example: There are 22 students in the class, 15 choose the structured inquiry, 5 choose the guided inquiry, and 2 choose the self-directed inquiry.

3. Part of the "Communicating New Knowledge" segment involves encouraging students to critique and securitize the evidence presented in defense of claims made by others. How can you foster this skill without having the process become a shouting match?

4. Chapter 3 ended with identifying three areas where teachers can differentiate: content, process, and products. Choose a lesson or unit of study familiar to you. Describe how you could differentiate your lesson or unit for these three areas.

9

Methods and Effective Practices for Increasing Student Achievement

Gayle H. Gregory and Elizabeth Hammerman

Once the classroom climate for effective instruction is created, the goals and standards for science for each grade level are identified and understood, and information is known about student learning styles, personal intelligences, and cultural perspectives, teachers can design instruction to meet the needs and interests of their students. Instruction is a creative process involving an array of multisensory activities and experiences that challenge the mind, stir the emotions, provide social interaction and physical challenges, and satisfy the human needs to learn and to know oneself. Instruction should mirror life and offer learners a wide range of opportunities to construct an understanding of the natural world. Prior knowledge of what students know and are able to do will provide a starting point from which teachers can build concept understanding and develop skills by utilizing methods and practices that are most appropriate for their students.

METHODS FOR TEACHING AND LEARNING SCIENCE

What are they? Methods are the various ways we can approach learning in the classroom. They are the choices that are made by teachers (or by students) about how students will learn. The methods that are selected and used by teachers are linked to their belief systems and self-efficacy as well as to the expectations of administrators, parents, and students. High quality instruction includes the use of a variety of methods. Instruction in science is a function of the interaction of five basic methods:

- **Expository**—lectures, media presentations, guest speakers, text material, pictures, CDs, audio and video tapes, trade books, and such.
- **Discussion**—student to student or teacher to student exchange of ideas and information.
- **Demonstration**—presentation by teachers, students, or invited guests with or without interactions and discussion.
- **Guided inquiry**—student- or teacher-generated questions and activities with varying degrees of structure leading to a range of predictable or fairly predictable outcomes or expectations.
- **Open inquiry or problem-based learning**—student- or teacher-generated inquiry questions or ill-structured problems without predicted outcomes or expectations.

Why do we use them? Methods are the means to the end, that is, they are the ways that instruction is designed to successfully address and meet goals and objectives for learning. Varying methods throughout instruction provide the greatest opportunity to capture and maintain student interest, motivate students, and maximize learning.

What do they look like?

Expository learning: Expository learning takes the form of receiving facts or information; reading stories, articles or text material; copying information; viewing a film or videotape; or listening to a lecture.

Discussion: Discussion engages students in dialog related to facts, findings, or opinions. Environments that encourage discussion are non-threatening and respectful of students' thoughts and ideas and understandings or misunderstandings. Discussions are especially useful following investigations or research for reflecting on processes, sharing and analyzing data, determining validity of conclusions, applying concepts, and creating meaning.

Demonstration: Demonstrations involve one or more persons giving a presentation to an audience that may vary in size from a small group to an entire class. Demonstrations may be valuable or necessary when

- The materials or equipment involved is costly or delicate.
- The equipment, materials, or process is not safe for students to use themselves.
- A visitor is showing or describing work or a small set of samples that are fragile or valuable.
- There is a person or animal involved.
- Safety is an issue.
- There is only one opportunity for an event to happen.

Demonstrations with interactions allow students to have input and to ask questions.

Guided inquiry: Inquiry is an active learning process that begins with one or more questions developed by the teacher or generated by students. The heart of inquiry is investigation, and investigations are rooted in "hands-on" or "minds-on" activities and experiences. Through the process of inquiry, data are generated that either support or do not support predictions or hypotheses. As students engage in discussion and reflection, they realize the role and importance of data for supporting their conclusions.

Inquiry investigations are, by nature, interdisciplinary. Science naturally integrates with mathematics, literacy, technology, social studies, the arts, and other areas of the curriculum. For example:

- Graphs can be used to display data sets.
- Reading can be enhanced through trade books and reference books that define concepts, provide information, and explain relationships between concepts.
- Notebooks can be used to record information, inquiry questions, background information, action plans, data, and explanations and summaries of learning, while providing opportunities for students to use vocabulary in meaningful ways.
- Technology and software programs offer novel approaches for learning, practice, relearning important concepts, and applying and extending learning.

Open inquiry and problem-based learning: In open inquiry, students generate questions and design action plans to access and use information, investigate and collect data, and draw conclusions based on their findings.

Inquiry questions may be generated prior to instruction as things they want to know or during instruction as new questions arise while learning occurs.

Sample Inquiry Questions

- Do marigolds that are kept in the light 24 hours per day grow taller than those that are kept in the light 8 hours a day?
- Which frozen liquid melts the fastest: water, milk, or soda? Which liquid evaporates the fastest?
- Does your pulse rate increase or decrease after listening to music?
- Do plants grow better if they are grown with music? Would the kind of music affect the results?
- Do batteries stored in the freezer power a toy car longer than those stored at room temperature?
- Do pumpkins that weigh five pounds or more contain more seeds than those that weigh less than five pounds?
- Does the size of the wheels on a toy car affect the distance it travels down a ramp?
- Does the temperature of water affect how fast salt crystals (or sugar crystals) dissolve or disappear?
- Do model airplanes with large wings fly farther than those with smaller wings?

Summary: All of the methods have a place in inquiry-based science. It is important that students understand that scientists use a variety of methods and strategies for discovering natural phenomena and constructing knowledge.

Expository methods are useful for providing interesting and relevant information, generating interest, and reinforcing or relearning concepts.

Demonstrations provide visual displays of phenomena that are often exciting for the observer. They may take the form of discrepant events that activate brain cells by causing cognitive conflict. Such conflict generates new inquiry questions.

Discussion that includes reflection on process and the sharing of ideas, data, conclusions, applications, and meaning is an important part of every investigation.

The process of inquiry focuses on questions that are of interest to students and capitalizes on the sense of wonder that motivates students to learn. A learning cycle approach begins with questions based on major concepts, issues, or problems. Students assume the role of "scientist" as they explore and investigate natural phenomena, collect and process data, formulate conclusions, create meaning, make connections and apply learning, and generate new questions.

In problem-based learning, "ill-structured" problems are posed by teachers or students and students are challenged to investigate and offer varied solutions based on their research. Problems may be designed to lead students toward content-rich investigations that have relevant applications leading to a deep understanding of issues, but not predetermined outcomes. Often alternative solutions are offered and considered.

The Roles of Teachers and Students in Methods

Figure 9.1 identifies the roles of teachers and students in the various methods. Note the methods that engage students in active versus passive ways of learning.

RESEARCH-BASED EFFECTIVE PRACTICES

What are they? Effective practices are instructional strategies that have been shown to increase student motivation, interest, and achievement. They are "brain-based" in that they capitalize on the brain's natural abilities and promote student learning. Effective science classrooms engage students in inquiry-based investigations, focus on developing understanding of important concepts and principles, develop student responsibility for learning, incorporate formative assessment, and encourage cooperative and collaborative approaches to learning.

Why do we use them? Research is critical to the practitioner in that it identifies practices that enhance student achievement and provide a strong rationale for the application of the practices to classroom instruction. Recently researchers have concluded that the most important factor affecting student learning is the teacher (Sanders & Horn, 1994, and Wright, Horn, & Sanders, 1997, in Marzano, Pickering, & Pollack, 2001; Wenglinsky, 2000). Research-based effective practices offer important messages to teachers about what works, providing valuable insights and information to guide them in planning instruction, monitoring and directing learning, and assessing the effectiveness of the instructional process.

Figure 9.1   Roles of Teachers and Students in Methods

Methods	What Teachers Will Do	What Students Will Do
Expository	• Lecture, provide information • Invite a speaker • Read or tell a story • Provide books, pictures, audio and video tapes, films, software, and other sources of information	• Read about a topic • Watch videotapes or presentations • Listen to a tape or music • Listen to a lecture or talk • Access and use information
Demonstration	• Conduct an experiment or activity, show a discrepant event, or explain a process or product while students observe • Engage in discussion with students during the demonstration (optional)	• Observe a product, process, or event • Observe and discuss a discrepant event
Discussion	• Ask questions • Interact verbally with students • Guide student-student verbal interaction	• Engage in conversation with the teacher or students • Listen • Ask and answer questions
Guided Inquiry	• Structure learning environment to meet needs of students • Engage students by creating a meaningful context and offering options • Ask or elicit inquiry questions • Design and facilitate activities and experiences • Check for misconceptions • Check accuracy of work • Guide instruction through questions and cues • Mediate and support • Challenge students to think and create meaning • Assess to monitor learning and guide instruction	• Participate in an activity or experience to answer one or more teacher or student-generated questions • Choose learning pathways and grouping patterns • Design action plans for investigating inquiry questions • Investigate and manipulate equipment and materials • Keep a notebook • Communicate, reflect, apply learning, create meaning • Apply and extend learning • Engage in research
Open Inquiry	• Encourage students to think, inquire, plan, research, and be involved in learning • Mediate and guide, as needed, to assure purposeful pursuits • Be flexible and supportive • Provide equipment, materials, resources, advice, and encouragement, as needed	• Ask questions, design action plans, engage in activities and experiences, share findings, and apply and extend learning • Confer with teachers, as needed • Investigate problems or issues • Keep a notebook • Take or share responsibility for learning • Share results and data • Consider alternative solutions • Ask new questions

What do they look like? The NSES identify effective practices for teaching science. Recommendations for teachers include the following:

1. Understanding and responding to student needs, interests, and strengths.

2. Learning science through investigation and inquiry.

3. Understanding concepts and developing abilities of inquiry.

4. Learning subject matter in the context of inquiry, science in personal and social perspective, technology, and history and nature of science.

5. Using activities that investigate and analyze science questions.

6. Designing investigations that focus on content and use process skills in context

7. Using evidence and strategies to develop or revise explanations.

8. Assessing what is most highly valued.

9. Continuously assessing student understanding and sharing responsibility for learning with students. (National Research Council, 1996, pp. 52, 72, 100, and 113)

A meta-analysis of research on instruction conducted at the Mid-continent Research for Education and Learning (McREL) identified nine strategies that have a high probability of enhancing student achievement for all students (Marzano, Pickering, & Pollack, 2001). The effective practices are as follows:

1. Identifying similarities and differences.

2. Summarizing and note taking.

3. Reinforcing effort and providing recognition.

4. Assigning homework and practice time.

5. Creating nonlinguistic representations.

6. Cooperative learning.

7. Setting objectives and providing feedback.

8. Generating and testing hypotheses.

9. Activating prior knowledge through questions, cues, and advance organizers.

The authors of the study made it clear that all strategies may not be effective for all students in all subject areas. They recommended that teachers rely on their knowledge of their students, their subject matter, and their situations to identify the strategies that are most appropriate for them.

STRATEGIES LINKED TO BRAIN RESEARCH AND CLASSROOM PRACTICES

The practices are rooted in brain-based learning and active inquiry. Figure 9.2 shows some ways that research can be used to inform brain-based instruction. The left column identifies the nine Marzano research-based instructional strategies by decreasing percentile rank. The center column describes findings from brain research that support the strategies as effective practices for learning. The right-hand column identifies characteristics of inquiry-based science that relate to the practices.

Gordon Cawalti (1995) edited a handbook of research on student achievement and identified effective practices for improving science instruction. These findings, compiled by Dorothy Gabel, include the following:

1. Using a learning cycle approach.

2. Using computers to collect and display data.

3. Using analogies, which enable the learner to compare the familiar to the unfamiliar

4. Using wait time and computer simulations.

5. Using student-generated and teacher-generated concept maps.

6. Using cooperative learning for classroom and laboratory instruction.

7. Using systematic approaches to problem solving and real-life situations.

8. Using a science-technology-society approach.

9. Using discrepant events for cognitive conflict and enhanced concept understanding.

Science Notebooks As Tools for Learning

Using notebooks in science has been shown to increase student achievement in science and other areas of the curriculum (Klentschy, Garrison, & Maia Amaral, 2000).

Figure 9.2   Effective Strategies, Brain Research, and Classroom Applications

Effective Strategies	Brain Research	Classroom Applications
Identifying Similarities and Differences	The brain seeks patterns, connections, and relationships between and among prior and new learning	• Classify objects and phenomena • Compare and contrast • Use Venn diagrams to compare characteristics of organisms or events • Write analogies for important concepts • Trace the history of inventions, theories, or technology; compare past with present • Describe relationships between prior knowledge (or misconceptions) and new learning • Create metaphors
Summarizing and Note Taking	The brain pays attention to meaningful information and deletes that which is not relevant	• Use notebooks to record information and summarize learning • Use jigsaw to emphasize important concepts • Differentiate between relevant and irrelevant data
Reinforcing Effort and Providing Recognition	The brain responds to challenge and not threat. Emotions enhance learning	• Provide a safe, comfortable, student-centered environment • Provide activities that are relevant, interesting and challenging • Provide continuous support and recognition
Assigning Homework and Practice	"If you don't use it, you lose it." Practice and rehearsal make learning "stick"	• Apply concepts and principles to student lives, technology, and society • Use games and puzzles to reinforce concepts • Reinforce learning through reading and extensions
Generating Nonlinguistic Representations	The brain is a parallel processor. Visual stimuli is recalled with 90% accuracy	• Create mind maps and graphic organizers, data tables and graphs • Draw pictures and illustrations to record observations of organisms and events and change over time • Create two- and three-dimensional models
Using Cooperative Learning	The brain is social. Collaboration facilitates understanding and higher order thinking	• Use lab partners and flexible grouping patterns • Create jigsaw experiences • Use and vary cooperative and collaborative strategies
Setting Objectives and Providing Feedback	The brain responds to high challenge and continues to strive with continuous feedback	• Communicate clear targets and learning goals • Use formative assessment strategies to monitor student learning • Provide continuous feedback • Use rubrics to guide instruction and for self-assessment • Maintain high standards and expectations
Generating and Testing Hypotheses	The brain is curious and has an innate need to make meaning through patterns	• Design standards-related inquiries based on student- or teacher-generated questions • Generate a hypotheses and create action plans for testing • Use questions to reflect on process and data and create meaning • Apply learning to personal lives and events within the local and global communities

SOURCE: Modified from Gregory and Parry, 2006

Notebook pages can be designed by the teacher or by students to record details of activities and experiences. Students can record their inquiry questions and observations; write action plans; draw pictures, illustrations, and graphic organizers; create data tables and graphs; explain understanding; and summarize learning and extended learning. The notebook is also a tool for formative assessment as it provides evidence of student work and learning throughout a unit.

A science notebook might include any or all of these components:

- Inquiry questions or problems of interest
  - Student- or teacher-generated.
  - Worthy of investigation.
- Prediction or hypothesis
  - Relates to inquiry question.
  - Relies on prior knowledge or experience.
- Action plan for investigating inquiry question
  - Relates to inquiry question.
  - Identifies equipment and materials needed.
  - Clearly identifies reasonable, sequenced steps.
  - Identifies variables, when appropriate.
- Observations and data
  - Qualitative and quantitative observations.
  - Data are relevant and shown on a table or chart.
- Graphics and graphs
  - Visual(s) to show process, change, or data and relationships between concepts.
  - Show relationships between variables in an experiment.
- Reflections and conclusions
  - Analysis of process and findings.
  - Insights or answers related to inquiry question.
  - Use of evidence to support conclusions.
- Applications and creating meaning
  - Link to prior knowledge and personal life.
  - Connections to technology and society.
- Summaries of learning
  - Frame thought.
  - Describe learning.
- New questions and next steps

Lab Reports

Lab reports may follow a standard framework or be designed to relate more specifically to certain laboratory activities. Lab reports may be separate from or part of a notebook, depending on the teacher's preference.

Lab reports reflect an understanding of content through the ability to design, conduct, and communicate the results of an experiment. In addition, the report communicates the purpose, background understanding, procedures, findings, and conclusions.

The components of a lab report are as follows:

- Title of the lab.
- The purpose, including the inquiry question, objective of the investigation, and the dependent and independent variables, if applicable.
- Background information or a survey of literature.
- Procedures: a step-by-step process that describes what will be done and how it will be done.
- Data and calculations: data should be shown on labeled data tables.
- Graphs of data: graphs should be appropriately labeled and clear.
- Discussion of results and the conclusions that can be drawn from the data; conclusions should be supported with logic and data; discuss the implications and meaning of the findings of the study.
- Suggestions for additional needed research if data are not conclusive.
- Applications to technology and society.
- New questions.
- Bibliography (if applicable).

Figure 9.3 shows an outline for a lab report.

Scoring Rubric for a Lab Report

Some components of the report may take several pages, such as background information, data tables and graphs, and applications. The framework will help to guide the students, especially if a rubric is provided. Figure 9.4 shows a sample scoring rubric for a lab report.

Grouping

What is it? Basically, there are four grouping patterns: whole group, small groups, partners, and individuals. There are times when instruction is suitable for large groups and times when activities are most effective when students work in smaller groups or with partners.

Figure 9.3 Lab Report

Name: _____ Date: _____

Title of Lab: _____

Description of Lab:

Inquiry Question:

Objective(s):

Background Information or Literature Review:

Procedures:

Data Tables, Graphs, and Calculations:

Conclusions and Additional Research:

Applications to Technology and Society:

New Questions:

Bibliography:

Figure 9.4 Scoring Rubric for a Lab Report

Part of Report	Exceeds Expectations (3)	Meets Expectations (2)	Does Not Meet Expectations (1)	Is Not Present
Title	Title is creative or unique	Title is shown and appropriate	Title does not fit investigation	Title is missing
Description	Identifies key concepts; is clear, detailed and accurate; identifies inquiry question and objective(s); identifies and explains variables	Identifies key concepts; is clear and accurate; identifies inquiry question, objective(s), and variables	Description is not accurate or is lacking detail related to inquiry question, objectives, or variables	Description is missing or inquiry question, objectives, or variables are not described or are missing
Background Information	Includes detailed information from two or more reputable sources of various types	Includes information from two reputable sources	Information is minimal or from a single source	Information is lacking or from an unreliable source
Procedures	Describes a detailed and accurate approach for safely gathering relevant data and addressing the inquiry question	Describes an accurate approach to gathering relevant data to address inquiry question	Description is lacking in detail or inappropriate; approach does not address inquiry question	Procedures missing
Data Tables, Graphs, Calculations	Tables and graphs are well-designed, accurate, and labeled; all calculations are shown and explained	Tables and graphs are accurate and labeled; calculations are shown	Tables and graphs are incomplete or inaccurate or labels or calculations are lacking	Tables, graphs, or calculations are missing
Conclusions and Research Needs	Conclusions are logical, data based, and explained; research needs are identified, if appropriate, and explained	Conclusions are logical and based on data; research needs are identified, if appropriate	Conclusions are not based on data; additional research needs are lacking or inappropriate	Conclusions or additional research needs, if relevant, are missing
Applications to Technology and Society	Concepts are applied to technology or society with detailed explanations and examples or resources	Concept(s) are applied to technology or society with examples and resources cited	Concept application is weak or minimal	Concept application is lacking
New Questions	Questions show insight or ingenuity	Questions relate to inquiry and are relevant to content	Questions do not relate to content being studied	Questions are missing
Bibliography	Exceeds required number and variety of relevant resources in appropriate format	Includes the required number and variety of relevant resources	Resources lacking in number, variety, or relevance	Resources are not cited

Instruction designed for a whole group may include brainstorming and decision making, demonstrations, guest speakers, video presentations, and anchor activities that include discussion for reflection and meaning making. Small groups and partners work well for lab activities and outdoor investigations, projects, stations, enrichment or relearning activities, tutoring, and peer review. Some students may prefer to work alone on projects, investigations, or research.

Why do we use it? Students are grouped to meet their instructional, emotional, and personal needs. Some students learn best while working alone while others work better in small groups or with partners. Grouping students by prior knowledge and skill levels (readiness levels), learning preferences, and interests offers multiple opportunities for success.

In a group, each student brings talents such as verbal fluency, creativity, empathy, or technical expertise, and students are provided an opportunity to share their talents. Goleman (1995) found that the most important factor in maximizing the excellence of a group's product was the degree to which the members were able to create a state of internal harmony. Altering grouping patterns throughout the instructional process maximizes the opportunities for meeting social needs and for this harmony to occur.

What does it look like? Because grouping is based on a number of different variables and is a dynamic process, there is no single way to do it. Flexible grouping is the best approach to capitalizing on each student's strengths and enhancing learning.

Some of the factors on which grouping can be based are as follows:

- Knowledge of content or readiness for learning based on preassessments or test data.
- Nature of the instruction.
- Types and amount of equipment and consumable materials.
- Availability of resources such as books, models, computers, tutors or aides, and the like.
- Learning profiles.
- Interest.

Cooperative Learning

When we put students in groups, there are many things that can go wrong. Students take over, don't work on task, talk about other things, become social loafers, or wind up dysfunctional and unable to resolve conflict. If we use the guidelines for cooperative group learning, students in groups usually work better together and actually accomplish the academic task and develop social skills.

What is it? Cooperative group learning is an instructional strategy where students work collaboratively to accomplish an academic task while also practicing a social skill.

Why do we do it? We know that the brain is social and needs to discuss and share ideas and perspectives. Discussion clarifies thoughts and checks for understanding. It is a great assessment tool as teachers 'eavesdrop' on groups and notice misconceptions that need to be clarified.

In a differentiated classroom, students will move in and out of a variety of partner and group situations and, therefore, need to know how to work well together. Cooperative group learning has a proven track record based on sound research that shows actual gains in student achievement (Johnson & Johnson, 1981, cited in Bellanca & Fogarty, 1991; Lou et al., 1996; Marzano et al., 2001).

What does it look like? Science instruction lends itself well to cooperative learning since many investigations and experiences are best accomplished in small groups or with partners. There are five elements (Johnson & Johnson, 1981, cited in Gregory & Parry, 2006) that need to be a part of cooperative learning experiences:

- **Positive interdependence:** Making sure that students need one another by giving them a common goal, shared resources, tasks or roles, a suitable environment, an outside force (i.e., time limits).
- **Individual accountability**: Every student must be accountable for the knowledge or skill practiced in the group (e.g., presentation, report, quiz).
- **Face-to-face interaction:** An environment conducive for learning.
- **Collaborative or social skills:** Practice one or more social skills that students need.
- **Group processing:** Discussing how well they did with the social skill.

Teachers should structure group activities and individual student roles around these elements in ways that enable all students to be successful.

Adjustable Assignments

What are they? In classrooms everywhere, we are examining how we can get a better fit for all students. Adjustable assignments allow teachers to help students focus on essential skills and understanding key concepts, recognizing that they may be at different levels of readiness. Some may or may not be able to handle different levels of complexity or abstraction. Although the assignment is adjusted for different groups of learners, the standards, concepts, or content of each assignment have the same focus and each student has the opportunity to develop essential skills and understanding at his or her appropriate level of challenge. The activities better ensure that students explore ideas at their level while building on prior knowledge and experiencing incremental growth.

Why do we use them? Using adjusted assignments allows students to begin learning where they are and to work on challenging and worthwhile tasks. If we were growing flowers and some of the seeds had sprouted and were ready to flower, we would not pull them out by the roots and make them start again from seed. It sounds a bit bizarre when we think about it. We of course would give the plants that were advanced in their growth the light, water, and food they need and would nurture the seedlings that were just sprouting to help them bloom and grow.

Adjusting assignments allows for reinforcement or extension of concepts based on student readiness, learning styles, or multiple intelligence preferences. Appropriate adjustments in the learning have a greater chance of providing a "flow" experience in which each student is presented with challenging work that just exceeds his or her skill level.

The chances of success for each learner are increased because success is within reach, and ultimately reaching success will be highly motivating. Adjusting assignments also decreases the chances of "downshifting" and the sense of helplessness that students feel when a challenge is beyond their capabilities.

How do we use them? Initially, as in any planning process, the concepts, skills, and content that will be the focus of the activity are identified and aligned with targeted standards and expectations.

Using some method of preassessment (e.g., quizzes, journal entries, class discussions and data collection techniques, learning profiles, etc.), teachers gather data to determine the prior knowledge of students for the new content or the skill that is targeted for learning. The preassessment data are compiled. Then the key standards and concepts to be taught during the unit are determined. The teacher then decides which parts of the study should be taught to the total class and how they will be presented. The appropriate places to teach these concepts or skills are determined. Then comes the time to make decisions about any adjustable assignment. Assignments are adjusted to meet the needs of learners based on their present knowledge or skill level. The following are questions the teacher will answer when making decisions about these assignments.

- What content does each of the groups already know?
- What does each group need to learn?
- What strategies should be used to facilitate the learning of each portion?
- What is the most effective way to group for each activity?
- What assessment tools will be used so that students will be accountable?
- Are the plans meeting the individual needs of the students?

What do they look like? Basic knowledge and experience vary among learners, so adjustable assignments may be needed. Here is an example that is typical of what teachers face every time they start planning for all of their students.

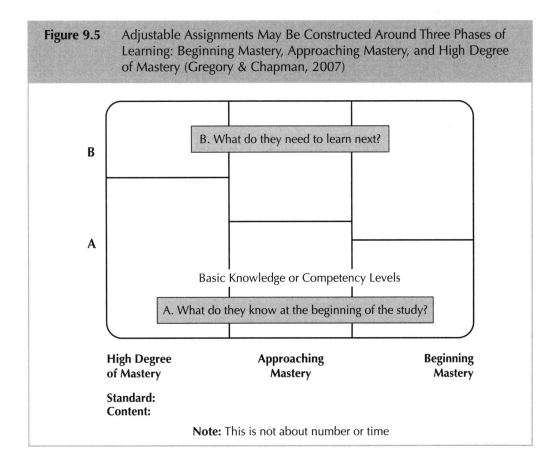

Figure 9.5 Adjustable Assignments May Be Constructed Around Three Phases of Learning: Beginning Mastery, Approaching Mastery, and High Degree of Mastery (Gregory & Chapman, 2007)

ADJUSTABLE ASSIGNMENTS FOR FORCE AND MOTION AT THE MIDDLE GRADE LEVEL

A unit of instruction dealing with force and motion at the middle grade level will require students to have a working knowledge and comprehension of basic terms such as force, motion, inertia, mass, acceleration, direction, magnitude, speed, and unbalanced forces. Students at a beginning mastery level may work in partners or small groups to operationally define these terms through hands-on activities or demonstrations at stations or centers. Other options for introducing important terminology include reading reference books, watching a videotape, or visiting a science center.

Students approaching mastery are ready to apply the terms to activities and investigations that relate directly to the key concepts found in state science standards. Such concepts are likely to be similar to those found in the NSES:

- The motion of an object can be described by its position, direction of movement, and speed.
- An object that is not being subjected to a force will continue to move at a constant speed and in a straight line.
- If more than one force acts on an object along a straight line, the forces will reinforce or cancel one another, depending on their direction and magnitude. Unbalanced forces will cause changes in the speed or direction of an object's motion (National Research Council, 1996).

As students test hypotheses and answer questions related to linear and nonlinear motion, they will learn about contributions of scientists like Aristotle, who attempted to clarify motion; Copernicus, who formulated a theory that the earth moved around the sun; Galileo, who supported the Copernican theory of the solar system through observation and experimentation; and Newton, who developed the famous three laws of motion.

Students with a high degree of mastery may already be familiar with the key concepts and are ready to apply these to more complex situations. For example, they may study force and motion in the context of amusement park rides, aerodynamics, or space exploration. They may study how the principles of force and motion apply to community problems or issues or to other areas of science, such as the dynamic forces in nature experienced through volcanic eruption, earthquakes, and mountain building, or forces that affect living things such as phototropism, geotropism, and gravity.

Curriculum Compacting

What is it? Curriculum compacting is a strategy first shared by Joe Renzulli of the University of Connecticut (Reis & Renzulli, 1992; see also Tomlinson, 1999, 2001). It provides for the student who is very capable and knowledgeable in a particular topic in a subject area. It is a way of maximizing time for the more advanced learner.

Why do we use it? Many students, because of prior experience, interests, and opportunities, may bring to the topic prior knowledge and skills that have been acquired over time. These may have been acquired through voracious reading, travel, and personal interest about a topic or from a mentor or role model who has had an influence on the learner. It is for these students that compacting may be used on occasion to enrich their curriculum, enhance and stretch their thinking, and help them develop into more self-directed learners. In many classrooms, where teaching to the middle is the norm, some learners are bored as they "repeat history," and others are lost because they don't have the background or experience they need to understand or be able to do what is expected of them.

Compacting or enriching may be used with the high-end or advanced learner(s) identified after a preassessment is given. It is important to allow all learners to move at their own pace, thus creating the "relaxed alertness" that Caine and Caine (1997) suggested. Challenging experiences that are perceived as "doable" in a learning situation put students into a state of "flow," thus engaging them at their level of challenge and not frustrating or boring them by giving them too difficult or too easy a task.

How do we do it? There are three phases that must be considered when using this approach:

Phase 1. In this phase, after an exploratory session where students are able to access prior knowledge and discuss their initial concepts and knowledge, a preassessment is given. This may be in the form of the following:

- A pretest.
- A conference where the learner shares knowledge and understanding about the topic.
- A portfolio presentation in which students show evidence of their comprehension and skill level (any or all of these may be used).

Phase 2. After the preassessment, the teacher analyzes the data and identifies what the student already knows and has mastered and what the student still needs to learn.

This additional knowledge or skill may be acquired by the following:

- Joining the total class group for that concept or information.
- Independent study.
- Homework assignments.
- Collaborating with a mentor or learning buddy in or outside school.
- Online learning.

Figure 9.6   Curriculum Compacting to Enrich Learning

Phase 1	Phase 2 Analyze data	Phase 3
Exploratory Phase	**Mastery:** skills, concepts What have they mastered?	**Advanced Level Challenges**
Preassessment: • Test • Confidence • Portfolio conference	**Needs to Master:** What do they need to know?	• Investigation • Problem-Based Learning • Service Learning • Project • Contract
To Find Out What the Learner • Knows • Needs to know • Wants to know	**How Will They Learn It?** • Gain with whole class • Independent study • Homework • Mentor/buddy in or out of school • Online learning	**Opportunities for Successful Intelligence (Sternberg, 1996)** • Analytical • Practical • Creative
		Assessment

Phase 3. Once the missing pieces have been added, the students may choose or be offered the following:

- An investigation or research project.
- An ill-structured problem to solve.
- A service learning opportunity.
- A project.
- A negotiated contract.
- A special assignment.

These assignments facilitate the challenge of applying their knowledge and skill in a practical and creative way. As we noted in Chapter 3, Robert Sternberg (1996) defined "successful intelligence" as including the aspects of being analytical, practical, and creative, not just knowing.

Implementing compacting: This approach not only allows learners to enhance their understanding but also enables them to obtain an added perspective on the subject matter. Used with academically gifted or talented students, compacting may be done as a pullout or partial pullout model or orchestrated in the classroom with the subject teacher. If students are pulled out, they should not miss other subject areas of study that they have not mastered. Teachers must be sure that students really do have full mastery of the concept, not just surface-level knowledge. Students should not be required to complete the regular classroom assignments in the subject for which they have compacted out.

References

Introduction

Huebner, T. A. (2010). Differentiated learning. *Educational Leadership, 67*(5), 79–81.

Tomlinson, C. (1999). *The differentiated classroom: Responding to the needs of all learners.* Alexandria, VA: Association for Supervision and Curriculum Development.

Chapter 1

Bloom, B. S. (Ed.). (1956). *Taxonomy of educational objectives: Book 1. Cognitive domain.* New York: David McKay.

Chapman, C., & King, R. (2008). *Differentiated instructional management: Work smarter, not harder.* Thousand Oaks, CA: Corwin.

Gregory, G. H., & Chapman, C. (2007). *Differentiated instructional strategies: One size doesn't fit all.* Thousand Oaks, CA: Corwin.

Renzulli, J. S., Leppien, J. H., & Hayes, T. S. (2000). *The multiple menu model: A practical guide for developing differentiated curriculum.* Mansfield Center, CT: Creative Learning Press.

Tomlinson, C. A. (1999). *The differentiated classroom: Responding to the needs of all learners.* Alexandria, VA: Association for Supervision and Curriculum Development.

Tomlinson, C. A. (2001). *How to differentiate instruction in mixed-ability classrooms* (2nd ed.). Alexandria, VA: Association for Supervision and Curriculum Development.

Trelease, J. (2001). *The read-aloud handbook* (5th ed.). New York: Penguin.

Chapter 2

Anderson, E. (1975). *Thoughts of our times.* Mt Vernon, NY: Peter Pauper Press.

Bigge, M., & Shermis, S. (1999). *Learning theories for teachers.* New York: Longman.

Bransford, J., Brown, A., & Cocking, R. (Eds.). (2000). *How people learn: Brain, mind, experience, and school* (Expanded ed.). Committees on Developments in the Science of Learning and Committee on Learning Research and Educational Practice, Commission on Behavioral and Social Sciences and Education, National Research Council. Washington: DC: National Academies Press.

Duke, N., & Pearson, P. D. (2002). *Effective practices for developing reading comprehension.* In A. E. Farstrup & S. J. Samuels (Eds.), *What research has to say about reading instruction* (3rd ed., pp. 205–242). Newark, DE: International Reading Association.

James, M. (2006). Teaching for transfer in ELT. *English Language Teaching, 60*(2), 151–159.

Kong, A. (2002). *Scaffolding in a learning community of practice: A case study of a gradual release of responsibility from the teacher to the students.* Paper presented at the Annual Meeting of the International Reading Association, San Francisco, April 28–May 2, 2002.

Meyer, D. (1993). What is scaffolded instruction? Definitions, distinguishing features, misnomers. In D. J. Leu & C. K. Kinzer (Eds.), *Examining central issues in literacy research, theory, and practice: Forty-second yearbook of the National Reading Conference* (pp. 41–53). Washington, DC: National Reading Conference.

Pearson, P. D., & Gallagher, M. (1983). The instruction of reading comprehension. *Contemporary Educational Psychology, 8,* 317–344.

Perkins, D. N., & Salomon, G. (1988). Teaching for transfer. *Educational Leadership, 46*(1), 22–32.

RAND Reading Study Group (RRSG). (2002). *Reading for understanding: Toward an R&D program in reading comprehension.* Washington, DC: RAND Corporation.

Vygotsky, L. S. (1978). *Mind in society: The development of higher psychological processes* (M. Cole, V. John-Steiner, S. Scribner, & E. Souberman, Eds. & Trans.). Cambridge, MA: Harvard University Press.

Chapter 3

Alber-Morgan, S. R., Hessler, T., & Konrad, M. (2007). Teaching writing for keeps. *Education and Treatment of Children, 30,* 107–128.

Atwell, N. (1987). *In the middle: Writing, reading, and learning with adolescents.* Portsmouth, NH: Heinemann.

Baker, S., Gersten, R., & Graham, S. (2003). Teaching expressive writing to students with learning disabilities: Research-based applications and examples. *Journal of Learning Disabilities, 36,* 109–123.

Blume, J. (1972). Tales of a fourth grade nothing. New York: Puffin Books.

Carle, E. (2004). *Mister Seahorse.* New York: Philomel Books.

DiSpirt, D. (2008). Strategies to summarize a narrative: Teaching the main ideas or events in a story. *Suite 101.com.* Retrieved December 17, 2009, from http://primary-school-lesson-plans.suite101.com/

Ellis, E. S., & Friend, P. (1991). Adolescents with learning disabilities. In B. Y. L. Wong (Ed.), *Learning about learning disabilities* (pp. 505–561). San Diego: Academic Press.

Engelmann, S., & Silbert, J. (1983). *Expressive writing 1.* Chicago: Science Research Associates

Gillingham, A., & Stillman, B. W. (1970). *Remedial training for children with specific disability in reading, spelling, and penmanship.* Cambridge, MA: Educators Publishing Service.

Goldberg, A., Russell, M., & Cook, A. (2003). The effect of computers on student writing: A meta-analysis of studies from 1992–2002. *Journal of Technology, Learning, and Assessment, 2,* 1–51.

Graham, S. (1983). The effect of self-instructional procedures on LD students' handwriting performance, *Learning Disability Quarterly, 6,* 231–234.

Graham, S., & Harris, K. R. (2003). Students with learning disabilities and the process of writing: A meta-analysis of SRSD studies. In L. Swanson, K. R. Harris, &

S. Graham (Eds.), *Handbook of research on learning disabilities* (pp. 323–344). New York: Guilford.

Graham, S., & Harris, K. R. (2005). *Writing better: Teaching writing processes and self-regulation to students with learning difficulties.* Baltimore: Brookes.

Graham, S., Harris, K. R., & Fink, B. (2000). Extra handwriting instruction: Prevent writing difficulties right from the start. *Teaching Exceptional Children, 33,* 88–91.

Graham, S., Harris, K. R., & Loynachan, C. (1993). The basic spelling vocabulary list. *Journal of Educational Research, 86,* 363–369.

Graham, S., & Miller, L. (1979). *Spelling research and practice: A unified approach. Focus on Exceptional Children, 12,* 1–6.

Graham, S., Olinghouse, N. G., & Harris, K. R. (2009). Teaching composing to students with learning disabilities: Scientifically supported recommendations. In G. A. Troia (Ed.), *Instruction and assessment for struggling writers: Evidence-based practices* (pp. 165–186). New York: Guildford.

Graham, S., & Perin, D. (2007). *Writing next: Effective strategies to improve writing of adolescents in middle and high school.* Washington, DC: Alliance for Excellence in Education.

Graves, D. H., & Rueda, R. (2009). Teaching written expression to culturally and linguistically diverse learners. In G. A. Troia (Ed.), *Instruction and assessment for struggling writers: Evidence-based practices* (pp. 213–242). New York: Guildford Press.

Greenwood, C. R., Delquadri, J. D., Hou, S., Terry, B., Arreaga-Mayer, C., & Abbott, M. (2001). *Together we can! Classwide peer tutoring learning management system teacher's manual.* University of Kansas: Sopris West.

Hagin, R. A. (1983). Write right—or left: A practical approach to handwriting. *Journal of Learning Disabilities, 16,* 266–271.

Hanover, S. (1983). Handwriting comes naturally? *Academic Therapy, 18,* 407–412.

Heron, T. E., Okyere, B. A., & Miller, A. D. (1991). A taxonomy of approaches to teach spelling. *Journal of Behavioral Education, 1,* 117–130.

Horn, E. (1954). Phonics and spelling. *Journal of Education, 136,* 233–246.

MacArthur, C. A. (1996). Using technology to enhance the writing processes of students with learning disabilities. *Journal of Learning Disabilities, 29,* 344–354.

MacArthur, C. A. (2009). Using technology to teach composing to struggling writers. In G. A. Troia (Ed.), *Instruction and assessment for struggling writers: Evidence-based practices* (pp. 243–268). New York: Guilford.

MacArthur, C. A., Graham, S., Schwartz, S. S., & Schafer, W. D. (1995). Evaluation of a writing instruction model that integrated a process approach, strategy instruction, and word processing. *Learning Disability Quarterly, 18,* 278–291.

Marchisan, M., & Alber, S. R. (2001). The write way: Tips for teaching the writing process to resistant writers. *Intervention in School and Clinic, 36,* 154–162.

Mason, L. H. & Graham, S. (2008). Writing instruction for adolescents with learning disabilities: Programs of intervention research. *Learning Disabilities Research & Practice, 23,* 103–112.

Okyere, B. A., Heron, T. E., & Goddard, Y. (1997). Effects of self-correction on the acquisition, maintenance, and generalization of the written spelling of elementary school children. *Journal of Behavioral Education, 7,* 51–69.

Persky, H. R., Daane, M. C., & Jin, Y. (2003). *The nation's report card: Writing 2002,* NCES 2003-529, Institute of Education Sciences. National Center for Education Statistics. Washington, DC: US Department of Education.

Reis, E. M. (1989). Activities for improving the handwriting skills of learning-disabled students. *The Clearing House, 62,* 217–219.

Rhoder, C. (2002). Mindful reading: Strategy training that facilitates transfer. *Journal of Adolescent & Adult Literacy, 45*, 498–512.

Santangelo, T., & Quint, W. (2008). Planning and text production difficulties commonly experienced by students with learning disabilities: A synthesis of research to inform instruction. *Insights on Learning Disabilities 5*, 1–10.

Schlagel, B. (2007). Best practices in spelling and handwriting. In S. Graham, C. A. MacArthur, & J. Fitzgerald (Eds.), *Best practices in writing instruction*. New York: Guilford.

Schoolfield, L. D., & Timberlake, J. B. (1960). *The phonovisual method*. Washington, DC: Phonovisual Products.

Sturm, J. M., Rankin, J. L., Beukelman, D. R., & Schultz-Muehling, L. (1997). How to select appropriate software for computer-assisted writing. *Intervention in School and Clinic, 32*, 148–161.

Troia, G. A., Lin, S. C., Monroe, B. W., & Cohen, S. (2009). The effects of writing workshop instruction on the performance and motivation of good and poor writers In G. A. Troia (Ed.), *Instruction and assessment for struggling writers: Evidence-based practices* (pp. 77–112). New York: Guilford.

Vaughn, S., Bos, C. S., & Schumm, J. S. (2006). *Teaching exceptional, diverse, and at-risk students in the general education classroom* (3rd ed.). Upper Saddle River, NJ: Pearson.

Wong, Y. L., Butler, D. L., Ficzere, S. A., & Kuperis, S. (1996). Teaching low achievers and students with learning disabilities to plan, write, and revise opinion essays. *Journal of Learning Disabilities, 29*, 197–212.

Wong, Y. L., Butler, D. L., Ficzere, S. A., & Kuperis, S. (1997). Teaching adolescents with learning disabilities and low achievers to plan, write, and revise compare-and-contrast essays. *Learning Disabilities Research and Practice, 12*, 2–15.

Chapter 4

Bender, W. N. (1996). *Teaching students with mild disabilities*. Boston: Allyn & Bacon.

Bender, W. N., & Shores, C. (2007). *Response to intervention: A practical guide for teachers*. Thousand Oaks, CA: Corwin.

Bryant, D. P., Bryant, B. R., Gersten, R. M., Scammacca, N. N., Funk, C., Winter, A., et al. (2008). The effects of tier 2 intervention on the mathematics performance of first-grade students who are at risk for mathematics difficulties. *Learning Disability Quarterly, 31*(2), 47–64.

Fuchs, D., & Deshler, D. D. (2007). What we need to know about responsiveness to intervention (and shouldn't be afraid to ask). *Learning Disabilities Research and Practice, 22*(2), 129–136.

Fuchs, L. S., Fuchs, D., & Hollenbeck, K. N. (2007). Extending responsiveness to intervention to mathematics at first and third grade levels. *Learning Disabilities Research and Practice, 22*(1), 13–24.

Fuchs, L. S., Fuchs, D., Powell, S. R., Seethaler, P. M., Cirino, P. T., & Fletcher, J. M. (2008). Intensive intervention for students with mathematics disabilities: Seven principles of effective practice. *Learning Disability Quarterly, 31*(2), 79–92.

National Mathematics Advisory Panel (2008). *Foundations for success: The final report of the National Mathematics Advisory Panel*. Washington, DC: U.S. Department of Education. Available online at http://www.ed.gov/about/bdscomm/list/mathpanel/index.html.

Sousa, D. A. (2008). *How the brain learns mathematics*. Thousand Oaks, CA: Corwin.

Tomlinson, C. (1999). *The differentiated classroom: Responding to the needs of all learners.* Alexandria, VA: Association for Supervision and Curriculum Development.

Wiggins, G., & McTighe, J. (1998). *Understanding by design.* Alexandria, VA: Association for Supervision and Curriculum Development.

Chapter 5

Delazer, M., Domahs, F., Bartha, L., Brenneis, C., Lochy, A., Trieb. T., & Benke, T. (2003). Learning complex arithmetic—A fMRI study. *Cognitive Brain Research, 18,* 76–88.

Ellis, E. S., & Lenz, B. K. (1996). Perspectives on instruction in learning strategies. In D. D. Deshler, E. S. Ellis, & B. K. Lenz (Eds.), *Teaching adolescents with learning disabilities* (pp. 9–60). Denver, CO: Love Publishing.

Fosnot, C. T., & Dolk, M. (2001). *Young mathematicians at work: Constructing multiplication and division.* Portsmouth, NH: Heinemann Press.

Fuchs, L., & Fuchs, D. (1986). Effects of systematic formative evaluation: A meta-analysis. *Exceptional Children, 53*(3), 199–208.

Gersten, R., Beckmann, S., Clarke, B., Foegen, A., Marsh, L., Star, J. R., & Witzel, B. (2009). *Assisting students struggling with mathematics: Response to Intervention (RtI) for elementary and middle schools* (NCEE 2009-4060). Washington, DC: National Center for Education Evaluation and Regional Assistance, Institute of Education Sciences, U.S. Department of Education. Retrieved December 22, 2010, from http://ies.ed.gov/ncee/wwc/pdf/practiceguides/rti_math_pg_042109.pdf

Gersten, R., Chard, D. J., Jayanthi, M., Baker, S. K., Morphy, P., & Flojo, J. (2009). Mathematics instruction for students with learning disabilities: A meta-analysis of instructional components. *Review of Educational Research, 79*(3), 1202–1242.

Hudson, P., & Miller, S. P. (2006). *Designing and implementing mathematics instruction for students with diverse learning needs.* Boston, MA: Allyn & Bacon.

Ives, B. (2007). Graphic organizers applied to secondary algebra instruction for students with learning disorders. *Learning Disabilities Research & Practice, 22*(2), 110–118.

Jitendra, A. K. (2002). Teaching students math problem-solving through graphic representations. *Teaching Exceptional Children, 34*(4), 34–38.

Marshall, S. P. (1995). *Schemas in problem solving.* New York, NY: Cambridge University Press.

Mercer, C. D., & Mercer, A. R. (1993). *Teaching students with learning problems* (4th ed.). New York, NY: Macmillan Publishing.

Miller, S. P., & Hudson, P. J. (2007). Using evidence based practices to build mathematics competence related to conceptual, procedural, and declarative knowledge. *Learning Disabilities Research and Practice, 22,* 47–57.

Montague, M. (2007). Self-regulation and mathematics instruction. *Learning Disabilities Research & Practice, 22*(1), 75–83.

National Council of Teachers of Mathematics (NCTM). (2000). *Principles and standards for school mathematics.* Reston, VA: Author.

Riccomini, P. J. & Witzel, B. S. (2010). *Solving equations.* Upper Saddle River, NJ: Pearson Education.

Sanjay, R. (2002). A new approach to an old order. *Mathematics Teaching in the Middle School, 8*(4), 193–195.

Stading, M., Williams, R. L., & McLaughlin, T. F. (1996). Improving academic performance through self-management: Cover, copy, and compare. *Intervention in School and Clinic, 32*(2), 113–118.

Swanson, H. L., & Deshler, D. D. (2003). Instructing adolescents with disabilities: Converting a meta-analysis to practice. *Journal of Learning Disabilities, 36*(2), 124–135.

Test, D. W., & Ellis, M. F. (2005). The effects of LAP fractions on addition and subtraction of fractions with students with mild disabilities. *Education and Treatment of Children, 28*(1), 11–24.

Tindal, G., & Ketterlin-Geller, L. (2004). *Research on mathematics test accommodations relevant to NAEP testing.* Washington, DC: National Assessment Governing Board.

Van Garderen, D. (2006). Spatial visualization, visual imagery, and mathematical problem solving of students with varying abilities. *Journal of Learning Disabilities, 39,* 496–506.

Witzel, B. S. (2005). Using CRA to teach Algebra to students with math difficulties in inclusive settings. *Learning Disabilities: A Contemporary Journal, 3*(2), 49–60.

Witzel, B. S., Mercer, C. D., & Miller, M. D. (2003). Teaching algebra to students with learning difficulties: An investigation of an explicit instruction model. *Learning Disabilities Research & Practice, 18*(2), 121–131.

Woodward, J. (2006). Developing automaticity in multiplication facts: Integrating strategy instruction with timed practice drills. *Learning Disability Quarterly, 29,* 269–289.

Xin, Y. P., & Jitendra, A. K. (2006). Teaching problem solving skills to middle school students with mathematics difficulties: Schema-based strategy instruction. In M. Montague & A. K. Jitendra (Eds.), *Teaching mathematics to middle school students with learning difficulties* (pp. 51–71). New York, NY: Guilford Press.

Xin, Y. P., Jitendra, A., & Deatline-Buchman, A. (2005). Effects of mathematical word problem-solving instruction on middle school students with learning problems. *The Journal of Special Education, 39,* 181–192.

Zrebiec Uberti, H., Mastropieri, M., & Scruggs, T. (2004). Check it off: Individualizing a math algorithm for students with disabilities via self-monitoring checklists. *Intervention in School and Clinic, 39*(5), 269–275.

Chapter 6

Sak, U. (2009). Test of the three-mathematical minds (M3) for the identification of mathematically gifted students. *Roeper Review, 31,* 53–67.

Tieso, C. (2005). The effects of grouping practices and curricular adjustments on achievement. *Journal for the Education of the Gifted, 29*(1), 60–89.

Winebrenner, S. (2001). *Teaching gifted kids in the regular classroom.* Minneapolis, MN: Free Spirit Publishing.

Chapter 7

Baker, S., Gersten, R., & Lee, D. (2002). A synthesis of empirical research on teaching mathematics to low-achieving students. *The Elementary School Journal, 103,* 51–73.

Baker, S., Gersten, R., & Scanlon, D. (2002). Procedural facilitators and cognitive strategies: Tools for unraveling the mysteries of comprehension and the writing process, and for providing meaningful access to the general curriculum. *Learning Disabilities Research and Practice, 17,* 65–77.

Butler, F. M., Miller, S. P., Crehan, K., Babbitt, B., & Pierce, T. (2003). Fraction instruction for students with mathematics disabilities: Comparing two teaching sequences. *Learning Disabilities Research and Practice, 18*, 99–111.

Ellis, E. S., Worthington, L., & Larkin, M. J. (1994). *Executive summary of research synthesis on effective teaching principles and the design of quality tools for educators.* (Tech. Rep. No. 6). Retrieved July 17, 2004, from University of Oregon, National Center to Improve the Tools of Educators website: http://idea.uore gon.edu/~ncite/ documents/ techrep/other.html.

Fuchs, L. S., Fuchs, D., & Karns, K. (2001). Enhancing kindergarteners' mathematical development: Effects of peer-assisted learning strategies. *Elementary School Journal, 101*, 495–510.

Gersten, R., Beckmann, S., Clarke, B., Foegen, A., Marsh, L., Star, J. R., & Witzel, B. (2009). *Assisting students struggling with mathematics: Response to Intervention (RTI) for elementary and middle schools* (NCEE 2009-4060). Washington, DC: National Center for Education Evaluation and Regional Assistance, Institute of Education Sciences, U.S. Department of Education. Retrieved from http:// ies.ed.gov/ncee/wwc/publications/practiceguides.

Hutchinson, N. L. (1993). Second invited response: Students with disabilities and mathematics education reform—let the dialog begin. *Remedial and Special Education, 14*(6), 20–23.

IRIS Center for Training Enhancements. (n.d.). *Effective room arrangement.* Retrieved on March 5, 2007, from http://iris.peabody.vanderbilt.edu/gpm/chalcycle.htm.

Miller, S. P., & Mercer, C. D. (1993). Using data to learn about concrete-semiconcrete-abstract instruction for students with math disabilities. *Learning Disabilities Research & Practice, 8*, 89–96.

National Mathematics Advisory Panel (NMAP). (2008). *Foundations for success: The final report of the National Mathematics Advisory Panel.* U.S. Department of Education Washington, DC. Retrieved March 2008 from www.ed.gov/MathPanel.

Owen, R. L., & Fuchs, L. S. (2002). Mathematical problem-solving strategy instruction for third-grade students with learning disabilities. *Remedial and Special Education, 23*, 268–278.

Riccomini, P. J., Witzel, B. S., & Riccomini, A. E. (in press). Maximize development in early childhood math programs by optimizing the instructional sequence. In N. L. Gallenstein & J. Hodges (Eds.), *Mathematics for all.* Olney, MD: ACEI.

Tournaki, N. (2003). The differential effects of teaching addition through strategy instruction versus drill and practice to students with and without disabilities. *Journal of Learning Disabilities, 36*, 449–458.

Wilson, C. L., & Sindelar, P. T. (1991). Direct instruction in math word problems: Students with learning disabilities. *Exceptional Children, 57*, 512–518.

Witzel, B. S. (2005). Using CRA to teach algebra to students with math difficulties in inclusive settings. *Learning Disabilities: A Contemporary Journal, 3*(2), 49–60.

Witzel, B. S., Mercer, C. D., & Miller, M. D. (2003). Teaching algebra to students with learning difficulties: An investigation of an explicit instruction model. *Learning Disabilities Research and Practice, 18*, 121–131.

Witzel, B. S., & Riccomini, P. J. (2007). OPTIMIZE your curriculum for students with disabilities. *Preventing School Failure, 52*(1), 13–18.

Xin, Y. P., Jitendra, A. K., & Deatline-Buchman, A. (2005). Effects of mathematical word problem-solving instruction on middle school students with learning problems. *Journal of Special Education, 39*, 181–192.

Chapter 8

Gregory, G., & Chapman, C. (2002). *Differentiated instructional strategies*. Thousand Oaks, CA: Corwin.

Gregory, G., & Hammerman, E. (2008). *Differentiated instructional strategies for science, grades K–8*. Thousand Oaks, CA: Corwin.

Llewellyn, D. (2005). *Measurement stations. Science Scope, 29*(1), 18–21.

Llewellyn, D. (2007). *Inquire within: Implementing inquiry-based science standards in grades 3–8* (2nd ed.). Thousand Oaks, CA: Corwin.

National Research Council. (1996). *National science education standards*. Washington, DC: National Academy Press.

Ogle, D. (1986). K-W-L: A teaching model that develops active reading of expository text. *The Reading Teacher, 39*(6), 564–570.

Robertson, W. (2002). *Force and motion: Stop faking it!* Arlington, VA: NSTA Press.

Tomlinson, C. (1999). *The differentiated classroom: Responding to the needs of all learners*. Alexandria, VA: ACSD.

Tomlinson, C., & Kalhfleisch, M. (1998). Teach me, teach my brain: A call for differentiated classrooms. *Educational Leadership, 56*(3), 52–55.

Chapter 9

Bellanca, J., & Fogarty, R. (1991). *Blueprints for thinking in the cooperative classroom*. Thousand Oaks, CA: Corwin.

Caine, R. N., & Caine, G. (1997). *Education on the edge of possibility*. Alexandria, VA: Association for Supervision and Curriculum Development.

Cawalti, G. (Ed.). (1995). *Handbook of research on improving student achievement*. Arlington, VA: Educational Research Service.

Goleman, D. (1995). *Emotional intelligence*. New York: Bantam.

Gregory, G. H., & Chapman, C. (2007). *Differentiated instructional strategies: One size doesn't fit all* (2nd ed.). Thousand Oaks, CA: Corwin.

Gregory, G. H., & Parry, T. (2006). *Designing brain-compatible learning*. Thousand Oaks, CA: Corwin.

Klentschy, M., Garrison, L., & Maia Amaral, O. (2000). *Valle imperial project in science (VIPS): Four-year comparison of student achievement data, 1995–1999*. El Centro, CA: El Centro School District.

Lou, Y., Alorami, P. C., Spence, J. C., Paulsen, C., Chambers, B., & d'Apollonio, S. (1996). Within-class grouping: A meta-analysis. *Review of Educational Research, 66*(4), 423–458.

Marzano, R. J., Pickering, D. J., & Pollack, J. E. (2001). *Classroom instruction that works*. Alexandria, VA: Association for Supervision and Curriculum Development.

National Research Council. (1996). *National science education standards*. Washington, DC: National Academy Press.

Reis, S., & Renzulli, J. (1992). Using curriculum compacting to challenge the above average. *Educational Leadership, 50*(2), 51–57.

Sanders, W. L., & Horn, S. P. (1994). The Tennessee value-added assessment system (TVAAS): Mixed-model methodology in educational assessment. *Journal of Personnel Evaluation in Education, 8*, 299–311.

Sternberg, R. (1996). *Successful intelligence: How practical and creative intelligence determine success in life*. New York: Simon & Schuster.

Tomlinson, C. A. (1999). *The differentiated classroom: Responding to the needs of all learners*. Alexandria, VA: Association for Supervision and Curriculum Development.

Tomlinson, C. A. (2001). *How to differentiate instruction in mixed-ability classrooms* (2nd ed.). Alexandria, VA: Association for Supervision and Curriculum Development.

Wenglinsky, H. (2000). *How teaching matters: Bringing the classroom back into discussions of teacher quality* [Online]. Available: http://www.ets.org/Media/Research/pdf/PICTEAMAT.pdf

Wright, S. P., Horn, S. P., & Sanders, W. L. (1997). Teacher and classroom context effects on student achievement: Implications for teacher evaluation. *Journal of Personnel Evaluation in Education, 11,* 57–67.

CORWIN
A SAGE Company

The Corwin logo—a raven striding across an open book—represents the union of courage and learning. Corwin is committed to improving education for all learners by publishing books and other professional development resources for those serving the field of PreK–12 education. By providing practical, hands-on materials, Corwin continues to carry out the promise of its motto: **"Helping Educators Do Their Work Better."**